AF522683

DEVELOPMENT OF WOMEN
Issues and Challenges

By

DR. G. SANDHYA RANI

Associate Professor
Department of Women's Studies
S.P. Mahila Visvavidyalayam
Tirupati-517 502

DPH

DISCOVERY PUBLISHING HOUSE PVT. LTD.

NEW DELHI-110 002

Published by:
Tilak Wasan

DISCOVERY PUBLISHING HOUSE PVT. LTD.
4383/4A, Ansari Road, Darya Ganj
New Delhi-110 002 (India)
Phone : +91-11-23279245, 43596064-65
Fax : +91-11-23253475
E-mail : parul.wasan@gmail.com
discoverypublishinghouse@gmail.com
web : www.discoverypublishinggroup.com

***First Edition:* 2012**

ISBN: 978-93-5056-013-6

Development of Women—Issues and Challenges

Printed at:
Shree Balaji Art Press
Delhi

Preface

The reality of women's lives remains invisible to men and women alike and this invisibility persists at all levels beginning with the family to the nation. Although geographically men and women share the same space, they live in different worlds. The mere fact that 'women hold up half of the sky'—does not appear to give them a position of dignity and equality. It is true, that over the years women have made great strides in many areas with notable progress in reducing some gender gaps. Yet, 'the afflicted world in which we live is characterized by deeply unequal sharing of the burden of adversities between men and women'. Sprawling inequalities persist in their access to education, healthcare, physical and financial resources and opportunities in the political, economic social and cultural spheres. The impact of inequalities is reflected in the status of women worldwide and in India.

For many years, Indian women have suffered in the hands of the men-folk, faced extreme levels of exploitation, have adhered to clearly defined norms of society and have been looked down upon as menial slakes. But with the help and support extended by feminists and other reformists, women have been able to uplift themselves by shedding their domestic tag. They have eventually managed to shake the brawny walls of social and economic exploitation. The modern woman of today is learning to break away the shackles of the past. The emerging new age woman has the ability to equip herself with education thereby seeking her own identity, confidence and not compromising on her self-respect at any cost.

Despite creating a dignified position in this male dominated society the struggle for each and every woman is far from over. Although it is evident that women have left nothing unaccomplished, the percentage of women achievers to men achievers is comparatively low. Women are subject to prejudice by the dominant patriarchy and are in turn left out from supremacy.

In fact, the plight of a married woman is still distressing. As most husbands want their wives to work, the woman is expected to perform household chores single handedly whereas the husband doesn't portray an iota of sensitivity in sharing responsibilities. There are few others who are supportive and understanding towards their spouse but this percentage is quite low in comparison to the autocratic men.

The position of Indian women today, is to examine as to how an average Indian finds herself in the social context. Is she on any way subordinate to her husband where by her personality is merged with that of her husband's or does she retain her individuality, commanding a position of equal respect with man, or is it a mixture of the two. In recent years, the position of woman has been subjected to much analysis. It should not be ignored that for assessment of the social status Indian women could not be treated as a homogenous group. In fact, there is a wide range of contrast between the position of women among the different sections of society tribal, urban and rural.

The traditional concept of the woman's role being restricted to domestic chores is undergoing a change. They are increasingly taking up jobs in commercial and industrial establishments as well as in the administration. This state of affairs has made a profound impact on the attitude of the educated middle class women in three areas: (1) Higher Education; (2) Employment and all levels of industry, commerce and administration; and (3) Politics.

Due to the principles of democracy based on liberty a woman's began to change towards greater emancipation. The role of wife-mother was affected by this new freedom. In India, due to efforts of social reformers and social legislations, women were brought out of the confines of their home. The process of industrialization and urbanization had their share in the changes which followed. It was the 21st century that brought about dynamic changes and new concepts which affected the status of women giving them fresh dignity and importance.

Human Resource Development has taken up as one of the major thrust areas by the Government of India during the VIII Five Year Plan and efforts were directed towards mainstreaming men, women (and children) into the national development on equal footings, while the main thrust in respect of children was to ensure their 'survival' with special respect of women was to make them economically independent and self reliant. Empowerment of women is one of the major objectives of the IX Five

Year Plan too. The plan reiterates to create an enabling environment with requisite policies and programmes, legislative support exclusive institutional mechanisms at various levels and adequate financial resources to achieve this objective.

Economically rural women are in a state of drastic poverty, rural females are considered as consumers and not producers. They have no occupation, property, education or skills. A majority of women are at a disadvantage in gaining admittance to professional training because of unequal access to education at preparatory levels. As a result they hardly get into formal sector of employment. They are, however, a major work force in informal sector but suffer from wage discrimination. Women in rural areas have unequal control and access to financial resources.

Keeping all these in view in this book an attempt is made to present articles covering the various facets of women's development. All the 36 articles are arranged under four broad categories namely Status of Women, Violence Against Women, Empowerment of Women and Entrepreneurship for Women's Development.

All the articles have been covering a wide range of issues relating to women, particularly women living at grassroot level, downtrodden and helpless.

Section—I contains ten articles on Status of Women in India. The chapter 'Women in Higher Education—Issues and Challenges', the authors (Dr. Suguna Reddy and Dr. Sandhya Rani) analysed the literacy levels of women in India and compared the female literacy rate with males. The enrolment of women in Higher Education was also presented along with the factors affecting women student enrolment in Higher Education. The chapter 'Effects of Modernization on Joint Family System in India' by Dr. Sandhya Rani and Dr. Suguna Reddy dealt with the changes that have taken place in the traditional joint family system as a result of the westernization and modernization. Dr. G. Sandhya Rani in the chapter 'Indian Women Political Participation—A Critical Review' presents the status of women in Indian political sphere and examines the reasons for their low participation in parliament as well as assembly elections. The chapter on 'Status and Position of Women in the Family: Its Impact on Industrialization and Urbanization' by Dr. Suguna Reddy and Dr. Sandhya Rani attempts to delineate the impact of industrialization on the status of women in the family. In this chapter the authors tried to analyse how the status of women in the family is affected by industrialization. The chapter on 'Mobilising for Change: Possibilities and Challenges, Mathamma Cult in Chittoor District in Andhra Pradesh' by Dr. Sandhya Rani and Dr. Suguna Reddy throws light on the existence of Mathamma cult and examines how it is deep rooted in our society. They strongly stressed the need to react against this kind of uncivilized practices to protect young girls. In the chapter 'Consequences of Malnutrition on Mothers and Child: Future Strategies' the authors Dr. Venkamma and Dr. Sandhya Rani focuses on the nutritional status of mother and child and discusses in detail the consequences of malnutrition during various phases of women's life.

'Problems and Prospects of Aged Widows: Challenges before Women in the 21st Century' analyses the existing condition of aged women in the present day society. It also covers the major threats and challenges that aged women have been facing and suggests some recommendations to improve their status. The chapter on 'Indian Women in Political Sphere' by Dr.P.Neeraja presents the participation of and the existing status of women in politics. She has given the number of women contesters in the recent parliament elections. The chapter by Dr. Anuradha and Dr. Rajani on 'Life Skills Education for Gender Empowerment during Adolescence – Strategies' deals with the concepts of life skills, elements of life skills based education and strategies for development, implementation and evaluation of life skill education programmes than can serve as an indirect tool for gender empowerment through community based approach. The chapter on 'Rehabilitation of Child Mathammas—A study of Jeevakona School' written by Dr. Sandhya Rani and Dr. Suguna Reddy presents the miserable conditions of Child Mathammas in the society. This chapter focuses on the existence of a social evil—Mathamma cult in the District of Chittoor and highlights the role played by RISE organization in eradication of this system. This organization has been running a school for Child Mathammas where they are able to find a new life. These schools provide education as well as training in income generating activities to the students.

Section—II contains eight chapters on the main theme 'Violence Against Women and Plight of Women Victims'. In the chapter 'Forms of Domestic Violence', the authors Dr.P.S.Vijaya Lakshmi and Dr. G. Sandhya Rani discussed on the various forms of atrocities and domestic violence against women. They presented some statistics on raising crimes on women in India. The chapter 'Strengthening Women at Risk: A Case Study of State Home in Hyderabad' by Dr.G. Sandhya Rani and Dr. B. Suguna Reddy presented the functioning of State Home in providing shelter to the destitute women and victims of violence, orphans and homeless. They highlighted the role of State Home since they are also imparting training to women in difficult circumstances in income generating activities and helping them to become economically independent. In the chapter on the 'Role of Family Counselling Centres to Overcome Gender Violence—A Study of PASS in Tirupati' by Dr. G. Sandhya Rani and Dr. B. Suguna Reddy presented the significance and role of family counselling centres in present day situation. The Family Counselling Centre of PASS an NGO in Tirupati was doing remarkable service in this area by providing guidance and counselling to the women at risk. In the paper 'Violence Against Women Causes and Consequences' the authors Dr. Suguna Reddy and Dr. Sandhya Rani focussed on various types of violence that have been taking place against women in India. They presented in detail the causes as well as consequences of this type of violence on society particularly on women.

The chapter on 'The Perils of Female Infanticide—Sociological Dimensions' the authors Dr. Suguna Reddy and Dr. Sandhya Rani presented the sociological dimension of the violence. They stressed that female infanticide is a type of silent violence against women in our society. In the chapter 'Implementing the Beijing Platform for Action with Special reference to Violence Against Women in India', the authors Dr. Suguna Reddy and Dr. Sandhya Rani analysed the recommendations of Beijing platform for Action in the context of Indian situation. They discussed the recommendations of various committees and conventions organized to prevent violence against women. In the chapter on 'Atrocities on Women: Wife Battering—Break the Silence' by Dr. Suguna Reddy and Dr. Sandhya Rani envisages to delineate some unique cases of wife battering in Tirupati urban and rural setting and deduce the reasons therefore. Dr. G. Sandhya Rani's paper on 'Causes of Domestic Violence—Strategies and Interventions with reference to India' presents the causes for various forms of violence against women in the world and also the consequences of it on women, children and society. This chapter also suggests certain strategies to overcome violence against women in India.

Section—III deals with chapters on 'Empowerment of Women'. In this section there are nine chapters covering various aspects of development of women. The chapter on 'Dr.B.R.Ambedkar's Views on Women Empowerment' by Dr. G. Sandhya Rani deals with the ideas and views of Dr.Ambedkar on women. This chapter projects how Babasaheb Ambedkar protested against social evils in the society and supported women was presented in a detailed manner. The chapter on 'Women and Empowerment' by Dr.G. Sandhya Rani presents the concept, meaning, components and elements of women empowerment. This chapter gives an overall view of the concept of empowerment. The chapter by Dr. Suguna Reddy on 'Perception of Ambedkar towards Women's Development' analyses various factors responsible for women's subjugation and subordination in the society and presents the perceptions of Dr.B.R. Ambedkar towards women's empowerment. The status of women and the provisions given to women by the Constitution of India were also discussed. In this chapter an analysis of growth strategies adopted in recent Five Year Plans by the Government of India were presented. The transformation that has taken place after the announcement of new economic policy in 1991 and its impact on women was discussed.

The chapter 'Gender Mainstreaming in Budget—Constraints and Strategies' the authors Dr.Suguna Reddy and Dr. Sandhya Rani focuses on the various concepts of budget and stresses the need for gender mainstreaming the budget. They also discussed the constraints in this process and suggested some recommendations to overcome these constraints. Dr. Sandhya Rani and Dr. Suguna Reddy in the chapter 'Sericulture—A tool for the Socio-economic Development of Women' analyses the suitability of sericulture activity to women and aged persons in rural areas. They also highlighted the role of sericulture in the economic development of our country and the role played by women as potential contributors in the process of development. The chapter on 'Women and Social Forestry' discusses the active involvement of women in protecting the environment and in sustaining the ecological balance. The chapter on 'Environmental Education for Sustainable Societies—Global Responsibility' by Dr. Suguna Reddy analyses the need for environmental education and the elevation of systems required for sustaining environment.

Section—IV covers the chapters on 'Entrepreneurship development among Women'. In this section there are seven chapters presented on various aspects of entrepreneurship. The paper on 'Support Systems—A Ray of Hope in the Lives of Women Entrepreneurs' by Dr. Rajani, Dr. Sandhya Rani and Dr. Karima Ferhana discusses the increasing importance of the development of women entrepreneurship in recent years. In this chapter the authors mentioned about the supportive systems available for women entrepreneurs to motivate them towards entrepreneurship. The chapter 'Need for Entrepreneurship Development Training Programmes for Women' Dr.Sandhya Rani and Dr. Suguna Reddy presents the status of women in rural India and also stresses the need for EDPs for promoting entrepreneurship among rural women elevating their standard of living. The chapter on 'Appropriate Technologies to Save Rural Women from Drudgery' by Dr.Sandhya Rani Dr. Suguna Reddy discusses the importance of introducing appropriate technologies to save rural women from drudgery. The chapter on 'Development of Women Entrepreneurship—Role of Commercial Banks' by Dr. Sandhya Rani discusses the role of commercial banks in promoting women entrepreneurship. This chapter also presents some of the schemes offered by State of Bank of India and Union Bank of India exclusively for women entrepreneurs.

'Entrepreneurship Development through Modern Technologies' by Dr.Sandhya Rani and Dr. Suguna Reddy presents the close association of technology for entrepreneurship development and the need to provide training to women to adopt new technologies. The chapter 'Entrepreneurship Development among Women for Better Future' by Dr.Sandhya Rani and Dr. Suguna Reddy analyses the role of entrepreneurship for women's development and the myths and reasons why women in India hesitate to take up entrepreneurship. The chapter on 'Efficacy of Entrepreneurial Training Self Help Group Women' by Dr.Rajani presents the entrepreneurial training given to SHG women to equip them with all the skills required for the establishment and smooth functioning of their micro-enterprises. She has done a survey on SHG women and presented their responses during pre-training, training and post-training phases.

I hope that this book is highly useful to the students and researchers in Women's Studies and related fields. I am thankful to the authors for contributing scholarly papers on various issues of women's development with theoretical and empirical analysis. I derived encouragement and support from my colleagues and friends in finalizing these papers. My thanks are due to Shri Tilak Wasan, Director of Discovery Publishing House, New Delhi, India for his constant support and meticulous care in publishing this book.

DR. G. SANDHYA RANI

Contents

List of Contributors

- **Dr. G. Sandhya Rani** has been working as Associate Professor in the Department of Women's Studies, Sri Badmavathi Mahila Visvavidyalayam, Tirupati. She obtained her first Post Graduate Degree in Economics from Sri Krishnadevaraya University, Anantapur, Andhra Pradesh. She was awarded M.Phil, and Ph.D. degrees in the field of Economics of Sericulture from the same University. She has also obtained post graduate degree in Women's Studies and Education from Mother Teresa Women's University, Kodaikanal and University of Madras respectively. She has 16 years of P.G. teaching experience and vast research and extension experience. She has published 24 research papers in reputed journals and books. She has also participated and presented papers in 63 national and international seminars, workshops and conferences and published two books on Sericulture and Rural Development. Her academic interests include Women's Studies - Women and Entrepreneurship, Women and Education and Rural Economics.
- **Dr. B. Suguna Reddy** is Professor in the Dept. of Women's Studies of Sri Padmavati Mahila Visvavidyalayam, Tirupati. She has received M.A. Degree in Sociology and Doctor of Philosophy from Sri Venkateswara University, Tirupati. Later she has received M.A. Degree in Women's Studies from Mother Theresa Women's University, Kodaikanal. She has wide teaching and Research experience. She has published 70 research papers in reputed journals and books. She has published three books on
  - Working Women and Religion
  - Empowerment of Rural Women through Self Help Groups
  - Women's Movements

Besides, she has presented more than 100 research papers in various Seminars/conferences/workshops/Symposias organized by National and International organization. She has reviewed books. She held the positions of Registrar of Sri Padmavati Mahila Visvavidyalayam, Tirupati and Dean of Rajiv Gandhi University of Knowledge Technologies (APIIIT'S), Hyderabad.

- **Dr. N. Rajani** has received her bachelor's, Masters and M.Phil degrees in Home science from S.V. University, Tirupati, she received her Ph.D. degree from Sri Padmavati Mahila Visvavidyalayam. She joined Sri Padmavati Mahila Visvavidyalayam as Project Fellow in CIDA-SICI Project on "Female Empowerment through functional Entrepreneurship". She served as Junior Research Fellow in DBT Project on "Facilitating Micro Entrepreneurship involving innovative food technologies amongst SHG women". She received training in Entrepreneurship in Acadia University, Halifax, Canada. She has published seven research papers and two books, presented thirteen research papers in national and international conferences. She is presently working as Assistant Professor in Dept. of Home Science, Sri Padmavati Mahila Visvavidyalayam, Tirupati. She is Consultant and Resource Person to Government and NGO Programmes. She served as Assistant Warden, NSS Programme Officer, Staff Advisor of Home Science Association, Life Member of several national professional bodies.
- **Prof. Alahari Venkamma** obtained B.Sc. (Nursing) from Osmania University, M.Sc. (Nursing) from NTR Health University, and Ph.D. from Sri Padmavathi Mahila University. She also secured M.A. degree in Social Anthropology from Sri Venkateswara University. She has been teaching courses in various Government Institutions of Andhra Pradesh since 1980. At present she is working as Principal and Professor, Govt. College of Nursing, Visakhapatnam. She attended various workshops and training programmes related to Nursing Education. Her research interests are Bio-Social aspects of Aging and Health Education.
- **Dr. Karanam Anuradha,** M.Sc., M.Phil., Ph.D. is working as Associate Professor in the Dept. of Home Science, S.V. University, and Tirupati. Her branch of specialization is Human Development. She has fourteen years of research experience and nine years of teaching experience at post graduate level. At M.Phil she studied T.V. Viewing behaviour of Pre-school children and at Doctoral level TV Viewing behaviour of elementary school children. She worked in a NCERT Project on "Home work and children" at S.V.

University, Tirupati for two years. She worked as UGC Research Associate in the Dept. of Home science at Sri Padmavathi Mahila Visvavidyalayam for five years on "Adolescents life skills and TV viewing behaviour". Her book entitled "TV Viewing—Its effect on Children's' personal and Educational Development" was published by Discovery Publishers in 1994. She has published more than ten articles in peer reviewed journals and participated in several conferences and presented papers. Her fields of interest are Child and adolescent development, TV Viewing behaviour of children and Life skills education for adolescents.

- **Dr. P. Neeraja** has been working as a Project Officer in Centre for Women's Studies, Sri Padmavati Mahila Visvavidyalayam, Tirupati. She has completed her P.G. Degree in Women's Studies and awarded Ph.D for her work on Empowerment of Women: Prospects in Sericulture during the year 2005 from Sri Padmavati Mahila Visvavidyalayam. She has technical qualification also in the field of Computers and Completed Certificate course in the Entrepreneurship Development Programme. She published two papers in reputed Journals and presented 17 papers in National and International Seminars and Conferences. So far she completed 4 Research Projects and organized more than 40 Training programmes and Workshops on various issues such as Gender Sensitization, Women's empowerment, Self Help Groups Women and Entrepreneurship Development, Atrocities against Women, Stress Management, Capacity Building Training to Panchat Raj Functionaries especially Women and promotion, of literacy and Health programmes . Her areas of interests are Women's Empowerment and Violence against women.
- **Dr. P.S. Vijaya Lakshmi** is presently working as Guest Lecturer for the students of Applied Economics in the Department of Women's Studies, Sri Padmavati Mahila Visvavidyalayam (Women's University), Tirupati. She did her research work in the field of public finance in the University of Madras. Her areas of specialisation are Public Finance, Federal Finance and Micro economics. She has Published papers in reputed Journals and presented number of papers in National and International Seminars and Conferences.

SECTION–I
STATUS OF WOMEN

CHAPTER

1

Women in Higher Education
Issues and Challenges

Dr. B. Suguna Reddy
Dr. G. Sandhya Rani

The most noteworthy feature of ancient Indian education was that women were given equal importance and rights with when in all ways of life including education. In the Rigvedic times, complete educational facilities were made available to women and they attained high educational levels and distinguished themselves in art, literature and philosophy. There are women seers or authors, sages who had gone through the discipline of Brahmacharya. There were two classes of women students, Brahmavadinis who were life long students of theology and sadyodvahas who studied upto the age of 16 or 18 years and learnt vedic hymns and theological works. They were considered kasakritsnis (Altekar 1956, Mukherjee 1958).

Women had the freedom to remain single as well as freedom to select their life partners. But as condition changed, when girls started to lost the privileges of education, the marriage age came down, they lost equality and considered as mere possessions and by 100 A.D. i.e., Manu's time they were ascribed completely to dependant status.

During the Middle Ages seclusion or purdah was added to the subordinate and subservient status of women and in course of time, women completely became illiterates and entirely dependent on men-father, husband and son, socially, economically and culturally.

All over the world, the movement for improving women's status has always emphasised education as the most significant instrument for social change. The social reformers of the 19th century tried to use education more to ameliorate the position of women socially and they were able to awaken the consciousness of the nation to the evils of child marriage, sati, polygamy, enforced widowhood, dowry system etc. Some of the prejudiced to which women were particularly subjected in traditional society underwent gradual decline during the early part of this century under the campaigns carried out be social reformers for the social amelioration of women, but the proportion of women enrolled in educational institutions remained relatively low.

During the present century, the country has made spectacular progress in promoting the interests of women. The literacy rate went up from 7 per cent in 1901 to 7.9 per cent in 1951, 18 per cent in 1971 and 24.88 per cent in 1981. But there is still a wide gap between male and female literacy. This is obvious from the following table.

Table 1.1 : Literacy Rate In India

(In percentage)

Year	Male	Female	Total
1951	24.9	7.9	16.6
1961	34.4	12.9	24.0
1971	39.51	18.44	29.45
1981	46.74	24.88	36.0
1991	63.86	39.42	52.11
2001	75.85	54.16	65.38

Source : Census India, Part–III, 2001.

The disparity between male and female participation in education becomes greater at the more advanced levels of education. But the intake of females in technical and higher education is considerably low.

In recent years, momentum has been gathering all over the world, demanding gender equality and push for equal representation of women in all spheres of activity including political, cultural, economic and educational. Conscious and concerted efforts have been initiated for the advancement of women. However, the status and position of women in many countries is far from satisfactory. While the number of women participating in public life has increased, their participation is relegated to areas deemed suitable for women and at the lower levels of the occupational ladder. This has been corroborated by the study of Tilak (1980) and it has been shown that are gender differences in the earnings. These gender inequalities have been attributed to lack of educational opportunity and socio-cultural values, norms and attitudes which discriminate against women.

In India, female participation in education is very low and their participation in higher education is relatively low. Even where the female participation is high, they are in the so called 'female oriented' courses and their participation in professional courses like engineering and technology and in the memerging areas of science are very low. This can be seen from the following table.

Table 1.2 : Enrolment of Women in University Education—Faculty-wise in the Year 1988–89

Faculty	Total enrolment	Enrolment of women	Percentage of women in total enrolment
Arts	1,591,012	687,069	43.2
Science	777,740	253,427	32.6
Commerce	848,804	173,957	20.5
Education	90,803	47,557	52.4
Engineering/Technology	181,604	11,263	6.2
Medicine	142,125	45,054	31.7
Law	228,979	20,024	8.7
Agriculture	51,323	2,503	4.9
Vet. Science	11,844	625	5.3
All faculties	3,947,922	1,251,491	31.7

Source : U.G.C., Annual Report for the year 1988-89.

In this context, referring to the education for women's equality, the National Policy on Education (1986) said "Education will be used as an agent of basic change in the status of women. In order to neutralise the accumulated distortions of the past there will be a well conceived edge in favour of women. The National Education system will play a positive, interventionist role in the empowerment of women. It will foster the development of new values through redesigned curricula, text books, training and orientation of teachers, decision makers and administrators and the active involvement of educational institutions. This will be an act of faith and social engineering".

Women's access and participation in higher education is determined by several factors. Participation of women in higher education can be examined from four major levels i.e., as students, teachers, researchers, administrators and decision makers.

Enrolment of Women In Higher Education

The enrolment of women students in higher education has been increasing rapidly since independence and has shown significant progress in the past decade. The enrolment of women students in Universities and colleges was around 43,000 in 1950 – 51 constituting about 10 per cent of the total enrolment.

Table 1.3 : Enrolment of Women Students in Higher Education

Year of Enrolment	Total enrolment	Number of women	Percentage
1982 – 83	31,33,093	8,80,156	28.1
1983 – 84	33,07,649	9,40,253	28.4
1984 – 85	34,04,096	9,,92,136	29.1
1985 – 86	36,05,029	10,67,484	29.6
1986 – 87	37,54,409	11,48,849	30.6
1987 – 88	39,10,828	12,24,089	31.3
1988 – 89	40,74,676	12,91,672	31.7
1989 – 90	42,46,878	13,67,495	32.2
1990 – 91	44,25,247	14,36,887	32.5
1991 - 92	46,11,107	15,12,270	32.8

Source : U.G.C. Annual Report 1991-92.

Factors Affecting Women Students Enrolment in Higher Education

Participation of women students in higher education is dependent on the access and other factors. The factors can be broadly classified into availability of institutions and infrastructural facilities, socio-cultural factors, financial problem and academic issues.

As far as the establishment of colleges and universities are concerned, adequate provisions have been made and there are exclusive colleges available in all parts of the country including rural and backward areas.

Except for small states in the far east, all the states have a large number of exclusive women's colleges. However, it must be pointed out that mere establishment of the college without adequate infrastructural facilities would not facilitate the enrolment of women students.

There is a general feeling that the availability of hostels for women students would improve their enrolment in institutions of higher education. The National policy on Education also said that efforts would be made to provide hostel facilities for women students to improve their enrolment in colleges. Besides hostels, college students need certain basic facilities for their overall development. These facilities include a common room, sports facilities, toilet facilities and provision for extra curricular activities. Many colleges located in rural and semi-urban areas do not possess these minimum basic amenities.

There are several social factors which hinder the enrolment of women in colleges. The most significant factor is the attitude of parents, especially the uneducated parents towards their daughters. They do not show interest in supporting the education of women as there is a general feeling that the women will eventually get married and go away to their in-laws house. Unless there are exclusive colleges for women, parents hesitate to send their daughters to co-educational colleges.

Among the economic factors, the college education is expensive for women from low and middle class families. Responding to this situation, some states like Gujarat and Rajasthan have made education totally free for all girls upto the doctoral level. The agrarian economy and a high women labour intensive situation prevailing in rural areas prevents more women students from going for college education. Another related factor is the unemployment of educated women which is also an important consideration in the enrolment of women in colleges.

The parameters of empowerment have been identified as building a positive self image and self confidence, developing ability to think critically, ensuring equal participation in the process of bringing about social change, providing for economic independence, encouraging group action in order to being about change in the society. All these are major challenges to higher education system in equipping women to derive maximum benefit to tackle the various issues.

It has been recognised that provision of educational opportunity is a vital component of the overall strategies of securing equity and social justice. Differential access of women to the educational system is a matter of concern. In order to rectify this situation and work towards the goal of advancing the status of women, several co-ordinated activities have to be undertaken and the national system has to play a positive and

Table 1.4 : State-wise and Location-wise Distribution of Women's College

State	No. of College			Total
	Urban	Semi Urban	Rural	
Andhra Pradesh	33	28	10	71
Arunachal Pradesh	0	0	0	0
Assam	7	3	3	13
Bihar	18	34	15	67
Delhi	17			17
Goa	1	0	0	1
Gujarat	11	7	2	20
Haryana	8	10	11	29
Himachal Pradesh	1	0	0	1
Jammu & Kashmir	3	4	2	9
Karnataka	23	19	1	43
Kerala	12	4	9	25
Madhya Pradesh	85	11	5	101
Maharashtra	26	6	5	37
Manipur	0	0	0	0
Meghalaya	1	0	0	1
Mizoram	1	0	0	1
Nagaland	0	0	0	0
Orissa	13	11	4	28
Punjab	27	12	17	56
Rajasthan	14	10	10	34
Sikkim	0	0	0	0
Tamil Nadu	40	18	10	68
Tripura	0	0	0	1
Uttar Pradesh	55	17	11	83
West Bengal	33	4	5	42
Total	**430**	**198**	**120**	**748**
Union Territories				**Total**
Andaman & Nicobar				0
Chandigarh				8
Daman &Diu				0
Lakshadweep				0
Pondicherry				2
Dadra & Nager Haveli				0
Total				**10**

interventionist role. In addition, efforts have to be made to adopt such value in society that give respect, dignity and recognition to women's education. Taking the perspective of human capital formation, it should be recognized that half of the available resources will be lost unless women are also included in this efforts as they constitute nearly fifty per cent of the population. Ensuring equal participation of women at all levels of higher education is fundamental to promote the status of women both for the well being of the individual and that of the society and the Nation at large.

In brief, it may be pointed out that while considerable efforts have gone into the enhancement of access to higher education opportunities for women students, there are still several issues that need to be taken to achieve the ultimate objective of empowering women. Conscious and deliberate efforts need to be made to provide opportunities for women students to fully actualize the potential available, to enable them to move smoothly into leadership positions of influence and decision making.

REFERENCES

1. Sharma. B.M., *Women and Education*, Commonwealth Publishers, New Delhi, 1994.
2. Murugkar. L., Development Goals and Women's Higher Education, *Journal of Higher Education* 8 (3) September, 1993.
3. Neera Desai, The Pattern of Higher Education of Women and Role of a Women's University, *Journal of Higher Education* 3 (1) Mansoon 1997.
4. Ahmad Karuna, Equality and Women's Higher Education, *Journal of Higher Education* Vol. 5 No. (1) Monsoon 1979.
5. Pearson. C.S., Shavlik. D.L. Touchton. J.G. *Educating the Majority*, Macmillan Publishers, London, 1989.

CHAPTER

2

Problems and Prospects of Aged Widows Challenges Before Women in the 21st Century

Dr. B. Suguna Reddy
Dr. G. Sandhya Rani

Introduction

Aging is a biological process experienced by mankind in all times. It is well known fact that life is a perennial process of growth right from infancy to old age through childhood and terminates with the death of an individual. Old age is a universal phenomenon. The optimum age fixed for treating a person as aged vary from country to country. The census of India stipulated 55 years as the age for treating a person aged whereas in USA, UK and other Western countries it ranges from 60 to 65 years. The number of old people is increasing all over the World both in absolute terms and in proportion to the population. The changes in the demographic structure of societies during the last few decades, particularly since the beginning of the 20th Century have made the aged a socially more visible section of the population. The recorded population of the 20.19 million aged in the 1951 census has been increased to 54.68 million in 1981 and is expected to increase to 75.70 million by 2001. surveys show that there are 50 million widows in India.

The life of aged widows full of tables of woe, is a fright and death seem to be the only escape. That is why each one with some grit and determination clutches on to her salvation. Abandoned by the families and ostracised by society a large number of widows are caught in an act of survival. The hollowness of society custom is a metaphor for their decadent state. Yet decade after decade tradition are maintained and the widow is associated with ill luck and held responsible for her husband's death and alienate herself from all family gatherings and any auspicious event. They have no one to support or speak for them and hence the dire need to rehabilitate them.

In the traditional Indian society the aged women occupied the high pedestal of prestige, power and privilege and enjoyed enhanced status and authority in the joint family system. But this has gradually declined from generation to generation. Urbanisation and industrialisation have struck the root values and at present, the Indian traditional to modern. Now-a-days the aged women are not given the same status and respect as they were in the days of yore and denied all the care and attention by their family members. The attitude of the children towards their aged parents too leaves a lot to be desired. The aged women specially the aged widows have become totally subservient on their children and are facing social, economic, health and other attendant problems.

Major Threats and Challenges Facing the Aged Widows

The images of aged widows particularly child widows have always evoked pity, awe and horror and are often perceived to be a burden and associated with ill luck.

- Isolated on the death of the husband, she is a parayadhan and has no rights in her parental home.
- Since Hindu marriage is only a sacrament and not a contract there is no compulsory registration of marriages. A deserted and separated women's plight is as bad as a widow.
- The life of a widow focuses a range of subjects and issues surrounding widowhood customs, the issue of an identity crisis and external relationship of widows.
- From time to time changes in society have influenced the status of widows and societal attitudes.
- The formidable challenge is inheritance laws, property rights, social security and identity with special reference to residence, maintenance, employment links between poverty and old age between mortality and old age.
- Facing a bleak feature these aged widows constitute a special concern group not only in the family but among the general population structure.

The present paper therefore makes an ardent bid at highlighting the social security measures and consequent avenues thereof for their rehabilitation.

The changing socio-economic scenario of our traditional society has altered the nature and dimension of the needs of different groups particularly of the aged widows. Owning to the dynamic socio-economic structure of the society traditional social security system can no longer provide comprehensive social support to the aged widows. Therefore, an urgent need to supplement the traditional family support system with infrastructure alternatives, community and social support systems entailing the aged widows to live with dignity and respect within the family.

Article 41 of the Constitution of India enjoins upon the State to make effective provision within the limits of its economic capacity and development for public assistance in case of unemployment, old age, sickness and disablement and in other areas of undeserved want. The responsibility for providing relief to the disabled and unemployed is provided in the State list of the Seventh Schedule of the Constitution of India. Social security and social insurance, employment and unemployment find a mention in the concurrent list of the Seventh Schedule. Thus, the constitution specially vest with the state and the Central Governments for providing social security and social insurance and public assistance in the cases of unemployment and disablement including obligations towards the old. In pursuance of these commitments of the State towards the welfare of the aged, the State Government have been providing old age pensions and maintaining old aged homes for the destitutes besides providing grants-in-aid to the voluntary organisations maintaining such homes.

The Ministry of Welfare has initiated a scheme of assistance to voluntary organisations for programmes relating to the aged. The scheme aims at providing physical, social, emotional, psychological and economic support to the aged with a view to help them to continue to be useful active members of the community. The primary object of the scheme is to encourage voluntary organisations of the elderly in particular to provide old age homes, day care centres, health services and non-institutional services for the ages.

Coming to the Rehabilitation of widow, they need a varied kind of services depending upon their age, health status, family background, educational level, occupational status and dependent children. Broadly speaking, aged widows can be rehabilitating through education, vocational training, employment and welfare programmes for dependent children. More specifically, they require help in the areas of education and vocational training, employment and self-employment opportunities, education of children, marriage of daughters, legal aid for inheritance of property and other matters, financial assistance for destitutes, residential institutions, counselling and guidance, community education to bring about change in the social attitude towards aged widows.

The Department of Women and Child Development under the Minstry of Human Resource Development has responsibility of providing services and opportunities for the welfare and development of women. The following are some of the centrally sponsored schemes having direct relevance of the rehabilitation of young and aged widows:

- Women's training centres for the rehabilitation of women in distress. This scheme introduced in 1977–78, envisages short term training of women in distress including widows in the age group of 18–50;
- Short stay homes for women and girls;
- Hostels for working women;
- Rural development schemes;
- Central Social Welfare Board (CSWB) programmes:
  (*a*) Socio-economic programmes
  (*b*) Condensed courses of education for adult women and vocational training programme
  (*c*) Voluntary action bureau
  (*d*) Family counselling centres
- State Government programmes.
  (*a*) Social and moral hygiene and after care programme
  (*b*) Rescue homes
  (*c*) Grant of marriage allowance to destitute widows for remarriage of daughters of destitute widows
  (*d*) Grant of marriage allowance towards marriage of daughter of destitute widows
  (*e*) Sanjay Gandhi Niradharan Yojana (Financial assistance to destitutes and widows)

Suggestions

- Family counselling centres should be established at the district level with the facilities of free legal aid for poor and aged widows.
- A wide publicity of Government schemes for the welfare of women and widows should be made through mass media.
- Community education is a much needed service as far as attitudinal changes towards widows are concerned. Voluntary

organisations, Mahila mandals and the professional social workers can play a significant role in the area of community education in this regard.

- The state and Central Governments should have a uniform policy of providing jobs to the widows of their employees. Relaxation in age and other requirements should be made in such cases.
- Considering the magnitude of the problems of young and aged widows, the programmes for their rehabilitation need to be expanded. The rehabilitation of widows should be taken up as a joint venture of the State and Central Governments, voluntary organisations and the community at large.

To sum up, the challenges faced by the aged widows are related to the general position of women and socio-economic conditions in the country unless the status of women in general is not raised and the socio-economic conditions are not substantially improved, the plight of aged widows will remain more or less static. If widows are not to become a liability in old age, prevention has to begin much earlier in their life cycle. Equal opportunities and access to education, employment, compensation for their home maker role, support in their family and maternal roles will go a long way in reducing vulnerability in old age. Voluntary help like imparting vocational training to aged widows or donating clothes and medicines are the kind of requirement they really need in the evening of their lives and thus a new dream perhaps unfolding. The State and Central Governments should play an active role in the socio-economic rehabilitation of aged widows. The current drive of the Government of India is to enhance the status of women, the challenges related to the aged widows need to be met for an appropriate solution.

REFERENCES

1. Kuppuswamy, B. *Social Change in India*, Vikas Publishing House, Delhi, 1972.
2. Prakash, G., *After Colonialism: Imperial Histories and Post-colonial Displacement*, Princeton University Press, Princeton, 1995.
3. Rani, K., Role, *Conflict in Working Wives*, Chetana Publications, New Delhi, 1976.
4. Dr.S. Ram (edt) *Women—Socio-economic Problems*, Commonwealth Publications, New Delhi, 2004.
5. Dr. S. Ram (edt) *Women and Social Change*, Commonwealth Publications, 2004.

CHAPTER

3

Effects of Modernisation on Joint Family System in India

Dr. G. Sandhya Rani
Dr. B. Suguna Reddy

Introduction

Man is a social being and society is a group of people living together practicing some customs and traditions which are common to every one. Family is a unit in the society which consists of father, mother, one or more children and some times near or distant relatives. It is the social structure on which entire society is built. In an individuals life the family occupies a very important place. Through it has been considered as a smallest unit of society it has its own impact on the overall development of an individual as well as society. Right from birth down to death family exerts a constant influence on the lives of individuals. It is the first social environment to which a child is exposed. But due to rapid growth of industries, urbanisation has taken place in the society. The impact of this change is very high on the traditional joint family system in our country. It has gradually disappeared and nuclear families came into emergence. Therefore, in this chapter we made an attempt to highlight the effects of 'modernisation' on joint family system in our country.

Family—Meaning and Definition

In Roman Law the word 'Family' is denoted as a group of producers and slaves and other servants as well as members connected by common descent or marriage. 'M.F. Nimkoff, defined that' family is more or less durable association of husband and wife with or without child, or of a man or woman alone, with children.

Significance of Family

Of all the social organizations large or small family is of the greatest sociological significance. It has a prestigious place in our social structure. As per one study, there is no human society in which some form for he family does not appear. Especially in Indian society family system has been deep rooted and it is very closely grounded in emotions and sentiments. Joint family system was the unique feature of Indian society. This family system has been built upon sentiments of love, affection sympathy, co-operation and friendship. A family system with all these features, influences the overall development of a child. It shapes the personality and moulds the character of its members. Similarly each member in the family feels certain responsibilities and duties to be discharged towards his/her family member. Infact, the smooth running of the family depends on how best the family members discharge their duties and responsibilities in co-ordination with the other members of the family.

Joint Family System

The joint family system is also known as undivided family. It normally consists of members who belong to three generations atleast. In our society it has constituted the basic social institution. The joint family system is also known as undivided family. It normally consists of members who belong to three generations atleast. The joint family system of the traditional type is no more found in India. Due to the stress and strain of time it has undergone drastic changes. It is slowly tending towards disintegration. Rapid industrialisation urbanisation, influence of western culture, development of means of transport and communications, enlightenment of women, over population, problem of housing etc., are mainly responsible for this change. The impact of industrialisation is the another reason for the disintegration of joint family system. Industrialisation which led to mechanisation of the industries, also helped for the widespread of urban areas. People in search of job opportunities started leaving their families to far away places. This again led to over crowdness of cities, high demand for jobs and existence of slum areas in urban centres etc. Infact, the joint family system is most suited to agricultural families. India, today is on the way to achieve economic development through rapid industrialisation. With the establishment of large scale industries, production of commodities also gone up. The goods produced by the village artisans cannot compete in quality or price with those produced in factories. Slowly the village industries suffer loss and after some time most of them closed down. The people depending on these occupations moved to urban areas in search of jobs. Further, the effect of Westernisation is very high on Indian society. India today has been greatly influenced in her social outlook by western thought and ideology. Modernisation has taken place in almost all aspects of human life. Traditional values and customs did not find place in this fast growing modem society.

Recent Trends in the Family System

The family system infact has undergone radical changes in the past half of 20th century. The industrial revolution and modernisation affected the existence of joint family system in our country. Urbanisation and modernisation very often go together. As a result of this the joint family system has become nuclear in nature, consisting of people belong to only two generations. The family structure, nature and functions have been altered. Socio-economic, cultural political and technological changes that are taking place in the society also helped to faster this type of change in the family system. In this way the fascinating modern life tempted people's mobility and have changed their life styles and values, which have adversely affected the existence of joint family system. Increasing literacy rate among women accompanied by their employment in offices and factories leave no time for them to take care of the elders at home. Further the high cost of living and changing priorities intern affect the families distribution of income in favour of the younger generations. As a result the vulnerability of the old people has been increasing and leading towards disorganisation of joint families. The changes that have taken place in the structure and functions of family system are highly significant and they shook the roots of traditional family system in Indian society. More over most of the functions of the family are modified due to the influence of modernisation. Most of the responsibilities of family members have been distributed to other institutions like voluntary organisations, old age homes, hospitals, nurseries, etc., since individuals have become very busy with modern life.

Conclusion

At present India is passing through a rapid social transformation and sustained economic development. Many important changes have been taking place in the social profiles of people. Joint family system, a peculiar characteristic feature of Indian society is gradually disappearing. The rapid industrialisation has led to the migration of villagers to urban areas in search of jobs has been associated with shortage of housing facilities in the cities which reflected on the existence of joint family system.

Increased incomes and influence of western culture led to the modernisation of life styles. This has contributed much to the disintegration of joint families. Further most of the important ties that bind all family members together began to loosen. Due to economic independence most of the people are preferring to live in nuclear families. The joint family system under modern influence is weakening. Thus under the effects of modernisation there is no scope for the existence of joint families. Therefore what is needed to day is to find out the ways by which the virtues of the joint family system can be retained.

REFERENCES

1. Cornish H.D., The *'Hindu Joint Family'*, Cambridge University, Press, 1915.
2. K.M. Kapadia, *'Marriage and Family in India'*, Oxford University Press. New Delhi, 1980.
3. A.V.P. Ranga Rao, *'Urbanization, Occupational Mobility and Social Integration'*, New Delhi; 1989.
4. C.N. Shankar Rao, *'Sociology'*, S.Chand and Company Ltd., Ram Nagar, New Delhi, 1997.

CHAPTER 4

Indian Women Political Participation *A Critical Review*

Dr. G. Sandhya Rani

Introduction

The principle of gender equality is enshrined in the Indian Constitution in its preamble, Fundamental Rights, Fundamental Duties and Directive Principles. The Constitution not only grants equality to women, but also empowers the State to adopt measures of positive discrimination in favour of women.

Within the frame work of a democratic policy our laws, development policies, plans and programmes have aimed at women's advancement in different spheres. From Fifth Five Year Plan (1974–78) onwards there has been a marked shift in the approach to women's issues from welfare to development. In recent years the empowerment of women has been recognized as the central issue in determining the status of women. The National Commission for Women set-up by an 'Act of Parliament in 1990' to safeguard the rights and legal entitlements of women. The 73rd and 74th amendments (1993) to the Constitution of India have provided for reservation of seats in the local bodies of panchayats and municipalities for women laying a strong foundation for their participation in decision making at the local levels.

Empowerment

Empowerment is a process, The process of gaining control over the self over ideology and the resources which determine power is called empowerment.

The outcome of empowerment is redistributing power. Political Empowerment means to enable women to be politically more conscious, active and articulate.

Till the end of the 19th century women in India were trusted under the weight of evil costumes. They were socially week, economically dependent and politically powerless. A common belief even with regards to women's voting behaviour is that they are influenced by the male members of their family. They did not venture to stand for elections as contestants. Therefore the role of women in the political scene was very much negligible.

Ever since the first general elections in 1952 women's voter's participation in various elections has been increasing. But their representations in National Parliament have never crossed 10 per cent.

After the introduction of 73rd and 74th amendments to Constitution, a similar provision for one third reservation to women in the Lok Sabha and in the Legislative Assemblies of the States by the way of 81st Constitutional Amendment is under consideration of the Parliament. These provisions are basically to create more consciousness among women and to strike a greater gender balance in the decision making.

Political Empowerment

The percentage of women voters has increased from 46.63 per cent in 1962 to 55.48 per cent in 1967 and gone down to 49.15 per cent in 1971, when there was a general decline in participation of all voters. Again in 1977, elections it has raised to 54.96 per cent there was a small decline in the percentage of women in 1980 elections (51.22 per cent). The states of Orissa, Bihar, Madhya Pradesh, Rajasthan, Uttar Pradesh and Himachal Pradesh which are generally known for the educational and social backwardness of women have had persistently low mobilization of women voters during elections. There is a close relationship between literacy and voting. Literacy always stimulates political awareness. The States and Union Territories where literary rates are high, the mobilization of women voters is also high. Politics in the present day society is mainly a skill controlled area. Persons skilled enough to control the environment are definitely active in politics. Generally women are politically, socially and economically weak. But women who are politically active have a different background than the inactive. In most cases their politicization occurs in the family which served as a backbone to enter in to the politics. This type of background always helps women to have a smooth entry in politics. Further, sometimes leisure increases outside contracts and involvement in activities outside ones family and home. Besides to this economic viability to upper class accounted for higher rates of political participation. Low social status due to low education and income result in lack of self confidence. Therefore, their participation in politics is comparatively less.

Factors such as literacy, family background, family economic, involvement in politics, social conditions, campaign strategy and their own personality play vital role in the case women candidates. The combined result of all these factors is that very few women are given party tickets or can fight elections as independent members and out of them naturally even fewer can get seats in legislature. The details of men and women who have contested and succeeded in Lok Sabha elections since 1952 to 1996 are furnished in the following Table.

Table 4.1 : Contestants in Lok Sabha Elections since 1952 to 1996

Year	Total Seats	Men		Women	
		Contested	Succeeded	Contested	Succeeded
1952	499	*NA	*NA	*NA	22
1957	500	1473	467	45	27
1962	503	1915	459	17	34
1967	523	2302	490	67	31
1971	521	2698	499	86	22
1977	544	2368	523	70	19
1980	544	4478	514	142	28
1984	544	5406	498	164	44
1989	517	5462	502	198	27
1991	544	8374	492	325	39
1996	544	13,353	504	599	40

Source: Data Compiled from different Newspapers. *NA – Not Available.

The above table reveals that the successful women candidates number in eleven Lok Sabha elections never crossed two digits. There were only 19 and 44 women in Sixth Lok Sabha and Eighth Lok Sabha respectively. This is the highest number of women out of eleven Lok Sabha Elections. Even in the recent 12th Lok Sabha elections, the number of women candidates reduced by 50 per cent when campared to 1996 Lok Sabha Elections. In 1996, 599 women contested on behalf of main political parties.

2004 – Indian Elections—Lok Sabha

1.	Andhra Pradesh	42 seats	279 candidates, 21 were women
2.	Maharashtra	48 seats	412 candidates, 29 were women
3.	Karnataka	28 seats	172 çandidates, 29 were women
4.	Gujarath	26 seats	151 candidates, 11 were women
5.	Goa	2 seats	16 candidates, 2 were women

Although Indian women played a major role in the Freedom Movement, it did not translate into continued participation in the public life in the Post-Independence era. On the contrary, many women withdraw in to their homes.

Situation Analysis

One is not born but rather is made to become a woman. It is civilization that creates this woman. Political empowerment of women is one of the core issues in determining the status of women.

1. There is a general notion that politics is a male prerogative and that women are not suitable for politics.
2. Women are not able to enter politics owing to patriarchal culture, reproductive functions, religious taboos, cultural constraints and so on.
3. Illiteracy is one of the impediments that is coming in the way of political empowerment of women.
4. Generally women are dependants and even employed women have no economic independence and no access to and control over productive forces.
5. Women have not been considered as powerful voters/party members by political parties. The conservative attitude of majority of political parties and the docile nature of women have also been preventing women from contesting the elections.
6. There is character assassination of women who join the politics. In a way this also prevents women from entering into politics.

Political Empowerment

1. Equal opportunity to women in political fields.
2. Change in social attitude—patriarchal culture—reproductive functions—cultural constraints.

3. Removal of Illiteracy.
4. Women should be considered as powerful voters party members and by contesters political parties.
5. Proper recognition to Women's capacities in political field.
6. Transparency in politics
7. Women should posses leadership qualities.
8. Among women also awareness about political field must be developed.
9. Proper recognition to Women's work and proper place in decision making bodies should be give to women.

Measures to be taken to Ensure Effective Participation of Women

1. With the help of Govt. Machinery, NGOs and Media, Universities, NSS Bureaus, awareness on politics must be created.
2. Education with regard to politics, procedures of the broader political system and about various development policies and programmes etc. along with Gender sensitization training should be provided.
3. Proper Training is to be given to the elected women representative and also to the interested women. Preparing Training modules, giving Training to the Trainers, identifying the needs etc is to be done.
4. And at local self-government level the constitution of all women panchayats by means of legislation as a transitional measure to break through the traditional attitudes in rural society is another measure by which effective participation of women can be ensured.
5. Finally, Reserving 50 per cent of seats for women at parliament and State assemblies on the basis of their percentage in population.
6. Now-a-days criminalization of politics is a widespread phenomenon. The prevailing situation rather prevents women from contesting elections.
7. Women have not been encouraged in politics on the pretext that they do not possess leadership qualities.
8. Generally there is a notion that women lack awareness, knowledge, self image and autonomy. As a result they have been discouraged from entering politics.

9. Further those who have entered politics and are managing the situations in different capacities have not been projected for their achievements but termed as concessions shown for being women.

The indifferent attitude of men and illiteracy and ignorance of women, patriarchal family structure have made women invisible in political sphere.

Women's Reservation Bill

Discrimination, exploitation and struggles have been part of women's life in all phases of their growth and in India too, it is no exception. As this gender bias goes on unabatedly despite India achieving 60 years of independence, it is time to think of a corrective mechanism i.e. a policy on reservation for women in the highest decision making bodies i.e. Parliament and State Assemblies.

A closer look at the facts reveals that women are impoverished in every sphere of activity not by choice but by systematic exclusions from policy options and protective measures. This discrimination and under valuation of women's work at the household level reflects in the work place too. The denial of entitlement to family's resources/deprivation of power positions in work places (in Government especially) are two glaring examples in the day-to-day lives of women. Neither social legislations nor landmark judgments on these have had any effect to render gender justice on this count.

From 1975 to 1995 the world has witnessed Four Major UN International Conferences on Women. Women through their collective vision in all these four conferences formulated Forward Looking Strategies and Platform of Action in all critical areas of concern. Unmindful of long distances that they have had to travel, transcending barriers of illiteracy, ethnicity, class, hierarchies (whether elites or from the grass roots). Women met at these Conferences in Mexico, Copenhagen, Nairobi and finally at Beijing to voice their concern for equal opportunities and built up several Global net works. In spite of such cumulative efforts by women over the last two decades politicians divide women's interest just to scuttle the passing of the currently proposed women's reservation bill. Not only for these politicians attempted to divide women but have also shown a sheer disrespect to the collective vision/global effort of women. Therefore the current Government in power should not allow such rested interests to neutralize the efforts of women/their concern but take full responsibility to pass the women's reservation bill in the parliament at least now without any further delay.

The objection of the political parties to this women's reservation bill is divided on caste/class lines. A question raised to them is what have these political parties done for women who have been victims of caste and class bias at the grass roots for ages? For instance, the women workers engages in the leather processing work or in the manual scavenging work are confined mostly to the schedule caste who are stratified as the lowest in the social hierarchy in India today. Have these political parties contributed anything to do away with such class/caste bias that has been a bane on our society for years? Then why should they bring up this issue on women's reservation bill in the parliament agenda? Why should they demand for the reservation within the quota of 33 1/3 per cent for women of OBC/SC/ST? Why do they want to waken women by further fragmenting then?

With absolutely no change in the living/working condition of OBC/SC/ST who still are living in despicable and / vulnerable conditions as ever, this new demand of the politicians towards their welfare does seem to be a ploy to scuttle the presentation of the current bill in the parliament.

It is an everyday occurrence that more and more new political parties are emerging like mushrooms either on single case lines or on the basis of sub-caste or division. When there is no understanding/unity between them where will they place the women's issue? Therefore, it is time for the political parties to understand clearly that the present bill for women's reservation is a provocation and outcome of the failure of the political parties to nominate women candidates in their own political party. Therefore now these political parties should ignore all differences and be magnanimous to support the bill in the parliament.

One of the land mark events in history during the women's movement particularly in the late 80s was the vision of former Prime Minister Shri Rajiv Gandhi who incorporated the 73rd and 74th amendment in the constitution providing 33 1/3rd seats in the Panchayats and Nagarpalikas for women. Several voluntary initiatives took it up then as a rare opportunity for themselves to reach the grass root helping and oriented several rural/urban women's group to avail of this political empowerment process. Today such orientation of voluntary initiatives has ensured women at the grass root a prominent position in the Panchayats and Nagarpalikas to take decisions for their own life and for their rural/urban communities on many issues of their concern be it on poverty or any other women issues. Despite women gaining 12 years of political experience through direct political participation in Panchayats and Nagarpalikas, why not they be given a chance to voice their concern in highest decision making body in Legislature and Parliament?

The tactics of delaying the women's bill and controversy surrounding the way it is being dealt have been symptomatic of the devaluation of democratic values in the country. If it has to happen that way, it is perfectly logical and democratic even to vote against the bill if it is inadequate in representing the views of the existing parliamentarians and the concerns of the political parties. But action of stalling a progressive legislation that no other country in the world has so far dared even to think of, is a clear indication of current day politician's scant respect for women.

There is also another argument that reservation of seats for women alone cannot solve the complex problem of gender injustice. But shouldn't this be the first step in gender equality that has been denied to them for years? Undoubtedly this proposed legislation on women's reservation in parliament requires political will and commitment on the part of the Government in command to stand unfettered during rough whether and pass the bill in the same form as envisaged by the visionaries who formulated the bill without any amendment. Otherwise woman have to start their struggle process all over again to achieve this 33 1/3 per cent reservation and occupy positions/powers.

Recently the Social Security Bill benefiting the working class on conditions of work and Livelihood Promotion Bill did not pass through the Parliament despite the creation of National Commission for Enterprises in the Unorganized Sector with enormous expenditure from the Government's exchequer to prepare for this bill. Unfortunately the Bill did not pass through because the bill was expected to benefit mainly the workers in the unorganized sector where 89 per cent of this sector is female entrants who out numbered the male workers. This is nothing but politics of gender and denial of gender justice. The Government in power should remain as a watchdog of women's interest and see that the bill is passed as a first effective step toward the political participation of women in the country's affairs.

Probable Reasons

The following are the for low participation of women in Lok Sabha Elections:

1. Generally, women have little interest in politics and want to confine themselves in the domestic circle;
2. Indian women traditional role demands their full attention to home, husband and family. The traditional norms, customs and social environment naturally result in a low level of political participation of women;

3. Women took active roles in freedom movement; they enjoyed the feeling of doing a sacred duty for the Independence of country. After Independence, they lost their links with the participation of the freedom struggle and are unable to locate their place in a competitive male dominated politics;
4. Political participation of women is influenced by psychological elements also. For Indian women, political activity is not on her priority list. They give top priority to their home;
5. The amount to be deposited has been raised to ₹ 10,000 recently;
6. The Bill which provides 33 per cent of reservation to women has not seen light till today;
7. Achieving success in elections has become the main criteria. Hence the main political parties also allotted less seats .to women candidates;
8. While there has been a substantial number of a new entrant among women, a large number of older ones have also dropped out from active participation in politics;
9. The other reasons which come in the way of women are economic dependency, increased expenses, low level of public life for women at all levels, threat of violence and character assassination.

Conclusion

Generally women are more likely to abstain from voting than men. This could be particularly expected in India, where3e social conventions and taboos, low economic states, illiteracy have to keep women more about from public activities. However, in recent years the level of awareness among women on the constitutional provisions given to them has increased. Further, there is a steady increase in the participation of women as voters. But still there is a need to mobilize women in large numbers into political main stream so as to rural and urban difference in voting participation of women in getting down. But most of the rural women are not aware of their rights to contest as candidates in elections. They are confining their roles as voters alone. The factors like increasing expenses of elections (because majority of women do not command any independent means), threat of violence and character assassination. The later two factors have recently developed and prevented women from contesting elections. Women's groups and women's organizations have to take a leads to reduce this type of unhealthy trends in politics. Apart from this, most of the women are not interested in politics due to a reason the 'politics' are no way useful for finding problems like price rise, water scarcity, housing problem, family welfare, etc. As long as this situation continues the proper involvement of women in political of India cannot be seen. Therefore necessary educational opportunities, raising political awareness and removal of threat of violence is necessary to ensure effective participation of women in politics.

REFERENCES

1. Baviskar, B.S., Impact of Women's participation in Local Governance in India in Jain, B.C. (ed), *Decentralization and Local Governance—Essay for George Mathew*, New Delhi, Orient Long Man, 2005.
2. Brilliant, F., *Women in Power*, New Delhi, Lancer Publication, 1987.
3. Chandrasekhar, B.K. (ed), *Panchayat Raj in India: Status Report 1999*, Task Force on Panchayat Raj, New Delhi, Rajiv Gandhi Foundation, March, 2000.
4. Chetana Kalbaugh, (Edt), *'Women and Development'* Vol. 4, Discovery Publishing House, New Delhi, 1991.
5. Govt. of India, *Census of India, 2001*, New Delhi.
6. Manikyamba, P., *Role of Women in Panahcyat Raj Structures*, New Delhi, Gyan Publishing House, 1989.
7. Mehta, G.S., *Participation of Women in Panchayat Raj System*, New Delhi, Kanishka Publishers, 2002.
8. Neera Desai, M. Krishna Raj, *'Women and Society in India'*, Ajanta Publications (India) Delhi, 1990.
9. Newpaper Reports – *The Hindu, Indian Express.*
10. Panchayat Raj updates.
11. Ruth Alsup and Brayn Kurey, *Local Organizations and Decentralized Development*, Washington, The World Bank, 2005, p.4.
12. Sharma, B.M. (Ed), *'Women and Education'*, Global Education Series-6, Commonwealth Publishers, New Delhi.
13. Towards Equality, *Report of the Committee on the Status of Women*, Government of India, 1994.

CHAPTER 5

Mobilising for Change Possibilities and Challenges– Mathamma Cult in Chittoor District of Andhra Pradesh

Dr. G. Sandhya Rani
Dr. B. Suguna Reddy

Introduction

Any hierarchal system of dominance and subordination victimises the weaker sections, and this victimisation can vary from subtle pressures through the power of ideology and socialisation or open brutal oppression. The aim is always to induce the subordinate group to comply with the wishes of the stronger.

Violence always accompanies power. It is committed to prove or feel a sense of power. Violence against women takes many forms and these forms vary between cultures, regions or religious communities in the world. Women have been the victims of violence all through the ages, there are various types of violences which are specifically directed at women : rape, sexual harassment, sexual exploitation and abuse as in prostitution domestic violence and pornography. All these forms of violence have increased greatly in recent years. 'Devadasi system' or 'Mahathmma cult' is one such form of violence against women existing even in this modern society.

Therefore in this chapter an attempt has been made to draw attention on the prevalence of Mathamma cult in chittoor district of Andhra Pradesh and some recommendations have also been given at the end of the chapter to improve the status of mathammas and for the removal of this uncivilized practice from the society.

Indian society is in transition period from traditional to modern. With the advent of industrialization and modern technology, the social transformation has taken rapid strides in many aspects of human life. But the existence of certain systems like 'Mathamma' makes us to think about the direction of our progress either backward of forward? The culture of dedicating girls to temples was once upon a time a common practice among a certain class of people. Even in this computer age also this system existing in various forms. This is still prevalent among some scheduled castes who offer their very young girls to the temple. The victims of Mathamma cult are inducted to prostitution with social sanction.

The female dancers and singers attached to temples are generally referred to by the term 'devadasis' which literally means 'female slaves of the deity'. They are not allowed to marry any mortal man and their dedication to temple service is considered as constituting a marriage with the deity. The cult of dedicating girls to temple is prevailing all over India in different forms and names such such as 'Maharis' in Kerala, 'Natis' in Assam 'Murali' in Maharashtra, 'Bogams' in Andhra Pradesh and 'Jogatis' 'Basavis' in Karnataka 'Thevardiyar' in Tamil Nadu.

The slaves of deities were said to be experts in music and dance in mediaeval period. As centuries passed their services shifted from gods to earthly gods and lords. The women so dedicated to the deity as Devadasis, usually lead a life of prostitute with religious sanction.

According to an estimation, girls dedicated as Devadasis to Yellamma, Hanuman, Khandoba temple in Maharastra—Karnataks border area number about 2.5 lakhs. Majority of them belong of the lowest strata of the society. These girls are leading miserable lives and looked down by the society. They are sexually exploited and not eligible for marriage.

In India, Hindu society is organized on the basis of a unique form of social stratification called 'caste'. The caste is all pervasive and it plays an active role in all spheres of life. It is common knowledge that one's birth in a particular family belonging to a particular caste. This system has successfully compartmentalized families in groups which are hierarchically organized with Brahmins at the apex and the untouchables who are now purity, pollution, occupation etc. have been placed in between these two extreme points in the social hierarchy.

In this system the highest group enjoyed all the privileges while the lowest and near lowest suffered all the disadvantages and they virtually became slaves of the upper and cleaner castes. The Constitution of India, in its 'Directive Principles of State Policy' contained in Article 46 emphasises, that "the state shall promote with special care the educational and economic interest of the weaker sections of the people and in particular of the Scheduled Caste (SCs) and the Schedule Tribes (STs) and shall protect them from social injustice and all forms of exploitation". In spite of all this it is observed that the developmental a programmes initiated by Government have not reached the SC's to the desired extent, part because of defective implementation of the programmes, prevailing social structure and evils in villages and lack of programme awareness and the absence of united and effective leadership among them. Further the traditional rivalries and rites among the different castes within SC category have been affecting the implementation of developmental programmes resulting in the flow of benefits to the much politicized and organized castes among them.

In Andhra Pradesh the practice of Mahathamma cult is still existing intensively in 14 district out of 23 districts. As per the study conducted in 1999 there were 16,799 Mathammas in Andhra Pradesh out of which 364 were living 19 mandals (14 in Tirupati division, 4 in Chittoor Division) of Chittoor district. For this present study, Tirupati, mandal has been taken. It is interesting to note that the age composition of Mathammas range between few months babies to 60-year old women. Out of 60 Mathammas idenitified in this area 25 per cent in the age group of 15 to 20 years. Another 20 per cent are in the age group of 10 to 15 years and some of them are going to schools.

With regard to caste composition though majority of Mathammas belong to Scheduled caste community, other caste people also have the practice of dedicating their young girls to god or goddess. Especially, tribal community people and Backward caste people have more faith on the system of Mathamma when compared to other castes. In this area 50 per cent of Mathammas belong to SC caste, 20 per cent STs and 20 per cent Backward Castes (BCs) and the remaining 10 per cent belong to Other Caste (OCs).

Education is till beyond the reach of most of Mathammas. Young Mathammas who are now attending schools also not keen about their continuation of education. Out of 364 Mathammas 40 per cent are illiterates. 18 per cent have studied up to primary school i.e., 5th standard and 22 per cent of Mathamma are studying at different levels of high school education and no single mathamma is found with college education. This is only because of the negative and unfavourable reaction of the society towards these girls. Hence they are dropping even in between of their studies without completing.

When the occupational structure of the Mathammas is observed, most of them are working as child labourers. Mathammas have to get their own income for their own maintence and for their dependants like father, mother brother, children etc. Young and elderly Mathammas though occupied in the activities like agricultural labourers, dancing at celebrations, maintaining petty businesses, sheep rearing, begging and finally prostitution. Their regular income never exceed ₹ 20 per day.

In this Mathamma cult the crucial component is that dedicated Mathammas are not supposed to marry any person. In the beginning they are treated with high social respect like inviting them for various women celebrations as a good sign. But in the course of time, caste heads and heads of the shephered community are having control over the mathammas, and also use to tie up the sacred thread around their neck. Even though, mathammas are not legally married to any one, they are permitted to live and maintain matronage with others. Since the community recognized the Mathammas as a community property, the entire community has control over them. So, the unwritten cultural practice is so much accepted and internalized within the society.

When the reasons for dedication of girls by parents is observed it revealed interesting results. Most of the reasons are related with health problems and there is no single case of hereditary. Parents usually dedicate their girls during the age of a month baby to 7 to 8 years. Nearly 80 per cent of dedications took place at the age of below one year. The health reasons vary from person to person ; Even for simple health problems like cold, cough and fever, abdomen pain, jaundice, chicken pox, illness of family members, fits, unable to suck milk, wounds etc. they dedicate girls to God. Therefore proper health education is an immediate necessity especially to the Dalit women.

In the Mathammas community, most important event is celebrating Mathamma festival. In this district, it is usually celebrated during the months of April to June. Villagers collect donations to celebrate Mathamma festival. In some other villages, when they overcome the natural and other critical situation then only they celebrate the Mathamma festival. By dancing in these festivals mathammas would get an amount of ₹ 2000 to ₹ 20,000 as well as kind depending upon the skill and grace of dance. They have to maintain their lives with these things throughout the year.

Caste Studies: For clear understanding of socio-economic position of Mathammas in Chittoor District, two case studies are presented here:

Case—I

Case—I is a daughter of one farmer who lives in Tirupati rural mandal. He offered his daughter to Goddess Mathamma when the girl was nine months old. Then this girl suffered with small pox. Her parents prayed

Mathamma and took an Oath to dedicate the girl to the Goddess. When this girl reached 10 years, her parents performed pooja and tied sacred thread around her neck. Since then this girl became village property and everybody has a right on her.

She gave birth to two children but nobody knows about their father. Her father died and her mother is living with her. She is earning for her livelihood by performing dances and working on daily wages. Her sons are going to school. But she expressed that she is leading a pathetic life without any one's care and concern.

Case—II

Case—II refers to the story of a young Mathamma who is dedicated by the parents when she was ill during her childhood days. She got married at the age of 15 years with a person who was working as watchman. They led married life for some years. She got two children, suddenly her husband become indifferent towards family and stopped coming to home. He underwent another marriage forced by his relatives and parents. She tried her best to bring him back to home but in vain. He left his job and went to some other village along with his new wife. Now, this women is working in the fields of others as labourer and rearing her children. The village people are against to her and kept them isolated. But the village men continued to use her to fulfill their lust and she is also forced to dance during Mathamma festivals.

In this context, the following crucial issues arise for serious discussion:

- To consider the rationale behind the entire system of Mathamma, the superstitions surrounding it and also the exploitation which has driven hundreds and thousands of women into this deplorable state;
- To explore the possibilities of weaning mathammas from this shameful and dreadful life and rehabilitate them in a more honourable and humanistic way;
- To nip the problem in the bud and present future deterioration and add to the dignity of womanhood and altogether eradicate this social evil from our soil.

The above issues call for systematic approval to educate the parents and also the exploter and exploited. The task ahead is stupendous and requires the attention of the government, voluntary organisations and social workers. Strategies have to be worked out to bring about a total change and reform so that the damage already done may be rectified.

As this system is in some measure spread out in almost all the districts of Andhra Pradesh, it becomes absolutely necessary that legislative measures are to be stringently initiated to wean the women away from falling a piety to this custom.

Recommendations

1. Sincere and committed efforts should be initiated to remove this kind of Mathamma systems from the society.
2. Proper Health education, awareness about various Governmental programmes must be given.
3. Especially Dalit community people must be given economic and social support for not allowing their girl children to become preys of this age old customs.
4. For the Mathammas who are already dedicated should be provided rehabilitation with the help of governmental and non-governmental agencies.
5. Interested child and young Mathammas must be given education free of cost.
6. Local NGO's should organize awareness camps for Dalit women, and general public in order to break through the cultural myth in the society.
7. As the Mathammas are suffering from ill-health and severe gynic problems, health camps should be organized and treatment must be given to the diseases such as STD, Aids etc.,
8. Local NGO's should organize counselling with Mathammas and their men and persuade them to have a legal marriage in order to have a good and normal social life.

Conclusion

In India, incidentally, the influence of modernization is overshadowed by religious rites and values. Progressive legislations have prohibited certain religious practices by branding them as social evils. In this 21st century also, when the entire world is moving towards scientific and technological revolution on the other side of the society it is still in primitive stage with regard to culture and religious aspects. Society, religion and blind beliefs and meaningless superstitions are dominating and degrading the human values. The existence of 'Mathamma cult' is the best example for such kind of systems.

With some honourable expectations even today these beliefs are found to be in practice among Hindus especially among Dalits. As long as such beliefs persist and customs revolve around women, so long will exploitative systems continue to crush Indian women. Hundreds of girls children will be punished as victims of the 'Mathamma' cult.

By providing alternative measure we could bring change in their life styles. Poverty, ignorance and inability force the parents to other their child as mathamma. By making them aware about the miserable life of mathammas we can bring change in the attitudes of the people. Imparting education and training in traditional and not traditional occupations definitely leads towards economic stability. Economic stability leads towards an increase in the social as well as educational status. A raise in the quality of life attitvdiual change among people. Therefore necessary measures are to be taken by the authorities concerned, for providing opportunities to improve the socio-economic and health status of people. Then alone our Indian society will come out of the barbarious practice of Mathamma cult.

REFERENCES

Books

1. *Encyclopaedia of Religion and Ethics, 1930 Vol-1* (Ed) James Hastings, Second Impression T&T clark Edinburgh.
2. Chandra Mouli V. *'Jogin' : Girl Child Labour Studies,* Sterling Publishers Pvt. Ltd. New Delhi, 1992.
3. Dubois, Abbe, J.A. *'Hindu Manners, Customs and Ceremonies'*, Third Print Asian Educational Services, New Delhi, 1985.
4. Gurumurthy, K:G., *'Devadasi Custom in Peasant Context in India Peasantry'*, B.R. Publishing Corporation. Delhi, 1982.
5. Krishan Reddy B, and Sujana Mallika. J, 'Welfare Measures for the Emancipation of Basavis of Kurnool District of Andhra Pradesh, in Chakrapani.C and Vijayakumari.S (ed) *'Changing Status and Role of Women in Indian Society'*, M.D. Publications Pvt Ltd, New Delhi, 1994.
6. Punekar, S.D and Kamala Rao, *'A Study of Prostitutes in Bombay'*, Allied Publishers Ltd. Bombay, 1962.
7. Surya Kumari. A "The Temple in Andra Desa, Siddhartha Publishing House to Use, Madhurai 1982.
8. Thomas. P. 'Indian Women through Ages', Asia publishing House, New York 1964.

Journals

9. Aloka Parasher and Usha Naik 'Temple Girls of Mediaeval Karnataks'. *The Indian Economic and Social History Review,* No. 1, 1986.
10. Gurumurthy, K.G., *'Devadasi Custom',* March of Karnataka, Bangalore, Karnataka Government Publication Division, August, Vol. XXI, No. 8. 1983.
11. Patil, B.R. *'The Devadasis', The Indian Journal of Social Work,* Vol. XXXC, No. 4, 1975.
12. Sadasivan. K, *'Origin of the Devadasi System',* South Indian History Congress, Proceedings of the Third Annual Conference, 1982.
13. Shan, Jyotsna, H, 'Devadasis in India', *Social Welfare,* March, Vol. 18, No. 12,1972.

CHAPTER 6

Consequences of Malnutrition on Mother and Child Future Strategies

A. Venkamma
Dr. G. Sandhya Rani

Introduction

In any community, mothers and children constitute a priority group. They comprise approximately 70 per cent of the population of the developing countries. In India, women of child bearing age (15 – 44 years) constitute 19 per cent and children under 15 years of age about 40 per cent of the total population. Together they constitute nearly 59 per cent of the population (Park, 1997).

Mothers and children not only constitute a large group but also a 'vulnerable' segment. This vulnerability is connected with child-bearing in the case of women and growth and development and survival in the case of infant and children. It is evident from the literature that infant, child, maternal mortality rates are higher in developing countries. Further, much of sickness and mortality among mothers and children is largely preventable. By improving the health of mother and children, we can contribute to the health of the population and the society. The problems affecting the health of mother and child are multifactorial. However, the main health problems affecting the health of mother and child are malnutrition, infection, and the consequences of unregulated fertility besides poor health services. Hence, in the present chapter an attempt has been made to understand the consequences of malnutrition on mother and child and to suggest the suitable preventive measure in order to improve their nutritional status.

Consequences of Malnutrition

1. Pregnancy

The well-known fact that for most of women in Third world, pregnancy and lactation are the most stressful periods. During this period the mother requires additional nutrients requirement for the babies well-being. Some of the consequence of under nutrition on the mother are:

(*i*) Chronic deprivation of food during the period of growth and development, results in short stature particularly among the adolescent pregnant girls;

(*ii*) A high incidence of micro nutrient deficiency has been observed among the women. These are markedly aggravated during pregnancy. Some of the common micro nutrient deficiencies are anaemia, angular stomatitis, glossities etc.;

(*iii*) Maternal malnutrition is a major determinant of high maternal mortality;

(*iv*) In recent years, evidence has accumulated to demonstrate an impairment in placental function in maternal malnutrition;

(*v*) Foetal wastage has been observed due to maternal malnutrition.

2. Foetus

It is known that during the antenatal period the foetus is a part of mother. During this period the foetus obtains all the building materials and oxygen from the mother's blood. Hence, the child health is closely related to maternal health. If the pregnant mother does not take good diet it has severe impact on the development of foetus. The adverse effects of maternal malnutrition on the foetus are :

(*i*) The dietary deficiency contribute to higher incidence of congenital malformations particularly neural defects due to the deficiency of folic acid;

(*ii*) Low birth weight babies are born to mother;

(*iii*) A high incidence of perinatal deaths is observed in various studies;

(*iv*) The early infants suffer from lower values for several nutrients are observed among the foetus born to the poor income group mothers of India (for example Iron deficiency, deficiency of folic acid, B_{12}, Vitamin A);

(*v*) Affects the brain development and poor mental function.

3. *Lactation*

The impact of undernourished women particularly energy and protein leads to poor lactation performance and it increases infant mortality among them.

4. *Consequences of malnutrition on child*

Malnutrition is the most widespread condition affecting the health of children. Malnutrition makes the child more susceptible to infection, recovering is slower and mortality is higher. Undernourished children do not grow to their full potential of physical and mental abilities. Malnutrition in infancy and childhood leads to stunted growth. It also manifests by clinical signs of micronutrient and vitamin deficiencies. Some of the specific nutritional deficiencies are:

(a) Protein energy malnutrition (PEM)

Protein-energy malnutrition has been identified as a major health and nutrition problem in India. It occur particularly among children under 5 years of age belonging to the poor underprivileged communities. This condition is particularly serious during the post weaning stage and often is associated with infection. Apart from contributing to high child mortality, severe malnutrition can lead to permanent sequelae those who survive. These include stunted growth, poor learning abilities and reduced work performance. Kwashiorkor, Marasmus are some the problems associated with the PEM.

(b) Micro nutritional malnutrition

It refers to group of conditions caused by deficiency of vitamins and minerals. It is estimated that about 2 billion people affected by micro nutrient malnutrition. To mention a few Vitamin A deficiency is still the most common causes of childhood blindness worldwide. Iodine deficiency can cause goitre, cretinism and brain damage and anaemia results from insufficient Iron intake.

Future Strategies for Improving the Nutritional Status of Mother and Child

In order to avoid the consequences of malnutrition on mother and child the following strategies are to be employed:

(*i*) Maintenance of Balanced diet is necessary to safeguard the population from nutritional deficiencies. Balanced diets formulated by the ICMS (1990) are given in table 6.1 for mother and child;

Table 6.1 : Recommended Dietary Intakes for Women, Infant and Child (ICMR – 1990)

Group	Particulars	Body Weight in Kg.	Net energy Kcal / d	Protein g / d	Fat g / d	Calcium mg / d	Iron mg / d	Vit. A. mg / d		Thiamin mg / d	Ribo-flavin	Nicotinic kacid mg / d	Phyrid-oxin mg / d	Ascor-bic acid mg / d	Folic acid	Vit. B – 12
								Retinol	B-carotene							
Woman	Sedentary		1875							0.9	. 1.1	12				
	Moderate work	50.0	2225	50	20	400	30	600	2400	1.1	1.3	14	2	40	100	1
	Heavy Work		2925							1.2	1.5	16				
	Pregnant woman	50.0	+300	15	30	1000	38	600	2400	+0.2	+0.2	+2	2.5	40	400	1
	Lactation 0-6 months		550	+25		1000	30	950	3800	+0.3	+0.3	+4		80	150	1.5
	0–12 months	50.0	+400	+18	45				.	+0.2	+0.2	+3	2.5			
Infants	0–6 months	5.4	108 /kg	2.05 /kg		500		350	1200	55 mg/ kg	65 mg/ kg	710 mg/ kg	0.1	25	25	0.2
	0–12 months	8.6	98/ kg	1.65/ kg						50 mg/ kg	60 mg/ kg	650 mg/ kg	0.4			
Children	1–3 years	12.2	1240	22		.	12	400		0.6	0.7	8			30	
	4–6 years	19.0	1690	30	25	400	18	400	1600	0.9	1	11	0.9		40	0.2.
	7–9 years	26.9	1950	41			26	600	2400	1.0	1.2	13	1.6	40	60	1.0

(*ii*) Fortification and enrichment of food to improve nutritional quality of the population;

(*iii*) Avoidance of multiple pregnancies;

(*iv*) Supplementary feeding programmes should be encouraged. For example Iron and Folic acid supplementation can tackle the nutritional anaemia among the women and young children;

(*v*) Immunization to the child and TT to the mother during pregnancy;

(*vi*) Improvement of environmental sanitation;

(*vii*) Provision of clean drinking water;

(*viii*) Hygienic food;

(*ix*) Health education;

(*x*) Nutrition education;

(*xi*) The Integrated Child Development Schemes provide a package of services to control nutrition and health problems of the child;

(*xii*) Encouraging mothers to give breast-feeding.

Conclusion

It is clear from the above that the child health is closely related to maternal health. A healthy mother brings forth a healthy child. Hence, good nutrition is required for the promotion, protection and maintenance of health in mother and child and ultimately it contributes the well-being of the society.

REFERENCES

1. ICMR, *Recommended Dietary Intakes of Indians*, Indian Council of Medical Research, New Delhi, 1990.
2. Mahtab S. Bamji, *Text Book of Human Nutrition*, Oxford and IBH Publishing Company Pvt. Ltd., New Delhi, 1998.
3. Park, K., Park's *Text Book of Preventive and Social Medicine*, M/s Banarasidas Bhanot Publishers, Jabalpur, 1997.

CHAPTER

7

Status and Position of Women in the Family
Its Impact on Industrialization and Urbanization

Dr. B. Suguna Reddy
Dr. G. Sandhya Rani

Introduction

This chapter attempts to delineate the impact of industrialization and urbanization on the status and position of women in the family.

Industrialization and Urbanization

Urbanization is no longer unique only to certain regions, rather it has become a global phenomenon. The process of urbanization is commonly viewed as an inevitable consequence of general progress in Science and Technology. The rapid growth of towns and cities has become one of the striking features of development in the history of mankind. The urbanization process is the sequel of industrialization. After independence, the Government of India has paid special attention to industrial growth. As a result of fast industrialization, the process of urbanization too is growing fast which is having deep impact upon the society. It is on account of industrialization that there is a progressive rise in the population of Indian cities. Whatever social impact is due to urbanization is indirectly due to industrialization. Therefore, the impact of industrialization and the impact of urbanization are in fact, the facts of the same underlying process, namely industrialization.

Urbanization as a Factor of Social Change

Social change is a term used to describe variations in, or modifications of, any aspect of social process, social patterns, social interaction, or social organization. It is a change in the institutional and normative structure of society.

Urbanization is a world-wide process and it is considered not only as an index of economic development, but also as on important factor of social change. Modern society is gradually transforming into an urbanized society. Social organization of city is consistently getting modified in response to new needs and challenges. In fact the word city has been synonymous with 'Modern' and 'New'. The new ways of life originating in city become the dominant modes of life. Urbanization as a process can be said to have significant consequences for social change. Urbanization and urbanism in terms of structural and organisational aspects have induced the process of social change. In Indian context, the rapid urbanization process is looked among the other changes, that caste system will change into class system, nuclear families will emerge from joint family and religion will become highly secularised. Further, the process of urbanization will bring widespread social change in a society.

Urbanization with Reference to Family Structure and Functions

Two vital factors which intervene with urbanization may dramatically affect the 'Family life'. These are industrialization and modernization. Industrialization has contributed to the growth of cities and benefited from it. Modernization seems to be acquired through encounter with routine procedures of bureaucracy. One of the most far reaching effects of urbanization has been one of the structure of family. Assessing the impact of urbanization on family life is a complex task, because the growth of city is inextricably intertwined with industrialization and modernization. Changes in the population size, density and heterogeneity have varied effects upon family structure. The people who migrate from rural areas are influenced by urban environment in the form of acquisition of more education, higher income, devoid of the influence of old folk-religion and eventually identifying themselves with the 'Nation' than with villages they hail from. The reliance upon the industrial system disrupts the traditional extended family in two ways, namely: (*i*) the nuclear family becomes distinct from the extended family net-work; and (*ii*) the power of the nuclear units over its members decline, as women enter labour force and children find that their parents have greater status than in villages and the young people enjoy considerable freedom, develop their careers and choose their life partners.

As a result of twin effects of industrialization and urbanization, the function of the family has also considerably changed compared to present day, the family had much more functions in the past. Mutual interdependence of the family members is changed in the urban environment. Cooperative labour becomes no longer essential. Instead of working together, males seek out in widely varying locations and bring individual comparisons in the earning capacities of the family members. The traditional succession of sons to father's occupation is disrupted in the city and they are forced to find out alternate employment. Traditionally, an Indian family used to be centre of birth, rearing and education of children. The function of socialization is also performed by the family members. But in the new urban-industrial oriented society, the family is not required to perform these functions. It may be said that the functions and role of modern family are more formal than real. Urbanization coupled with industrialization has shattering effects on joint families. Traditionally, the family in India has been oriented towards agricultural occupations which encourage the joint or extended family structure. The migration of people to urban areas distorts the very basis of joint family system upsetting the very economic stability. Further, due to rapid industrialization, the technology of agriculture changes with the result, agriculture becomes commercialised, rural family undergoes changes a kin to the urban family. Besides, in urban areas, the family trades and professions have almost been eliminated. The members of the family may differ widely in socio-economic levels which gives scope for individualism. As a consequence thereof, the joint family system has been virtually eliminated in the cities. Although the cultural pull of a tradition of extended families is still strong, the hold is no longer absolute.

Change in the Status and Functions of Women

In the past, the status enjoyed by women in Indian society was at a very low ebb from socio-economic stand-points. The woman enjoyed no freedom. Some times, her role has been dual looking after the family and contribution wherever possible to the earning capacity of the family. The extent and nature of contribution has varied from time to time, and society to society. In Indian, to day, one sees hotch-potch in the women's role, her relation to environment which is characteristic of a society in transition from tradition to modernity. Industrialization has however brought about new phenomenon. Except the difference in biological roles, the equality of sexes has been well established. The woman is no more an object adoration, pleasure and joy; she is no more subservient to her master-husband, but has an individuality of her own and can play an independent role as a member of the society. Rise of women's movements resulted in attack on the privileged position of men, specially in economic and political roles. Not only this, the increasing nature of demands in families, loss of security provided by joint or extended family, individualisation of earnings, nuclearisation of families and the inability of only one person in many cases to earn enough for the whole family has drawn out the woman from the nursery and kitchen to the world outside home to study and work shoulder to shoulder with men. In free India it is seen that women have been entering salaried, remunerative occupations and professions in increasing numbers.

With the advent of industrialization and urbanization, the role of women in the family has considerably changed. On the one hand, the city and industry provides ample scope for employment, and on the other, it has certain effects on the status of women in the family. The migration of families from the tradition oriented villages and subsistence agriculture to urban areas for wage employment has a telling effect on the status of women. In village context, both men and women participated in the production process and had valued roles. However, these traditional agriculture and domestic roles have started to decline in value with growth urban-industrial emphasis. In cities, most of the women take up jobs and provide the needed economic generation to maintain their family status, but a large chunk of women found fulfilment and satisfaction in their work through careers that were intrinsically rewarding. Women are therefore, becoming independent economically. Their status and respect in society has therefore improved effectively. In modern times women consider themselves equal, at times superior to men. As a result of this feeling many women tend to abstain from marrying. The employment of women further necessitates the redefinition of household roles. While socialization of children could be affected adversely by the employment of mother, there is an increasing evidence that working per-se does not have an adverse effect. The role of the husband in the family is perhaps directly influenced by urban life. In all levels of society, the husband is a part-time member of the family, who must seek some how integrate the work with demands of the family life.

Conclusion

In the light of the above discussion, it may be concluded that the twin process of urbanization and industrialization have brought the nation into an era from which there was no return. The urbanization process has brought a revolutionary change in the whole process of social life. In modern time the family has also lost its character of economically productive agency and has turned as a consumer unit. These changes have not only altered the family structure and functions, but also have affected its composition. There are unmistakable signs that traditional conceptions regarding the place and role of women are slowly changing in contemporary Indian society. Increasing opportunities for modern education, greater geographical and social mobility and the emergence of new economic patterns are in the main responsible for this trend. Women has become aware of the fact that if she wishes to be independent and to contribute to the well-being of her family she has to become a wage earner. By working she can promote not only the family welfare, but can attain personal status and an independent social standing. It may be critically pointed out that women are gradually realising that they have personalities of their own, and that their mission in life does not end with good wives and mothers, but also in realising that they are all members of the civic community and of the body-politic.

REFERENCES

1. Dept.of Social Welfare, Govt. of India, *Report of the Committee on Status of Women in India towards Equality*, New Delhi, 1974.
2. Good W.J., *World Revolution and Family Pattern*, Collier Macmillan, London, 1963.
3. Hate, C.A., *Changing Status of Women in Post-independence India*, Allied Publications, Bombay, 1970.
4. Indrani Chatterjee, *Gender Slavery and Law in Colonial India*, Oxford University Press, New Delhi, 1999.
5. Kuppuswamy, B., *Social Change in India*, Vikas Publishing House, Delhi, 1972.
6. Motilal Banarasidas, *The Position of Women in Hindu Civilisation*, Varanasi, 1962.
7. Prakash, G., *After Colonialism: Imperial Histories and Post-colonial Displacement*, Princeton University Press, Princeton, 1995.

CHAPTER

8

Life Skills Education for Gender Empowerment During Adolescence *Strategies*

Dr. K. Anuradha
Dr. N. Rajani

Introduction

Adolescents, belonging to the age group 10-19 years constitute 22.8 per cent of India's population. They are going to represent the future of the country and their predicaments cannot be easily overlooked. Within the paradigm of population and development related issues, the role of adolescents in general and adolescent girls in particular cannot be overlooked.

'Adolescence' is a crucial period for healthy development in both psychological and physical terms. During this period, attitudes, beliefs and values tend to settle in to a pattern, out of which emerge the shape and direction of one's life-style. Physical changes emerge during this period pose additional complications to adolescent girls' status in society. Across the developing world, adolescents only recently have been recognized as a distinct group with needs that differ from those of adults or children. In India, the health needs and rights of adolescent girls, particularly those who are unmarried, are inadequately addressed. Social norms and restrictions deprive adolescents of knowledge and access to information about their rights and their bodies, leaving them unable to make informed reproductive health choices. If they become pregnant, girls bear the consequences of it to a much greater extent than boys. In the short term, pregnant school girls and unmarried teenage mothers are often forced to drop out of school, and relations with their parents and guardians may become severely strained. In the long term, the lower level of education reduces their economic prospects. In some settings, girls who have been sexually abused are more likely to become pregnant at an early age.

Defining Life Skills

Skills development has formed a part of adolescents programming around the world. But with the move towards a comprehensive programming that addresses multiple behaviours and competencies, the life skills approach is beginning to be recognized as an effective unifying framework.

The World Health Organization has defined life skills as, "the abilities for adaptive and positive behaviour that enable individuals to deal effectively with the demands and challenges of everyday life" (WHO, 1999).

UNICEF defined life skills as "a behaviour change or behaviour development approach designed to address a balance of three areas: knowledge, attitude and skills". The UNICEF definition is based on research evidence that suggests that shifts in risk behaviour are unlikely if knowledge, attitudinal and skills based competency are not addressed (UNICEF, 2004).

UNICEF, UNESCO and WHO (1999) listed the ten core life skill strategies and techniques for promotion of health and well-being of children and adolescents as :

Decision making	Interpersonal relationship skills
Problem solving	Self awareness
Critical thinking	Empathy
Creative thinking	Coping with stress
Effective communication	Coping with emotions

Decision Making: involves resolving a problem/issue by selecting a most suitable approach from the several alternatives placed before the adolescent. Any decision has its flip side always, like the two sides of a coin. There is a need to pick a solution that outweighs the negative aspect. Once a decision is taken, it is necessary to learn to face the consequences. Decision making helps to deal constructively with decisions about one's lives. This can have consequences for health if young people actively make decisions about their actions in relation to health by assessing the different options and what effects different decisions may have.

Problem Solving: Once a decision is made to resolve a problem, the practical application of the option chosen and the process used to achieve the desired output is problem solving. All young persons face problems in their everyday life. It may be at home, school, or in peer group. To effectively solve a problem one needs to be open-minded and flexible. Some people may achieve it without much difficulty, but some may have to develop the art of solving problems by constant practice, looking at other similar problems and improvising on the available solution. There are several ways of solving a particular problem. It is what is suitable at that particular time. Problem solving enables individuals to deal constructively with problems in daily living. Significant problems that are left unresolved can cause mental stress and give rise to accompanying physical strain.

Creative Thinking: Problem solving skills involve both critical and creative thinking. Both types of thinking are interdependent. In reality, they operate together and hence difficult to differentiate one from the other. Creative thinking is defined as generation of new ideas by modifying or combining ideas from existing ones. Creative thinking contributes to both decision making and problem solving by enabling one to explore the available alternatives and various consequences of actions or non-action. It helps to look beyond direct experience, and even if no problem is identified, or no decision is to be made, creative thinking can help adolescents to respond adaptively and with flexibility to the situations of daily lives.

Critical Thinking: Critical thinking is an ability to analyze information and experiences in an objective manner. Critical thinking can contribute to health by helping one to recognize and assess the factors that influence attitudes and behaviour, such as values, peer pressure, and the media.

Effective Communication: is the ability to express oneself both verbally and nonverbally in an appropriate manner. This means being able to communicate well the thoughts, desires, beliefs, opinions, fears, and seek assistance and advice in times of need. This means being able to express opinions and desires, but also needs and fears. And it may mean being able to ask for advice and help in a time of need.

Interpersonal Relationship: is a skill that is necessary to interact with people around. Interpersonal relationship skills help to relate in positive ways with the people around. This may mean being able to make and keep friendly relationships, which can be of great importance to one's mental and social well-being. It may mean keeping good relations with family members, which are an important source of social support. It may also mean being able to end relationships constructively.

Self Awareness: is essentially trying to understand one better. Self-awareness includes recognition of one selves, character, strengths and weaknesses, desires and dislikes. Developing self-awareness can help youth to recognize when they are stressed or feel under pressure. It is also often a prerequisite for effective communication and interpersonal relations, as well as for developing empathy for others.

Empathy: is the capability to listen and understand the feelings of another person. Empathy is essentially to put oneself in the other person's shoe and experience the situation that is totally unfamiliar to us. Empathy is the ability to imagine what life is like for another person, even in a situation that we may not be familiar with.

Coping with Emotions: Emotions can be classified under four broad categories namely happiness, sadness, fear, and anger. One needs to recognize emotions with others. Each person reacts to these emotions differently under varying circumstances. There is a need to identify the cause of a particular emotion. One person's happiness may be another person's sadness. Similarly, one person's anger may not necessarily bring anger to another person. Coping with emotions involves recognizing emotions in ourselves and others, being aware of how emotions influence behaviour, and being able to respond to emotions appropriately.

Coping with Stress: A pressure or force on the body and its reaction to the same is called stress. It is an emotion that is experienced by everyone several times in their lives. It need not necessarily have a bad impact on body. It depends on how one handles the situation. Stress can be effectively used to achieve a desired goal.

Coping with stress is about recognizing the sources of stress in one's lives, recognizing how this affects, and acting in ways that help to control levels of stress. This may mean that taking action to reduce the sources of stress, for example, by making changes to the physical environment or lifestyle. Or it may mean learning how to relax, so that tensions created by unavoidable stress do not give rise to health problems.

Life skills are thus distinctly different from physical or perceptual motor skills, such as practical or health skills, as well as from livelihood skills, such as crafts, money management and entrepreneurial skills. Ultimately, the interplay between the skills is what produces powerful behavioural outcomes, especially where this approach is supported by other strategies such as media, policies and health services. Health and livelihood education however, can be designed to be complementary to life skills education, and vice versa.

Importance of Life Skills Development for Adolescents

A child's holistic development is one wherein he/she develops an ability to cope with real life situations outside of a support institution; where they are able to take conscious, confident decisions about their life and are enabled to successfully integrate into mainstream society.

Most institutions support vulnerable youth, primarily through basic needs such as food, shelter, education and primary health care; leaving a huge gap in the child's comprehensive development and growth. In recent years, youth have to be multi-faceted. They face severe competition in all spheres of their life. Peer pressure is extremely high and an expectation to succeed in all activities that one pursues like studies, sports, music, and so on. In some of the developing countries, young girls from economically weaker sections work harder as they are expected to give a helping hand in running the household along with their studies, thus putting their health at risk.

Adolescents grow up in a mixed environment regarding violence, alcohol, and smoking. They are exposed to a wide range of negative issues. They are not in a position to decide what is right and what is wrong. Their thoughts and actions need to be channelized in the right direction. While education gives one knowledge and literacy, it does not train one to handle the pressures of life. A life skill programme could include content about friendships, bullying, sexual relationships, anger management, and perceptions about drug use.

Unlike the past, when education only catered to a single specified area, the life skills-based education encompasses and evaluates the skills of a student, and thereafter provides necessary support in the form of tools and materials to enhance the respective skills.

Theoretical Background

Theories about the way human beings, and specifically, children and adolescents grow, learn and behave provide the foundation of a life skills approach. These theories are not mutually exclusive and all contribute to the development of a life skills approach.

Though several theories describe child and adolescent development, social learning theory explains link to the development of life skills.which has found that people learn what to do and how to act by observing others and that their behaviours are reinforced by the positive or negative consequences which result during these observations. In addition, many examples from educational and behavioural research show that retention of behaviours can be enhanced by rehearsal. As Albert Bandura, one of the leading social psychologists in the area has explained, "When people mentally rehearse or actually perform modelled response patterns, they are less likely to forget them than if they neither think about them nor practice what they have seen" (Bandura, 1977).

Life skills learning is facilitated by the use of participatory learning methods and is based on a social learning process which includes: hearing an explanation of the skill in question; observation of the skill (modelling); practice of the skill in selected situations in a supportive learning environment (scaffolding); and feedback about individual performance of skills.

Social Learning Theory had two profound influences on the development of life skills and social skills programs. One was the necessity of providing children with methods or skills for coping with internal aspects of their social lives, including stress reduction, self-control, and decision-making. Most life and social skill programmes address these skills. The second was that, to be effective, life and social skills programmes need to replicate the natural processes by which children learn behaviour. Thus, most life and social skills programmes include observation, role-play, and peer education components in addition to plain instruction.

Some theoretical perspectives view life skills as a way for adolescents to actively participate in their own process of development and the process of constructing social norms. By teaching young people how to think rather than what to think, by providing them with the tools for solving problems, making decisions and managing emotions, and by engaging them through participative methodologies, skills development can become a means of empowerment.

Life Skills-based Education (LSBE)

Life skill-based education (LSBE) is an approach to education that can facilitate and can contribute to gender equity in teaching and learning. It can enhance the value of traditional subjects, such as literacy and numeracy, as well as address topics of increasing relevance to young people, including gender, equality, human rights, HIV/AIDS and sustainable development. Around the world, Life Skills-based Education (LSBE) is being adopted as a means to empower young people in challenging situations.

LSBE refers to an interactive process of teaching and learning which enables learners to acquire knowledge and to develop attitudes and skills which support the adoption of healthy behaviours. UNICEF defines LSBE as "an interactive process of teaching and learning which enables learners to acquire knowledge and to develop attitudes and skills which support the adoption of healthy behaviours" (UNICEF, 2004).

Life skill based education equips a person to handle challenging situations in a better way and see things in a better perspective. This is where Life Skill-based Education will play a good part. Life skills-based education is now recognized as a methodology to address a variety of issues of child and youth development and thematic responses including as expressed in United Nations Special Session (UNGASS) (2002), UN Decade on Education for Sustainable Development (2005), 51st Commission on the Status of Women (2007) and the World Development Report (2007).

Life skills education promotes mental well-being in young people and equips them to face the realities of life. By supporting mental well-being and behavioural preparedness, life skills education equips individuals to behave in a pro-social ways and it is additionally health giving (Birell Weisen and Orley, 1996). To achieve health giving pro-social behaviour a life skills programme must have effect on the mental well-being and behavioural preparedness. Consequently, life skills education can be seen as empowering youth and thus enabling them to take more responsibility for their actions (Orley, 1997).

Life skills education is particularly important in such critical areas a HIV prevention, care and support, child protection and emergencies. The goal is to arm children with every available weapon for their defense in the face of potential harm. Around the world, *Life Skills-based Education (LSBE)* is being adopted as a means to empower young people in challenging situations.

Life Skills-based Education (LSBE) for Gender Empowerment

Gender empowerment is a process of awareness and capacity-building leading to greater participation in transformative action, to greater decision-making power and control over one's life and other processes. Empowerment of women as a policy objective implies that women legitimately have the ability and should, individually and collectively, participate effectively in decision-making processes that shape their societies and their own lives, especially about societal priorities and development directions.

The life skills-based education programme gives young people a chance to learn from one another and equips them to improve their lives, build their self-esteem and make well considered decisions.

Life Skills-based Education is now recognized as a methodology to address a variety of issues of child and youth development. Life Skills-based Education Include a wide variety of participatory and interactive techniques to achieve the key goal of attitudinal and behavioural change in adolescents. Teaching methods that can be used are youth-centered, gender-sensitive, interactive, and participatory. Common Teaching

Methods include small group discussions, role-playing, debating, brain storming, community partnerships etc.

Identifying Strategies for Life Skills-based Programme

The following elements can be included for Life Skills Education for gender empowerment:

- Content that includes a balance of knowledge, values, attitudes and skills to gender issues;
- Using interactive and learner-centered teaching methods for both boys and girls;
- Including behaviour change/development;
- The programme should be based on participant needs (i.e. based on situation analysis and relates to real life).

Development of Life Skills-based Programme

While developing life skills-based programme, the full range of available strategies that may contribute to the main goal must be considered. Research must be conducted to identify credible sources and pertinent data, the most effective and relevant strategies have to be chosen and effective programmes whenever possible must be adapted. Baseline data on attitudes, settings and practices relating to gender in contexts where life skills-based education is planned has to be obtained. The strategies for developing LSBE for adolescents are the relationship between knowledge, attitudes and life skills should be considered and the desired behavioural determinants and behaviours, including measurement techniques must be chalked out.

The dichotomy between in-school life skills-based education and programming for especially vulnerable children and adolescents who are not in school must be planned. Appropriate teaching methods and standards for training and support must be promoted. Promotion of interest and responsibility among duty bearers for life skills development, especially among vulnerable children and adolescents is also essential.

Management of Resources for LSBE

In order to have an effective implementation of life skill education there is a need for professionally trained and skilled personal from within the country. Professional training requires a purposely planned programme of study prepared by experts which has the approval of a competent authority. There is an urgent need to train and prepare a large contingent of 'trainers of trainers' (TOTs). The TOTs will require adequate training on all aspects of the subject. They have to be expert in this field of study in order to be effective in performing their task.

Pilot Testing LSBE and Training

Pilot testing is important for identifying mistakes and gaps of the programme planned.

Implementing LSBE

During and after the planning process, all young people, regardless of sex, should be given the opportunity to express their opinions within the educational context. Throughout the learning process, equal responsibilities should be delegated to both boys and girls, e.g. roles of leaders and followers are alternated equally among boys and girls. Empathy-oriented approaches for both sexes, particularly with relation to HIV/AIDS should be incorporated. Recommendations include small group discussions audio-visual material and empathic listening as key strategies for developing empathy.

Evaluation of LSBE

Evaluating the effectiveness of a life skills programme requires a clear program design that is the overall purpose of the programme and the measurable goals. It should also include the expected outcomes in terms of improvement in skills, changes in behaviour, or changes in attitude or beliefs in the adolescent.

Programme objectives, processes, and outcomes should be assessed using realistic, relevant indicators. Enough time should be given for results to be accurately observed. Appropriate monitoring and evaluation processes that will assess knowledge, attitudes, skills, and behaviours must be done. Assessment of life skills-based education (LSBE) at the local level and individual level must be based on observed changes in a learner's acquisition and use of knowledge, the expression of values and attitudes, development of skills interactions with the social and physical environment.

Two important dimensions are coverage and quality. Extent of provider training, fidelity to the programme design and programme duration are just some of the components of implementation that may affect intervention outcomes.

The Outcomes

Life skills-based education (LSBE) can empower young boys and girls to:

- Think about their own gendered behaviours and expectations;
- Reflect on ways women/girls and men/boys see themselves, each other, and the prevailing gender norms or 'rules' to which they are expected to conform their families or communities;
- Exchange experiences, views and opinions, and discuss gender-based differences and contradictions that will be regarded with a sense of respect and stimulate thinking;
- Address issues of sexual safety and risk within sexual health education and HIV/AIDS prevention education.

Strategies for Policy Makers

The policy makers can help in implementing LSBE by:

- Providing information on incorporating gender-responsiveness in life skills-based education approaches as a useful methodological tool for teachers;
- Actively advocating gender-responsiveness in life skills-based education;
- Using measures that focus on openness in discussions within the context;
- Training teacher for gender-sensitive life skills-based approaches.

Conclusion

The present chapter throws light on Life skills-based education, elements of LSBE, method of development, implementation and evaluation of programme for gender empowerment of adolescents. Adolescents are active individuals. Their life experiences suggest that they learn best by doing rather than by talking. A Chinese proverb best describes the ideal way of teaching life skills—*"I listen and forget, I see—and remember, I do—and understand"*. Hence, the programmes aimed empowering adolescents on life skills should be long term and learning should be through active participation. Life skill management for adolescent is the need of today's world. Life Skills Education makes a person 'a balanced adult' who contributes meaningfully to society and also definitely helps to become future empowered citizens. There is a great need to conduct base line surveys and develop strategies for life skills education, in Indian setting, especially in Andhra Pradesh.

REFERENCES

1. Bandura, A. (1977). *Social Learning Theory.* New York: General Learning Press.
2. Orley, J. (1997). *Promoting Mental Health and Teaching Skills for Life*: The WHO Approach. [online] www.healthchildrennetwork.lu/pdf/conference/1997.
3. UN Decade on Education for Sustainable Development (2005).
4. http://unesdoc.unesco.org/images/0014/001416/141629e.pdf.
5. UNESCO (2001). *Life Skills in Non-formal Education: A Review.* Indian National Commission for co-operation with UNESCO, Ministry of Human Resource Development, New Delhi.
6. UNFPA, (2003). *Adolescent Skills Building for Sexual and Reproductive Health* http://www.unfpa.org/upload/lib_.pdf.
7. UNGASS on Children (2002), United Nations Special Session (UNGASS). http://www.unicef.org/specialsession.
8. UNICEF (2004) Report on the Regional Forum on Life Skills-based Education for Behaviour Development and Change. *Adolescent Education News letter*, 7 (2). Weisen and Orley (1996). Chapter Four Life Skills.
9. http://www.actionresearch.net/living/rawalpdf/Chapter4.pdf WHO (1999). Life Skills Education for Children and Adolescents in Schools.Geneva: World Health Organization (WHO) (1999). Adolescence: The Critical Phase, New Delhi.

CHAPTER

9

Rehabilitation of Child Mathammas
A Study of Phooley Learning Centre at Jeevakona

Dr. G. Sandhya Rani
Dr. B. Suguna Reddy

Indian society is in transition period from traditional to modern. With the advent of industrialization and modern technology, the social transformation has taken rapid strides in many aspects of human life. But the existence of certain systems like 'Mathamma' make us to think about the direction of our progress either backward or forward?

The culture of dedicating girls to temples was once upon a time a common practice among a certain class of people. Even in this computer age also this system is existing in various forms. This is still prevalent among certain class people mainly in Dalit Community. They offer their very young girls to temples. The victims of mathamma system are inducted to prostitution with social sanction.

The social reformers, freedom fighters, women activists have tried to enact legislation to put an end to this practice. They not only fought for the abolition of the system but also encouraged the youth to marry the girl dedicated to God or Goddess.

In India, even after 54 years of independence this evil cult is practiced in almost all states with different names. The Government now thought about eradicating this evil through awareness development especially among rural people and providing rehabilitation to the victims.

Therefore, in this chapter an attempt has been made to throw light on the rehabilitation programme of RISE—A Voluntary Organisation in Tirupati, Chittoor District.

Mathamma culture is in practice in several parts of Chittoor district. As per the survey conducted by the SC Welfare Corporation in the year 2001, there are 336 mathammas in this district. Out of them 175 mathammas are below the age of 18 years. The 'Child Mathammas' are identified in the 19 mandals of the district namely B.N. Kandriga, K.V.B. Puram, Nagalapuram, Puttur, Renigunta, Satyaveedu, Sri Kalahasti, Tirupati rural and Urban ..... Majority of them are in the age group of 1-12 years. They all belong to Dalit community.

When we talk about the need for rehabilitation of mathammas, we have to remember that we are at the threshhold of the third millennium. We are enjoying the advantages of all the technological innovations. But on the other side of this development, there is dark area, with full of blind beliefs and practices. The existence of mathamma culture is a standing example of this. The lives of mathammas are very pathetic. Though they earn some money when they are young, during old age they have to lead miserable lives without anybody's care and concern.

Child Mathammas are another painful part of mathamma culture. These girls are dedicated to Goddess 'Mathamma' for simple reasons like:

Common cold, continuous fever, stomach ache, wounds etc.

Some times:

(*i*) if they have two daughters they dedicate one daughter to the temple;

(*ii*) If they do not have son, they promise Goddess that they will dedicated their daughter to the temple for want of son;

(*iii*) In the case of no children they promise to dedicate their first daughter.

Majority of these people belong to either weaker sections or marginalized by the society. Centuries together they are leading lives under the umbrella of traditions. Illiteracy, ignorance, poverty, fear of God, lack of awareness make these people to follow these customs.

Child mathammas and mathamma children are the worst victims of this culture. For no fault of them they are ill-treated and insulted by the society. Since there is no healthy family atmosphere and negligence of the society make these children to develop frustration, jealous, anger and criminal mentality. In future they will turn into anti-social elements.

Therefore there is an urgent need to rehabilitate child mathammas and mathamma children. With a view to provide them formal education and to bring them into the main stream of society. Some voluntary organizations have started schools with the financial assistance of National and International agencies.

The 'Phooley Learning Centre' established at Jeevakona of Tirupati town is one such school functioning under the supervision of RISE.

This school was started on 25th of August 1999, with 48 students. The main objective of this school is:

"To arrest totally the cultural practices of dedicating girls in future and converting them to normal living conditions by enhancing awareness among people".

The other specific objectives are:

1. To make the mathamma children and child mathammas as potential to understand the socio-economic conditions in order to enhance self dignity;
2. To create an opportunity for them to continue further schooling and subsequently link up with main stream of education;
3. To impart the skills of relevant trades for them to develop self - confidence and to provide self-employment opportunities;
4. To protect the children from the blind cultural practices of dedication and make them to develop a critical look on cultural practices.

This is residential type of school with co-education. Food and accommodation will be provided to the students free of cost. There are five teachers and one Vocational Training instructor. They also stay within the school campus. At present there are 81 students from I to X standard. Out of them 66 are girls and 15 are boys. Among 66 girls 50 are child mathammas. The organizers of the school visited villages identified child mthammas and convinced their parents to join them in this school. While admitting into school these girls are given new names.

The medium of instruction is telugu. Apart from formal education, vocational training is also given to both boys and girls. At present they have weaving and tailoring classes. They weave towels, their school uniform cloth etc. students undergoing tailoring course stich uniforms, frocks and shirts. They also learn stitching, bag making, fabric designing etc.

Students are also given training in growing vegetable and flower garden in the school campus. These vegetables are used for cooking purpose. The organizers and the staff members irrespective of their cadre responding in a very positive way towards these children and encouraging them to participate in the competitions conducted by various institutions.

In the following table the distribution of students according to their educational standard is presented:

Standard	Girls	Boys	Total
I.	9	1	10
II.	8	3	11
III.	9	3	12
IV.	7	1	8
V.	8	5	13
VI.	7	1	8
VII.	12	0	12
VIII.	3	1	4
IX.	1	0	1
X.	2	-	2
Total	**66**	**15**	**81**

****Source**: Annual Records, Phooley Learning Centre, Jeevakona, 2001

It is clear from the table that the majority of students are girls. This once again highlights the severity of this evil practice. Out of 66 girls, 50 are child mathammas. Remaining boys and girls are mathamma children.

The organizers have been receiving funds from HEKS, Jurich, Switzerland to meet the expenditure, for supporting the students and to provide food, accommodation and for giving vocational training. They have constructed permanent buildings for school and hostel.

The atmosphere in the school campus is very healthy. This kind of environment helps students to develop positive outlook towards future. When students are interviewed they reacted enthusiastically and expressed their views about future.

Students Response

When the students are interviewed they responded actively. The responses of the students are furnished herewith:

1. The facilities available in the school are better than their houses;
2. They preferred to live in the hostel rather than in the house, as

they have to face many problems, heavy works and some times food is also not available for them;

3. They expressed their sorrow about the prevalence of superstitions and blind beliefs which motivate people to dedicate their children to temples;
4. They are very happy and confident about their future since they are receiving formal education and also undergoing vocational training;
5. They said they want to continue their education and would like to become police officers, teachers, doctors, etc.;
6. They told that whenever they go to their homes, they are demotivating their parents and the other public dedicating children to Gods or Goddesses.

When the parents of these children are interviewed they felt very happy with the school, its organization and they too want to continue their children's education in spite of many odds.

Conclusion

Though there may be some people who are against to the establishment of separate schools for these children, I think that this kind of starting is necessary to motivate mathammas and parents of child mathammas to send their children to have education without any inferiority complex. In this type of schools at present education is available upto school level. For collegiate education they have to join in the mainstream of education either formal or non-formal. Therefore by the time they join into colleges they will group up to a level to understand their status in the society and with the help of education already received they will be in a position to face the society with courage and confidence. To train them and to motive them towards developing positive outlook imparting education upto school level in separate schools is advisable.

Unless the magnitude of poverty and high rate of unemployment is reduced imbalances in the distribution of wealth assets and existence of social injustice are property checked people will not come out of these blind beliefs and practices. Till then there is a need of rehabilitation programmes to contine.

REFERENCES

1. *Annual Reports,* Phooley Learning Centre, Jeevakona, Tirupati, 2000-2001
2. Bela Rani Sharma, *Women, Marriage, Family Violence and Divorce*, 1997.

3. Chakraborty, *Atrocities on Indian Women,* APH Publishing Corporation, New Delhi, 1999.
4. Chetana Kalbagh (edit), *Women and Development,* Discovery Publishing House, New Delhi, 1999.
5. D'Mello, Flavia, *Domestic Violence*, SNDT Women's Centre Publication Bombay, 1984.
6. Lellamma Devasai and Devasia, V.V., *Girl Child in India*, Ashish Publishing House, New Delhi, 1991.
7. Niroj Sinha, *Women and Violence*, Vikas Publishing House, New Delhi, 1990.
8. Sharma O.C., *Crimes against Women*, Ashish Publishing House, New Delhi, 1994.
9. Sushma Sood, *Violence against Women*, Ashish Publishers, Jaipur, 1990.

CHAPTER

10

Women in Political Sphere

Dr. P. Neeraja

Indian women have a long history lifestyle and witnessed a remarkable transition from the ages of Vedic period. It is a fact that the women in India are playing a significant role in politics prior to India's independence, on the call of Mahatma Gandhi they too participated and contributed on par with men in the country in the country's independence movement. Thereby it is aptly observed that social and economic justice alone could not bring success to democracy until there is political empowerment among women which could get only when and where mass participation takes place significantly.

Bringing women into power will not only a matter of equity but it broadly means of correcting an unjust and unrepresentative system. Women elected peoples representatives in local bodies viz., Panchayats, Municipalities etc, play a dynamic role in not only in rightly understanding civic needs, problems but also solving them successfully and more efficiently, they can empower rural women largely if they are empowered to do so.

Political empowerment of women is crucial for the emancipation of women from household bondage. Prior to 73rd Constitution Amendment Act, participation of women in politics at grassroots level was unknown. But the new dispensation has changed the situation and women have been freely participating in the decision making processes through their representation in the PRIs.

For further development of women politics is an avenue for upper mobility and higher level of participation in decision making. Participation in the political process certainly sharpens the identity of a group in relation to others in the society.

Historically women have had fewer or no opportunities in exercising her leadership in the different spheres of social life. With the engendering of the governance structure through the 33 per cent reservation, women have opportunities for participation in politics and express their voice in shaping public policies. But the conservative nature of people in rural areas, the lack of education and access to the media, poor exposure to the outside world, the patriarchal nature of the family, economic dependence on men etc. render the women representatives vulnerable and make them feel powerless and unequipped to participate effectively in process of local governance.

Women constitute almost half of the voters in almost all the countries and exercise their right to vote in nears proportion to men but not holding equal power anywhere including in India, though the Constitution assured equal rights for both men and women in all spheres. Women's rights and equality cannot be achieved unless women in large number are offered fair opportunity to take part in politics by way of their representation in the national and state assemblies and other decision making bodies at highest levels.

One of the major components of human development is the empowerment of people to participate and benefit from development process. The issue of women's empowerment is central to the achievement of the goals of equality, development and peace, the theme of the Beijing Conference (1995). To achieve these goals, it is essential for the women to be in decision making in critical numbers. It is through equal participation of women that a transformation in politics can be brought about.

The year 2009 witnessed the History written moments when Smt. Mira Kumar became the first Indian women to hold the office of the Lok Sabha Speaker. She is an ex-IFS officer and hails from the Bhojpuri land clearly indicating the women power in politics. It can be said that the image and involvement of women in Indian politics has increased by many folds and some of them have successfully reached the top posts but a lot more has to be done in order to increase their presence, works towards the betterment of the women society and taking India parallel to the world's developed countries. Despite the improving participation of women in Indian politics, there are some bigger challenges which still need to be worked upon. For the better understanding of their participation let us have a glance on the following tables.

Table 10.1 : World and Regional Averages of Women in Parliament

(In percentage)

Countries	Single or Lower House	Upper House or Senate	Both Houses Combined
World Average	17.9	16.7	17.7
Nordic Countries	41.4	—	41.4
Europe OSCE (Nordic countries included)	20.9	17.9	20.3
Americas	20.7	20.1	20.6
Europe OSCE (Nordic countries not included)	19.0	17.9	18.8
Sub-Saharan Africa	17.3	21.2	17.7
Asia	16.9	14.8	16.7
Pacific	12.9	31.8	15.0
Arab States	9.6	7.0	9.0

Source: National Parliaments—2008.

Table 10.2 : Representation of Women in the Central Council of Ministers, 2006

Sl.No.	Ministerial Rank	Central Council of Ministers			
		Female	Male	Total	Percentage Female to Total
1.	Cabinet Minister	1	28	29	3.45
2.	MOS	6	33	39	15.38
	Total	**7**	**61**	**68**	**10.29**

Note: MOS—Minister of State.

Source: www.parliamentofindia.nic.in

India, Ministry of Statistics and Programme Implementation, Central Statistical Organisation. (2007). Women and Men in India 2006. New Delhi.

A record 59 women MPs have been elected to the new Lok Sabha—the highest since independence, Before this verdict, the proportion of women MPs in the House had never crossed 10 per cent—it stopped at 9.02 per cent in 1999. The first Lok Sabha had 4.4 per cent women; the sixth, in 1977, had the smallest proportion ever, 3.5 per cent.

Table 10.3 : Number of Elected Total and Women Panchayat Representatives in the Three Tiers of Panchayati Raj State-wise as on 01.04.2006.

Sl.No.	India/ State/ Union Territory	Gram Panchayat		Intermediate Panchayat (Panchayat Samiti)		District Panchayat (Zilla Parishad)	
		Women	Total	Women	Total	Women	Total
1	2	3	4	5	6	7	8
	India	862069	2010528	49358	118054	5186	13038
1.	Andhra Pradesh	68736	208291	4919	14617	364	1095
2.	Arunachal Pradesh	2561	9046	577	2216	45	181
3.	Assam	7851	15620	746	1402	117	273
4.	Bihar	40553	116029	4065	11611	410	1162
5.	Chhattisgarh	41913	124211	906	2639	95	274
6.	Delhi						
7.	Goa	438	1450	***	***	15	50
8.	Gujarat	30680	109209	1394	4161	274	817
9.	Haryana	23897	66256	962	2833	135	384
10.	Himachal Pradesh	6822	18549	562	1658	87	251
11.	Jammu & Kashmir						
12.	Jharkand	$	$	$	$	$	$
13.	Karnataka	39318	91402	1519	3683	373	1005
14.	Kerala	4801	8458	629	1009	105	202
15.	Madhya Pradesh	106491	208356	2159	4297	248	486
16.	Maharashtra	77548	178132	1407	2877	658	1423
17.	Manipur	611	1111	***	***	22	39
18.	Meghalaya						
19.	Mizoram						
20.	Nagaland						
21.	Orissa	33602	93781	2188	6227	296	854
22.	Punjab	27108	48860	813	1667	89	190

...(Contd.)

1	2	3	4	5	6	7	8
23.	Rajasthan	39450	114282	1908	5257	364	1008
24.	Sikkim	316	905	***	***	28	100
25.	Tamil Nadu	36824	109308	1765	6524	227	656
26.	Tripura	1785	5352	106	299	28	82
27.	Uttarakhand	21337	53961	1169	3247	144	373
28.	Uttar Pradesh	230865	377518	18580	33290	0	788
29.	West Bengal	18150	49545	2953	8483	246	720
	Union Territories						
30.	Andaman & Nicobar Islands	261	498	25	42	10	20
31.	Chandigarh	55	162	6	15	3	10
32.	Dadra & Nagar Haveli	45	114	***	***	4	11
33.	Daman & Diu	21	73	***	***	3	20
34.	Lakshadweep	30	49	***	***	8	14
35.	Pondicherry	$	$	$	$	$	$

Note: Meghalaya, Mizoram and Nagaland are Traditional Councils. In NCT of Delhi, Panchayati Raj System is yet to be revived.

*** Intermediate Panchayat does not exist (2 Tier).

$ Elections to the local bodies are yet to be conducted.

Source: India, Ministry of Panchayati Raj. (2006). Panchayats and Elected Representatives in the Three Tiers of Panchayati Raj System Statewise as on 01.04.2006. New Delhi.

Table 10.4 : Women Representatives in Panchayati Raj Institutions (PRI),2006

Sl.No.	India/ State/ UT	Village Panchayats				Intermediate Panchayats				District Panchayats			
		No. of Panchayats	Total	Women		No. of Pancha-yats	Total	Women		No. of Pancha-yats	Total	Women	
				No.	%			No.	%			No.	%
1	2	3	4	5	6	7	8	9	10	11	12	13	14
	India	232913	2656476	975116	36.7	6094	156609	58094	37.1	537	15694	5779	36.8
1.	Andhra Pradesh	21825	208291	68736	33.0	1098	14617	4919	33.7	22	1095	364	33.2
2.	Arunachal Pradesh	1639	6485	2561	39.5	136	1639	577	35.2	14	136	45	33.1
3.	Assam	2223	22898	8977	39.2	188	2148	791	36.8	20	390	135	34.6

1	2	3	4	5	6	7	8	9	10	11	12	13	14
4.	Bihar	8471	117397	64152	54.6	531	11537	5671	49.2	38	1157	577	49.9
5.	Chhatisgarh	9820	157250	53045	33.7	146	2831	954	33.7	16	305	103	33.8
6.	Delhi	-	-	-	-	-	-	-	-	-	-	-	-
7.	Goa	190	1450	438	30.2	-	-	-	-	2	50	15	30.0
8.	Gujarat	13819	109209	36400	33.3	224	4161	1394	33.5	25	817	274	33.5
9.	Haryana	6187	66256	23897	36.1	119	2833	962	34.0	19	384	135	35.2
10.	Himachal Pradesh	3243	25352	8483	33.5	75	1667	559	33.5	12	251	86	34.3
11.	Jammu & Kashmir	-	-	-	-	-	-	-	-	-	-	-	-
12.	Jharkhand	3746	-	-	-	211	-	-	-	22	-	-	-
13.	Karnataka	5653	91402	39318	43.0	176	3683	1519	41.2	27	1005	373	37.1
14.	Kerala	999	16139	5701	35.3	152	2005	695	34.7	14	339	119	35.1
15.	Madhya Pradesh	23051	388829	131671	33.9	313	7164	2393	33.4	48	884	304	34.4
16.	Maharashtra	27918	223857	75148	33.6	351	3902	1317	33.8	33	1951	653	33.5
17.	Manipur	165	1707	625	36.6					4	61	21	34.4
18.	Meghalaya	-	-	-	-	-	-	-	-	-	-	-	-
19.	Mizoram	-	-	-	-	-	-	-	-	-	-	-	-
20.	Nagaland	-	-	-	-	-	-	-	-	-	-	-	-
21.	Orissa	6234	93781	33602	35.8	314	6227	2188	35.1	30	854	296	34.7
22.	Punjab	12447	88136	30875	35.0	141	2622	866	33.0	17	298	97	32.6
23.	Rajasthan	9188	113541	40012	35.2	237	5256	2013	38.3	32	1007	377	37.4
24.	Sikkim	166	905	352	38.9	-	-	-	-	4	100	32	32.0
25.	Tamil Nadu	12618	109308	36824	33.7	385	6524	2313	35.5	28	656	227	34.6
26.	Tripura	513	5352	1852	34.6	23	299	106	35.5	4	82	28	34.1
27.	Uttar Pradesh	52000	703294	273229	38.8	820	65669	24674	37.6	70	2698	1122	41.6
28.	Uttarakhand	7227	53988	20319	37.6	95	3152	1079	34.2	13	360	119	33.1
29.	West Bengal	3354	49545	18150	36.6	341	8483	3033	35.8	18	721	245	34.0
	Union Territories												
30.	Andaman & Nicobar Islands	67	759	261	34.4	7	67	25	37.3	1	30	10	33.3
31.	Chandigarh	17	162	53	32.7	1	15	6	40.0	1	10	3	30.0
32.	Dadra & Nagar Haveli	11	114	45	39.5	-	-	-	-	1	11	4	36.4
33.	Daman & Diu	14	77	30	39.0	-	-	-	-	1	20	7	35.0
34.	Lakshadweep	10	79	30	38.0					1	22	8	36.4
35.	Pondicherry	98	913	330	36.1	10	108	40	-	-	-	-	-

Source: India, Ministry of Panchayati Raj. (2006). The State of the Panchayats: A Mid-Term Review and Appraisal 22 November 2006. New Delhi, pp. 23-26.

Table 10.5 : Women's Representation in Parliament, 1952-2009

Sl.No.	Year	Lok Sabha (Lower house)			Rajya Sabha (Upper House)		
		Total Seats	Women Members	Percent-age Women	Total Seats	Women Members	Percent-age Women
1.	1952	499	22	4.4	219	16	7.3
2.	1957	500	27	5.4	237	18	7.5
3.	1962	503	34	6.8	238	18	7.6
4.	1967	523	31	5.9	240	20	8.3
5.	1971	521	22	4.2	243	17	7.0
6.	1977	544	19	3.4	244	25	10.2
7.	1980	544	28	7.9	244	24	9.8
8.	1984	544	44	8.1	244	28	11.4
9.	1989	517	27	5.3	245	24	9.7
10.	1991	544	39	7.2	245	38	15.5
11.	1996	543	39	7.2	223	20	9.0
12.	1998	543	43	7.9	245	15	6.1
13.	1999	543	49	9.0	245	19	7.8
14.	2004	545	45	8.2	245	28	11.4
15.	2009	543	59	11.0	245	30	12.0

Note: CSDS Data Unit

Source: 1. India, Ministry of Human Resource Development, Department of Women and Child Development. (2004). Government of India, II & III Periodic Report on the Convention on the Elimination of All Forms of Discrimination against Women : CEDAW Periodic Report. New Delhi, p. 86.

2. www.parliamentofIndia.nic.in

A record 59 women MPs have been elected to the 2009 Lok Sabha—the highest since independence, Before this verdict, the proportion of women MPs in the House had never crossed 10 per cent—it stopped at 9.02 per cent in 1999. The first Lok Sabha had 4.4 per cent women; the sixth, in 1977, had the smallest proportion ever, 3.5 per cent.

We can proudly say that the 'President of our country' is a woman, Speaker is a woman but it is shame on the world's largest democracy—even after 60 years of independence- despite 15 general elections, Indian women still have an abysmal representation in Indian Parliament . Surely we cannot be proud of just 9 per cent representation of woman in Indian parliament. When we compare this value with some of the developed countries like Germany, UK, France, US, Japan etc, we stand nowhere.

For example, Germany has 32 per cent of women in their parliament which is really amazing knowing that they don't have any reservation as such for woman.

This unequal representation of Indian women in national political parties is all the more disquieting given that the Indian constitution guarantees gender equality in the Articles 325 and 326.

India ranks 115th of 162 countries in terms of gender development. Indian patriarchal society not only harbors a culture of violence against women in the form of dowry, domestic violence and female infanticide, it also manifests even in government policies towards women

Women's participation in political decision making plays a crucial role in the process of enhancing women's participation in public life. But, inadequate representation of women in politics is a problem in all of the democratic countries of the world today. Despite the widespread movement towards democratization in most countries, women are largely underrepresented at most levels of government, especially in ministerial and other executive bodies. Globally, only 10 per cent of the members of legislative bodies are now held by women.

The 73rd and 74th Amendments (1993) to the Indian Constitution have served as a major breakthrough towards ensuring women's equal access and increased participation in political power structures. These Amendments provided for reservation of 33.33 per cent of elected seats for women at different levels of local governance in both rural and urban areas. However, the number of women representatives in both houses of parliament though steadily increasing continues to be very low. They represent only 8.2 per cent of the total Members in Parliament in 2005. The number of women in the Central Council of Ministers continues to remain extremely low, and there has been a decline in this proportion between 2002 and 2005.There is need for affirmative action to ensure that women's concerns gain political prominence and a fairly representative number of women are in position not only at grass root level, but also at the state and national levels.

The path of the women's bill, which seeks 33 per cent reservation for women in Parliament and State Assemblies, has been pending since 1996. Successive governments have placed it on the table of Parliament, but only to shelve it in the absence of a political consensus. Giving representation to women in Parliament is not only a question of giving fair representation to women in working of the nation, but also a question of social justice, gender balance and gender equality. Moreover, as it is a matter of right for women to ask for fair representation, for they constitute 50 per cent of the demos.

Though women of today are more thoughtful, more independent, they also are dependent on men in some way or the other, which influences their behavioural pattern. This leads to a feeling of low self esteem among women. There is a need to make women more aware of their rights be it social, political or economic. The under representation of women in high level political decision making structure is an universal phenomenon and therefore their inclusion is considered essential. But globally women constitute only 10 per cent of legislative bodies and less in parliamentary positions.

The status of women is the right yardstick of the society to assess the nature and directions of social change. If we look into the matters related to the position that women have, the rights and privileges they enjoy, their freedom and choice on different matters, access to and control over resources and earnings, we can see the wide gap between male and female in all the matters. The reason lies in apathy towards women's problem, lack of gender sensitization at the decision making levels, limited number of women in such bodies and the constraints in over all social structures.

Empowerment means the right to dignity, respect, security and self fulfillment. Politics is an avenue for upper mobility and higher level of participation in decision making. Participation in political process certainly sharpens the identity of women.

Constraints

Women feel that the proper place for women is within the four walls of her home and her chief duty is to look after her domestic chores. No doubt the traditional position of women has been greatly affected by the various steps in the direction of the emancipation by the grant of equal legal rights. Apart from the traditional position, there are certain practical hurdles also. The burden of child bearing and child rearing keeps the Indian women so engrossed in her domestic spheres that she hardly gets any time to enter public life and seek elections. In many cases women who have the means and the ability to participate in the active public life, are reluctant to offer themselves. Some of the major constraints for their marginal participation are

- Illiteracy
- Social mobility
- Family responsibilities
- Prevalence of violence
- Non-cooperation from the family members

- Poor exposure to outside the world
- Access to media
- Patriarchal nature of the family
- Economic dependence/lack of control over resources
- Role of money power in elections
- Lack of infrastructural facilities etc

No doubt the 73rd constitutional Amendment has brought about one million women into politics by virtue of one third reservation. There are around 86 thousands elected women representatives cutting across three tires of PRIs constituting 38 per cent of total elected representatives in Andhra Pradesh. But most of them remain inactive and most of the times and the vacuum created are being filled by their kith and kin.

Strategies to encourage women's representation

Government of India also taking various steps from time to time to change the status of women. In order to make political participation of women we should certainly exert pressure on political parties to open up opportunities for women as contestants for elections and political executives. The following are some of the strategies to be taken into consideration for the effective participation of women in politics:

- A Mass awareness programme has to be launched to change the mindset of the people and leaders on the role of women in politics in socio-economic transformation of society;
- The candidates must be given training in legislative technique so as to get a clear perspective of their role and responsibility as members of democratic bodies;
- Spreading legal literacy among the community and elected representatives is another measure that can accelerate women's political participation in equal proportion to men;
- Another need is to provide support services like easing out domestic responsibilities, child care duties;
- The political parties can ensure better women's participation in politics by providing political education on sensitive issues having implications on gender relations;
- Non-Governmental organizations can play a dominant role in identifying suitable/acceptable candidates for each position in local bodies;
- Mass media is also a vital agent in accelerating the participation of women in political process.

Conclusion

For the growth of genuine and sustainable democracy, women's participation in politics is essential. This will not only uplift their personality but will open the way for their social and economic empowerment. Emergence of women as a strong group would change the prevailing political practices, the nature and content of debates in the legislature and women's issue can be taken care of from feminist perspective both in policy formulation and implementation. As the well known phrase says that 'if you educate a man only a man is educated but if you educate a women, the whole family will be educated', similarly if you are able to make at least one women politically aware, they will be able to sensitize many people to the issue. Political participation of women could give women a sense of dignity as an individual. But till now, there was never really an active participation of women in Indian politics except a few stars here and there. The grass root levels still suffer with poverty and discrimination which avoids them from joining active politics. When there is everyday struggle to gain livelihood, one cannot expect them to contribute socially.

REFERENCES

1. M.R. Biju, (2006), *'Women Empowerment'*, Mittal Publicatins, New Delhi.
2. George Mathew (1995), 'Will Reservation Ensure Participation' *Social Welfare*, Vol. 42, No. 5-6.
3. National Commission for Women, (1997), *Knocking at the Male Bastion: Women in Politics.*
4. Rajasekharan (1996) 'Reservation: Boon or Bane', *Social Welfare*, Vol. 43, No. 1.
5. *The Grassroots* Government Journal (2008) Vol. VI, No. 1.

SECTION–II
WOMEN AND VIOLENCE

CHAPTER

11

Forms of Domestic Violence

Dr. P.S. Vijayalakshmi
Dr. G. Sandhya Rani

Introduction

The problem of violence against women is not new. A woman's life lies between pleasure at one end and danger at the other end. Atrocities on women are not a myth, but reality. The type, frequency, and intensity of atrocities on women may vary from time to time or place to place, but it is there everywhere. Even in India where women are thought to be highly esteemed, the problem of violence against women is as old as Sita who was abducted by Ravana or Droupadi who was publicly tortured by Kauravas. Even today various forms of atrocities are prevalent in the society. Sadly no statistics on crimes against women collected separately till 1988. It was only from 1989 data began to be collected which related to:

(*a*) The incidence of crimes committed

(*b*) The number of persons arrested

(*c*) Cases disposed by police/courts

(*d*) Social background of the victims

Definition of Violence against Women

The term 'violence against women' is not defined under the Indian laws. The United Nations Declaration on the Elimination of Violence against Women defines violence against women as:

"Any act of gender-based violence that results in, or is likely to result in, physical, sexual or psychological harm or suffering to women, including threats of such acts, coercion or arbitrary deprivation of liberty, whether occurring in public or in private life."

In other words Violence means "Injurious and destructive behaviour which damages the victim physically, mentally or financially"

As per the definition found in the Social science Encyclopaedia, violence 'entails inflicting emotional, psychological, sexual, physical and or marital danger. It involves the exercise of force or constraint perpetrated by individuals on their own behalf of for a collective or state sanctioned purpose.

In spite of the long list of legislations protecting women, there is an alarming increase in the number of offences committed against women. As per the recent statistics released by National Crime Records Bureau (NCRB), reported 16,075 Rape cases in the country. The following statistics by the NCRB illustrates the magnitude of the violence being perpetrated against women under various heads. It is needless to emphasis that these are only official statistics and in India many cases go unreported due to various reasons such as lack of awareness, fear, shame, long delay's in disposal of cases etc. As per the available statistics:

- A woman is sexually harassed every 40 minutes
- A rape occurs every 36 minutes
- A woman is kidnapped every 42 minutes
- A woman is molested every 24 minutes
- A dowry death every 100 minutes

Victims of Violence are Mainly

(*a*) The low caste women

(*b*) Destitute woman

(*c*) Women with disabilities

(*d*) Migrant women

(*e*) Elderly women etc. are more vulnerable to violence when compared to other women.

Violence against Women Includes

- Physical, sexual and psychological violence occurring in the family
- Sexual abuse of female children in the household
- Dowry-related violence
- Marital rape

- Other traditional practices harmful to women
- Violence related to exploitation
- Acts of violence against women also include forced sterilization, and forced abortion, and forced use of contraceptives.

Impact of Violence against Women (VAW)

Violence crodes women's self esteem and shatters their self confidence. Because of the social stigma women are afraid to speak out openly on violence suffered by them. By swallowing and suppressing their emotions they spoil mental and physical health. Violence against women is an obstacle to the achievement of the objectives of equality, development and peace. VAW violates and impairs the enjoyment by women of their human rights and fundamental freedoms. In all societies, to a greater or lesser degree, women and girls are subjected to physical, sexual and psychological abuse. The low social and economic status of women can be both cause and consequence of violence against women.

Causes of Violence against Women

- Historically unequal power relations between women and men (patriarchy)
- Influence of certain culture-harmful effects of traditions
- Lack of access to legal information, aid or protection
- Insufficient laws to effectively prohibit violence against women
- Absence of means to address the causes and consequences of violence against women
- Media image of VAW eg. Depiction of rape, sexual slavery and use of women as sex objects, pornography
- Unemployment
- Strained familial relationships

The Tabe–11.1 depicts the various forms of violence that takes place in the different stages of a girl child/woman's life.

Women are highly vulnerable to violence. Because of their female sexuality they have fallen victims to rape, female genital mutilation, and domestic violence and dowry deaths. They are subject to violence not only in the family (battering, sexual abuse of female children, dowry related violence, deprivation of food, marital rape, female genital mutilation) but also in the community (rape, gang rape, sexual abuse, sexual harassment, trafficking in women) and the state as well (women in detention and rape during times of armed conflict). A number of incidents are reported in the press regarding the offences against women especially rape, molestation, kidnapping, family violence, dowry harassment, dowry deaths, wife beating, eve-teasing, etc. There has been a constant increase in the violence against women and hardly a day passes without reports in the newspaper or a magazine.

Table 11.1 : Various forms of violence against women

Life Phases	Type of Violence
Pre-birth	• Sex selective abortion • Coerced Pregnancy (for example mass rape in war, during riots, caste rapes etc.)
Infancy	• Female infanticide • Emotional and physical abuse of females • Different access to food and medical care for girl infants (death from malnutrition)
Girlhood	• Child marriages • Genital mutilation • Sexual abuse by family members and strangers • Child prostitution
Adolescence	• Courtship violence (if couple are from different castes, religions or strata, the male and at times even the female faces death, beating and ostracization). Sexual abuse in work place • Rape • Sexual harassment • Forced prostitution • Eve teasing • Exploitation and Abduction • Kidnapping
Productive/Marital Period	• Dowry harassment and murder • Bride burning • Partner homicide • Psychological abuse • Wife battering • Sexual abuse in work place • Sexual harassment • Rape • Pregnancies at small intervals
Elderly	• Abuse of widows (mother forced by sons to take the blame for dowry murder) • Cursing widow

The offering of any share of property in consideration of marriage, has also been made punishable. According to Dowry Prohibition Act 1961. Dowry means "Any property or valuable security given or agreed to be given either directly or indirectly.

Dowry

This is one of the most heinous crimes committed by the society on the young brides unfortunately this crime is prevalent only in India. The practice of giving dowry to a daughter is an old institution in our country. In the early days parents used to give some part of their property at the time of marriage to help her to setup a new home out of concern and affection. Gradually it became a demand and compulsory on the marriage. Dowry is an amount of consideration (be it in cash or in kind) paid to the groom by the bride's family for marriage. Social scientists consider dowry as a major reason for increasing domestic violence against women. In order to combat this menace, the Government has enacted the Dowry Prohibition Act, 1961 and it has been amended further to make punishment for offences under the Act more stringent. Accordingly the burden of proof that there was no demand for dowry has been shifted to the person who is alleged to have taken or abetted the taking of dowry.

Giving and Taking of dowry both are offences, punishable,

Agreements for giving or taking of dowry are void and punishable.

Even *Dowry Negotiations* before or after the marriage are punishable offences under the Act.

Whoever commits dowry death shall be punished with imprisonment which shall not be less than seven years but which may extend to imprisonment for life.

Some of the ingredients to construe dowry death are given as under:

- Women died under unnatural circumstances within seven years of marriage;
- That there is a demand for dowry and harassment by the accused.

The greed of the groom and his parents reached the Himalayan peak and any amount of offering was not sufficient. Even today this evil practice is persisting in many families. The parents of the girls are never in peace, since there is a constant threat to the life of a girl. According to one estimate in India more than 5, 000 women are killed each year because their-laws consider their dowries inadequate. Only a tiny percentage of murders are punished.

Impact of Dowry

1. It causes late marriages
2. Many girls are remaining as spinsters
3. It creates indebtedness to the parents of the bride
4. It results in suicides of many girls both married and unmarried
5. It results in concentration of wealth where rich become rich and poor become poorer
6. It leads to psychological distress to many girls

Domestic Violence

Domestic violence is violent victimization of women, with in the boundaries of family. Domestic violence can be in the form of physical torture, psychological torture, deprivation of basic needs and sexual molestation. Insufficient evidence and social barriers continue to make it difficult to acquire accurate data on domestic violence.

Since domestic violence takes place within the privacy of the household and inflicted by a person on whom the woman is dependent mentally and emotionally, and prove for want of witness, legal proceedings are rendered difficult. Victims do not bring the incidence to lime light for fear of social stigma.

All acts of gender-based physical, psychological abuse by a family member against women in the family, ranging from simple assaults to aggravated physical battering, kidnapping, threats, intimidation, coercion, stalking, humiliating verbal abuse, forcible or unlawful entry, arson, destruction of property, sexual violence, marital rape, dowry or related violence, female genital mutilation, violence related to exploitation through prostitution, violence against household workers and attempts to commit such acts shall be termed 'domestic violence'.

Further, 'Domestic violence' means any of the following acts committed on a woman by her husband or any of his or her relatives, namely:

- Any willful conduct which—
- Is of such a nature as is likely to drive the woman put of the house or commit suicide or to injure herself; or
- Causes; injury or danger to the life, limb or health (whether mental or physical) of the woman; or
- Harassment which causes distress to a woman; or
- Any act which compels the woman to have sexual intercourse

against her will either with the husband or any of his relatives or with any other person; or

- Any act which is unbecoming of the dignity of the woman; or
- Any other act of omission or commission, which is likely to cause mental torture or mental agony to the woman.

Legal Framework to Combat Domestic Violence in India

In India domestic violence on women is on the increase. Everyday hundreds of women are physically, mentally, psychologically abused and also thrown out of the homes. Many a times these take diverse forms and lead the woman to death. As per the National Crime Records Bureau (NCRB) statistics, there are 49,170 cases of cruelty by husband and relations and 6,851 cases of dowry deaths reported during 2001. It is needless to mention that many cases go unreported due to various reasons such as lack of awareness lakh of will, corruption, threat to life etc. Studies reveal that one of the main reasons for the increase in the number of cases of 'domestic violence' is the greed for money or demand for dowry, societal attitudes etc. It is in this background it is necessary for each one of us to understand the issue and the legal provisions for playing a reformist role to combat this growing menace.

Laws alone cannot put an end to the problem. The mind set of the people should change. Domestic violence against women has become a global issue with the increase in the number of cases.

Prostitution

Even though the law has prohibited prostitution in the country, it is prevalent in Indian society since long. In the early days prostitution was encouraged by the kings as a social institution. Now it became a social evil.

It was legally defined as "indiscriminate sexual inter course with men for hire weather in cash or in kind".

According to Dr. Rey, prostitution is "an act by which a woman allows the use of her body by man, without distinction and for a payment made or expects"

Reasons

- Poverty, bad working conditions
- Broken family, bad neighbourhood, illegitimate motherhood
- Rigid restrictions on widowhood

- Domestic causes including ill-treatment, neglect by the parents/husband
- Ignorance
- Desire for easy life. The victimization of rape religious and cultural factors etc.

Apart from industrialization and urbanization, certain social and religious customs and beliefs have contributed to prostitution. The Devadasi System in India is closely connected with prostitution in the country.

Problems of Prostitutes

Prostitutes suffer from a number of health problems, about 90 per cent of the women living in inferior type brothel houses suffer from sexually transmitted diseases, and (HIV&AIDS).

Many women try to escape from the clutches of the brothel keepers. But it is not possible because they do not allow them to go out till they earn 100 per cent of profit on their investment.

The survey conducted by the Central Social Welfare Board (1991) in six cities of the country found the total population of prostitutes as 70,000 to 1,00,000 and about 30 per cent of them are below the age of 20. Economic distress is found to be the major reason.

In 1998 in Culcutta prostitutes from various parts of the country gathered to discuss the problems that affected them. They felt that Legalisattion of their work will give dignity to them. Some of them view that they will be free from police harassment. But there is a counter argument to this demand. There is a fear that licensing could encourage more sex outside the family and more women into the trade.

Estimates suggest that more than 2 million women participate in sex work, and that 25 per cent of the women are less than 18 years old.

The major cause for prostitution is poverty. If children are to be prevented from adopting this, as a profession the larger problems of unemployment and poverty should be tackled. As long as these problem persist all measures to tackle the problem of prostitution will be found futile. It is a pity that child pornography is also on the increase.

Sexual Harassment

Definition of 'Sexual harassment at workplace' is as follows:

"Any unwelcome sexually determined behaviour (whether directly or by implication) like—

- Physical contact and advances;
- A demand or request for sexual favours;
- Sexually coloured remarks;
- Showing pornography;
- Any other unwelcome physical, verbal or non-verbal conduct of sexual nature".

The incidence of sexual harassment and eve-teasing are not new in India. Cases of Sexual harassment are reported from time to time. As early as in 1860 provisions were incorporated under the Indian Penal Code under Section 354, to deal with the offence of molestation and section 509, to address the offence of eve-teasing. However, there exists no legislation to curb the growing incidence of sexual harassment of women at workplaces. As per the recent statistics of the National Crimes Record Bureau (NCRB) a woman is: molested every 24 minutes and is sexually harassed every 40 minutes. The eve-teasing or sexual harassment of girl students many a times discourages the parents from sending their daughters for education and employment. Similarly, sexual harassment of women at workplace has adverse impact on the women employees. It is essential for the Government and the society at large to address this issue not only for safeguarding the dignity and person of women but also to realize the Constitutional goal of gender equality.

In the absence of effective guidelines/laws governing sexual harassment of women at workplace, the Supreme Court in its landmark judgment in Vishaka Case formulated the code of conduct to follow at the workplace and for the mandatory setting up of complaint redressal mechanisms in all Government, Private and other Public Sector undertakings. In recent years sexual harassment of girls by the close family friends and relatives also increasing.

Rape

Sec. 375 of IPC describes rape as sex with women against her will or with her consent, putting her in fear or death or hurt. According to it sexual intercourse with a woman under circumstances falling under any of the six following descriptions:

- Against her will
- Without her consent
- With her consent, when the consent has been obtained by putting her any person in whom she is interested in fear of death or hurt
- With her consent, when at the time of giving such consent, by reason of unsoundness of mind or intoxication or the administration

The Government with the assistance of Voluntary Organization and other bodies should organize seminars, symposia and discussions periodically and educate the public on various aspects of violence against women.

Statistics on 498A, 304B, 376 and 509 of the Indian Penal Code

According to statistics published by the National Crime Records Bureau (NCRB) in 2002 a total of 147,678 crimes against women were reported in 2002 compared 143,795 during 2001. This represents an increase of 2.7 per cent over the previous year and shows an increase of 12.3 per cent over 1998. These NCRB figures record crimes specifically categorized as 'Crimes against Women', although women may additionally be the victims of other crimes, robbery, murder etc. The proportion IPC crimes committed against women towards total IPC crimes increased continually during past years from 6.7 per cent in 1998 to 7.4 per cent during 2001 and 2002.

Table 11.2 : Crime Head-wise Incidents of Crime against Women during 1998-2002 and Percentage variation in 2002 over 2001

Sl.No.	Crime Head	Year					Percentage variation in 2002 over 2001
		1998	1999	2000	2001	2002	
1.	Rape						
2.	Kidnapping & Abduction	15151	15468	16496	16075	16373	1.8
3.	Dowry Death	16351	15962	15023	14645	14506	-0.9
4.	Torture	6975	6699	6995	6851	6822	-0.4
5.	Molestation	41376	43823	45778	49170	49237	0.1
6.	Sexual Harassment	30959	32311	32940	34124	33943	-0.5
7.	Importation of Girls	8054	8858	11024	9746	10155	4.2
8.	Sati Prevention Act	146	1	64	114	76	-33.3
9.	Immoral Traffic (P)	0	0	0	0	0	—
10.	Act Indecent Rep of Women (P) Act Dowry Prohibition Act	8695 190 3578	9363 222 3064	9515 662 2876	8796 1052 3222	1242 2508 2816	27.8 138.4 12.6
	Total	**131475**	**135771**	**141373**	**143795**	**147678**	**27**

Annual Records of NCRB, 2002

Table 11.3 : Annual Reports of NCRB, 2002

Sl.No.	Year	Total IPC Crimes	Crime against women (IPC cases)	Percentage to total IPC crimes
1.	1998	17,78,815	1,19,012	6.7
2.	1999	17,64,629	1,23,122	7.0
3.	2000	17,71,084	1,28,320	7.2
4.	2001	17,69,308	1,30,725	7.4
5.	2002	17,80,330	1,31,112	7.4

Conclusion

Violence means, injurious and distractive behaviour which damages the victim physically, mentally and financially. Inspite of a long list of legislations, protecting women, there is an alarming increase in the number of offences committed against women in recent years. Domestic violence can be described as a violent victimization of women, with in the boundaries of the family.

Domestic violence takes place within the privaces of the household and inflicted by a person an whom the women is dependent mentally and emotionally and prove for want of witness, legal proceedings are rendered difficult. More over victims hesitate to bring the incident in to lime light due to social stigma. Various forms of domestic violence is on raise in recent years and the recent introduction of Domestic violence (P) Act, should be implemented effectively to reduce these type of crimes against girl children and women.

REFERENCES

1. B&TI Foundation, *Report of Workshop on Children and Women Vulenarable to Violence Trafficking Sexual Abuse and HIV*, U.P. and Uttaranchal, p. 8, 2001.
2. *Crime in Marriages a Broad Spectrum*, by Poornima Advani, published by Gupushi Publishers, 1994.
3. *Death by Fire-sati, Dowry, Death and Female Infanticide in Modern India*, by Malasen, published by Rutgess University Press, 2002.
4. *Dowry and Protection to Married Women*, by Paras Diwas, Peeyush Diwan, Puf, by Deep & Deep Publications, 1987.
5. *Dowry Death* by Kamakshya Prasad, Jawaid Ahmad Khan, Harinath Upadhyaya, Published by Modern Law Publication, 2000.

6. *Dowry Murder—the Imperial Origins of a Cultural Crime* by veena talwar. Oldenburd, published by Oxford University Press, 4.5.2002.
7. *Encyclopaedia of Violence Against Women and Dowry Death in India*, by Kalpana Roy, Published by Aumol publications. Pvt Ltd, 1991.
8. *Human Development Report 2000-2001*, the World Bank.
9. K.N. Tiwari, Director, Disha Social Organization *Violence Against Women in India, Suffering Continues Despite Progress All Over.*
10. Poonacha, Veena and Divya Pandey, Response to Domestic Violence; Government Non-government acts in Karnataka and Gujarat, & Wnomi Card, Political Weekly, Vol. XXXV, p. 57.
11. Saman, Sathya Could You Be Sold for a Song? *Femina* April 07, 2000, p. 104.
12. Women are South Asia, *Dowry Death and Human Rights Violations*, by Pramod Kumar Mishra, Published by Authors Press, 2000.

CHAPTER 12

The Perils of Female Infanticide Sociological Dimensions

Dr. B. Suguna Reddy
Dr. G. Sandhya Rani

Introduction

Violence against a Person Means 'Assault by Somebody' or 'Assault Against Somebody'

Widening inequality, poverty and environmental collapse are accelerating the process of dispossession, destitution and migration across the country. Weakening family and community ties in the modern era have not been replaced with alternative modes of human commitment and social organization. As psychologist Mary Clark notes, the denial of human emotional needs such as bonding, trust, affection and a shared spiritual orientation to life in the modern world has resulted in a plethora of pathological behaviours ranging from "greed, dominance, wife-beating, child-abuse, indescent representation of women, sex determination test, rape, kidnap and abduction, sexual harassment at workplace, prostitution and socially sanctioned prostitution like Mathamma, Basavi, Jogini, Devasi system, etc.

Everywhere women are the victims of sexual assault and family violence and in India we have a unique situation of co-existence of all forms of violence. Not withstanding enormous socio-economic changes, question of violence against women in all spheres of life continues to evade solutions.

It is believed that the home is the only safe place for a woman. This is given as an excuse for not allowing woman to go outside their homes.

However, most acts of violence are committed on women in the home itself and the incidence of violence of all forms within family has also gone up.

According to a study published by 'Peoples Union for Democratic Rights (PUDR), the number of unnatural deaths of women has been rising in the last few years and most of these are a result of domestic violence.

Female Infanticide is a Silent Violence Against the Female

- Female infanticide is an act of the killing of a new born baby by their parents or by others with their consent.
- Killing of the female foetus in the mother's womb itself is foeticide (Amniocentesis)

These two are the tragic trauma of female life in this society. Discrimination between a boy and girl begins even before birth.

Pre-natal diagnostic tests are meant for the detection of foctal abnormalities and prevention of the birth of defective children. But unfortunately in India where sons are preferred over daughters these tests are misused for the detect of the sex of the foetus (Amniocentesis)

The pre-natal Diagnostic Technique (Regulation and prevention of Misuse) act 1994 was passed in 1996. But effective monitoring is difficult due to the vastness of the country and the sheer size of the population. Law alone cannot mitigate the problem and it is clear from the recent estimates which say that two million abortions are performed after sex determination tests in a year. If female infanticide is also taken into account, then the actual figure may increase to around five million a year.

Though the Indian penal code has defined infanticide as 'Murder' (IPC Sec 102), offenders go unpunished. Even in the very few cases where police action has been initiated, it is the mother who had been arrested and punished and not those people who induce her or force her to commit the act of killing "Research studies indicate that some of the women who committed the act of Female infanticide justify it saying that they had enough of sufferings as 'woman' and they do not want their daughters to undergo the same pain, suffering and biased treatment from the society and by putting them to death they had actually helped them.

Main Reasons for Female Infanticide/Male Preference

1. Financial burden (marriage of daughter and the social stigma of having an unmarried daughter in the house.)
2. To keep (their property) the wealth with in the family.

3. To get rid off the illegitimate children.
4. Superstitious beliefs (if you kill a female child, the next one is sure to be a son; female child brings ill luck to family).
5. Believed that boys are economic asset to the family.
6. People believe that if they have no son, they are not eligible to attain moksha.

Because of all these reasons generally people look for son and they do not want female children.

Dowry

This is one of the most heinous crimes committed by the society on the young brides and unfortunately this crime is prevalent only in India. The practice of giving dowry to a daughter is an old institution in our country. In the early days parents used to give some part of their property at the time of marriage to help her to setup a new home out of concern and affection. Gradually it became a demand and compulsory on the marriage. Dowry is an amount of consideration (be it in cash or in kind) paid to the groom by the bride's family for marriage. Social scientists consider dowry as a major reason for increasing domestic violence against women. In order to combat this menace, the Government has enacted the Dowry Prohibition Act, 1961 and it has been amended further to make punishment for offences under the Act more stringent. Accordingly the burden of proof that there was no demand for dowry has been shifted to the person who is alleged to have taken or abetted the taking of dowry. Any advertisement, which relates to dowry, also comes under a punishable crime.

Strategies to Combat Violence against Women

- Developing a holistic and multidisciplinary approach to the challenging task of promoting families, communities and states that are free of violence against women is necessary and achievable.
- Educational systems should promote self-respect, mutual respect, and cooperation between women and men.
- Absence of sex segregated data and statistics on the incidence of violence against women.
- Boys and girls should be brought up equally without discrimination from the childhood without assigning a stereotyped role.

- Parents should be role models by sharing work and responsibility equally.
- Property should be jointly owned by parents.
- Ensure joint decision-making in upbringing of children.
- Educate family members not to give or take dowry.
- Son preference syndrome should be changed through awareness programmes.
- Ensure implementation of existing legislations to provide equal opportunities in employment.
- Till prevention of sexual harassment act is enacted, S.C. guidelines should be compulsorily implemented in all sectors.
- Equal opportunities for women in decision making bodies in all institutions must be mandatory.
- Women's reservation bill should be passed immediately.
- Ensure equal representation for women in all political parties and its decision making bodies.
- Gender neutral terms to be used in all spheres.
- Gender bias should be eliminated from curriculum.
- Women and men can be mobilized to overcome violence in all its forms and that effective public measures can be taken to address both the causes and consequence of violence.

Conclusion

Violence against women is endemic in India. The reason is women in the country are highly vulnerable because of poor quality of life indicated by rampant poverty, lack of education, high under five—mortality, poor health status, high fertility rate and high maternal mortality rate. Also contributing to the violence against women is societal mindset about women that have not changed much.

Violence is papetuated on women both inside and outside her home.

The Government and vouluntary organizations are making efforts towards ending/minimizing violence against women. The efforts of the governments are in the shape of enacting relevant legislations, issuing orders and launching various women welfare schemes. But their implementations remains tardy, as the low level government functionaries are not gender sensitine. On the other hand the voluntary organizations are taking both preventive as well as reactionary measures. But efforts of the voluntary organizations suffer from paucity of funds and infrastructure.

REFERENCES

1. B&TI Foundation, *Report of Workshop on Children and Women Vulenarable to Violence Trafficking Sexual Abuse and HIV*, U.P. and Uttaranchal, 2001, p. 8.
2. *Crime in Marriages a Broad Spectrum*, by Poornima Advani, Published by Gupushi Publishers 1994.
3. *Death by Fire-sati, Dowry, Death and Female Infanticide in Modern India*, by Malasen, Published by Rutgess University Press, 2002.
4. *Dowry and Protection to Married Women*, by Paras Diwas, Peeyush Diwan, Puf, by Deep & Deep Publications, 1987.
5. *Dowry Death* by Kamakshya Prasad, Jawaid Ahmad Khan, Hari Nath Upadhyaya, published by Modern Law Publication, 2000.
6. Dowry Murder—*The Imperial Origins of a Cultural Crime* by Veena Talwar. Oldenburd, Published by Oxford University Press, 4.5.2002.
7. *Encyclopaedia of Violence Against Women and Dowry Death in India*, by Kalpana Roy, Published by Aumol Publications. Pvt Ltd, 1991.
8. *Human Development Report 2000-2001*, the World Bank.
9. K.N. Tiwari, Director, Disha Social Organization *Violence Against Women in India, Suffering Continues Despite Progress Allover.*
10. Poonacha, Veena and Divya Pandey, Response to Domestic Violence; Government Non-government Acts in Karnataka and Gujarat, & Wnomi Card Political Weekly, Vol. XXXV, p. 57.
11. Saman, Sathya Could You Be Sold for a Song *Femina,* April 07, 2000 p. 104.
12. Women in South Asia, *Dowry Death and Human Rights Violations*, by Pramod Kumar Mishra, Published by Authors Press, 2000.

CHAPTER 13

Strengthening Women at Risk
A Case Study of State Home in Hyderabd

Dr. G. Sandhya Rani
Dr. B. Suguna Reddy

The State Home (Rashtra Sadan) in Andhra Pradesh is located in Hyderabad. This was constructed by the Directorate of 'Women and Child Welfare', Andhra Pradesh in the year 1958. The main objective of this home is to rehabilitate women at risk viz., unmarried mothers, orphans, women in moral danger, deserted, destitutes and economically backward.

It provides free accommodation for 100 girls/women. It has an established building both for administration and the hostel. The State Home offers technical training to the inmates in different trades and courses. Government provides necessary finance for the purchase of raw materials, machinery etc.

In view of this background information an attempt has been made in this chapter to highlight role of State Home at Hyderabad in providing necessary assistance, help and guidance to women at risk.

The home provides shelter to all girls/women who are in need of immediate shelter. The admission is voluntary and some times the field staff at the district level and block level investigate the cases and recommend for admission. A thorough study of case history is made with the help of the case workers and then they will be allotted to different units to which she is found fit or in which she is interested.

The period of stay is normally three years. But girls are rehabilitated even earlier than that period. The following procedure shall be followed in respect of the newly admitted inmates:

- They are first received at the receiving unit and thoroughly checked;
- They are given disinfected clothes, bedding according to the existing rules;
- They are given medical treatment whenever necessary.

The age composition of inmates range between 16 to 45 years. They came from various districts of Andhra Pradesh.

The available courses and trades for the inmates are:

Trades	-	Tailoring
	-	Book-binding
	-	Glassware making
Courses	-	Auxillary and Mid-wife nursing
	-	Vocational training (sericulture, weaving, etc.)

Eligibility

According to the educational qualifications the training will be given to the inmates. For example for undergoing training in tailoring, just basic skills of literacy are enough. For book-binding, the minimum educational qualification is 7th standard. For teacher training and auxillary, nurse mid-wife course, S.S.C is the minimum requirement.

For the interested inmates coaching for 7th class and 10th class examinations will be given. The home consists of the following teaching staff:

Graduate trained teachers—2

Secondary grade trained teachers—5

Part time teacher—1

Readymade Garment Making Unit

The inmates are given training in tailoring and that they are rehabilitated as dailywage workers in the unit.

Glass Ampoules Unit

The inmates are trained in ampoules making and some are employed in outside units. Since there is no demand for handmade ampoules making, the unit is imparting training in glassware making. One manager and one glass blower who are technically qualified are working in this unit.

Old Age Home

The home for the aged women has been started in February 1979 with a sole aim of giving shelter to destitute women of 60 years age and no one to take care of them. The sanctioned strength of this home is 30. These women are provided with all facilities. They are also allowed to observe their religious customs and traditions. During evening they involve in gardening.

District Shelters

The homes established in district headquarters are only for short stay purpose. After investigation of the case the girls/women are sent to state home for rehabilitation purpose.

In State Home there is no compulsion of the stay of the inmates. If they find any support to live on their own they can take permission of the concerned authority (superintendent) and leave the home.

The State Home and the district shelter for women shall be under the administrative control of the Director of Women and Child Welfare.

The inmates that are to be admitted into the State Home means those discharged from correctional institutions discharge from jails, bostan schools, certified schools and other similar correctional institutions of this State.

The inmates that are to be admitted into the state home of the care home means those are discharged from non-correctional institutions like orphanages, service homes, government hospitals, poor homes, widow homes etc.

Women who are the victims of commericalised vice will require a fairly long period of care for rehabilitation. They can also be admitted in to the State Home after necessary enquiry if they are involved in any case or danger.

Generally these admission are taken-up by the managing committee. The director and the superintendent may also make admissions in emergency and obtains the approval of the managing committee immediately.

A child below 5 years of age in the care of its mother may also be admitted into the home along with the mother if the child cannot be placed with its relatives. If the child is born after her admission into the home it may remain with her. But no single child is allowed to be with its mother after completion of 5 years of age. It can be placed with its relative or be admitted into the children's home.

Classification and Treatment of Inmates

Separate sections will be there for grown up and adolescents. Each section will have house mistress who shall be selected by the superintendent from the teachers and instructors at home. A monitor may be chosen from the inmates to assist house mistress. They take care of the general behaviour and training of each inmates in their section and also about the maintenance of cleanliness of the rooms, clothing etc.

The inmates on admission shall be provided with two sets of clothes. The material for clothes shall be either woven in the Home or purchased in the local market.

Permission to Inmates to Absent for a Short Period

On the death of the parent or guardian or to visit parents or guardian who is seriously ill an inmate may be permitted to absent from the home for a period of one week. The welfare officer of the place to which the inmate goes on leave shall be given intimation of the leave.

Discharge

The inmates as soon as they are rehabilitated both socially and economically and when the superintendent with the consent of the managing committee feels that their stay in the home is not necessary they may be discharged.

The following case studies highlight the problems faced by the inmates which have compelled them to join in the State Home. Fictitious names are used in case studies to protect the identity of the inmates.

Case Study—1

The present case study refers to Radha a 20 years old girl. She belongs to a poor family. Her story resembles many such stories in rural areas of Andhra Pradesh. She is the first daughter or her parents. They belong to backward community. She is also having two brothers and two sisters who are younger to her. Her parents with the available land of half acre tried to provide atleast basic necessities to their children. Her younger brothers and one sister were going to school.

Once her father took an amount of ₹ 10,000 from a landlord for agriculture purpose. Due to failure of monsoon and other erratic conditions of nature he could not repay that loan. The landlord took away their land. Her father, committed suicide. Her mothers health deteriorated and combined with no medical treatment. She also died after two years. Her relatives brought all the children to Hyderabad city and kept Radha as a full time servant in one small family at Secunderabad. She was blamed that she has stolen a gold chain and bangles. She ran out of that house and with the help of one social worker and joined in home. She has to stay two more years in the home. She is undergoing training in tailoring.

Case Study—2

This case study refers to Rajani, who belongs to a middle class family. She has parents, two brothers and one sister. She studied upto X class. Her parents performed her marriage with a lorry driver. She got a son.

She led married life happily for four years. After that her husband started to harass her for more dowry. Her father is a retired watchman. They are not at all able to give even a single pie. Her husband pushed her out of their house and warned her to bring ₹ 10,000 from her parents. She stayed with her parents for some months. After understanding the miserable status of her father and problems they are facing to feed two more people she came out of their house and joined in State Home. Her son also got admission in Shishu Vihar. Now she is undergoing training in book-binding unit and she wants to continue her studies if possible.

Case Study—3

This case study refers to Rani, 16-year old rural girl. She studied upto 7th class. She belongs to an agricultural labourers family. When she was 12 years old her mother died and her father remarried. Her step mother used to torture her.

She was tempted by the attractions in city life and left home when she was 14-year old. She reached Hyderabad and worked as a construction worker for one year. Then she faced some bitter experiences with her co-workers and manager, mason etc. She left that job and joined as ayah in a private school. After some days one of that school staff members started harassing her. Accidentally she met one person who works in a voluntary organisation. He advised her to take shelter in 'State Home' with the help of some known people she sought admission and now she is confident about her culture. She is undergoing training in tailoring.

Case Study—4

This case study refers to the story of Rama a 23 year old women. She is an illiterate. She has born as third child in her family. Her father was doing petty business like vegetable and fruit vending. Her parents sent her to school and she studied upto IX class. When she was in VIII class her father performed her sister's marriage after one year her brothers marriage was also over. Her father met an accident and lost his two legs. Since then their family's economic condition deteriorated. Her brother went out of their house and set up separate family. She has to shoulder the responsibility of her parents. When her mother died no one helped her. She worked as servant maid and as a cook for some time. But there she had to face number of troubles. Her brother took away her father. He did not show any care or concern towards this girl. She once involved in a police case and was sent by them to the state home. Here as expressed by her she is leading a peaceful life and working as sales women in a cloth stores. She wants to stay in the state home itself as it is providing security for her life. She has also completed training in tailoring unit. Now she is earning for herself and sending money to her brother. She also visited her father six months ago.

Conclusion

The functioning of state home at Hyderabad is quite satisfactory and the staff are also more humane in discharging their duties. They are responding on humanitarian grounds and guiding the inmates in a right way to design their future life.

REFERENCES

1. Alban, K.M., *Women a Vulnerable & Lot*, Mumbai, 1985.
2. Alahazi, M.H., *Torture Against Women*, Surya Publications, Mumbai, 2000.
3. Dudley D. Cahn and Sally A. Lloyd (Ed.) *Family Violence from a Communication Perspective*, Sage Publications, London,1996.
4. Jain Jasbir, Supriya Agarwal (Ed.), *Gender and Narrative*, Rawat Publications, New Delhi, 2002.
5. Madhurima, *Violence Against Women—Dynamics of Conjugal Relations*, Gyan Publishers House, 1996.
6. Sharmila Rege (Ed.) *Sociology of Gender—The Challenge of Feminist Sociological Knowledge,* Sage Publications, 2002.

CHAPTER 14

The Role of Family Counselling Centres to Overcome Gender Violence

A Study of PASS in Tirupati Town

Dr. G. Sandhya Rani
Dr. B. Suguna Reddy

Introduction

The strength and greatness of a Nation is measured by the character, integrity and moral fiber of its individuals which are determined by the family being basic and important unit of the society. The strength and over all happiness of the society depends on the families. The family serves as an umbrella for socio-economic stability of the society.

The concept of the joint and extended family was the normal feature of our society. But in present day society the joint family system is disappearing. Emphasis on duties and respectable submission to the advice and commands of the elders which used to serve as a stabilizing factor in the families is giving place to emphasis on rights and expression of arrogance and mis-placed self-esteem. As a result the head and well – wishers of the family find it difficult to resolve the family disputes and such matters are now approaching the courts.

Further in recent years, the incidence of increasing violence, crimes and atrocities against women have been causing serious concern. It is observed that majority of the problems are related to the family. This may be with the husband due to the marital discord, cruelty or demands for more and more dowry or they may be because of maladjustment with the family environment. In order to preserve social fabric and prevent families from breaking up and to provide awareness about the prevailing laws related to women and children it is considered necessary to establish and strengthen family counselling centres (FCCs).

Family counselling may be defined as a process by which the parties to the family dispute, together with the assistance of impartial, dignified, independent and committed, person voluntarily and systematically isolate issues in need of consideration, develop a range of options to resolve those issues, consider alternative and reach to a confessional settlement that will take into account the interests and needs of all concerned. Family counselling is a co-operative problem solving process designed to help the parties to the family disputes to find constructive solutions of the problems. These solutions may or may not involve enforcement of legal rights of the parties.

The present article is a short introduction to the 'Family Counselling Centre' of PASS—A voluntary organization in Tirupati town.

People's action for Social Service (PASS) is a registered non-profit secular, welfare organization committed for the cause of community development.

PASS has established, FCC in 1991 with the following specific objectives:

- to provide preventive and rehabitative services to women and children who are victims of atrocities and exploitation;
- to provide counselling services to those who are having marital mal-adjustments and family disputes;
- to create awareness about the prevailing laws related to women and children; and
- to provide referral services like free legal aid, short stay, vocational training and medical treatment.

For the purpose of the counselling the family disputes may be classified as:

- Matrimonial dispute i.e., dispute between husband and wife;
- Parent adolescent dispute, i.e., dispute between parent and children;
- Custody of child, i.e., dispute between husband and wife, involving the question of custody of a minor child.

The family disputes lead to bitter fight between the parties and ruin their relationship and make the children who are at no fault worst sufferers. The bitterness ill-will, related tension of the litigating couples discard their children to criminal activities and they hold the society wholly responsible for their discard and a long line of anti-social persons is caused as a consequence. This situation can be remedied by early intervention, through family counselling centres. Counselling is usually cheaper, effective and quicker than approaching any other agencies for solution or settlement. This counselling must be arranged to suit the convenience of the parties and should focus on the future rather than on rights and wrongs of the past.

PASS has dealt about more than 1000 cases so for in different kinds like marital maladjustment with husband/in-laws and with other family members etc. Out of all these cases a few case studies are furnished below:

Case—I

Mrs. P. Komala is a 25-year old woman. She got married Mr. P. Ramesh Kumar at the age of 22. Mr. P. Ramesh Kumar is working as a supervisor in Spartek Company. They have one daughter of 3 years old. At the time of their marriage, the parents of Komala have given a sum of ₹ 10,000 and 10 soverigns of gold as a dowry. They were very happy until they give birth to their child. They also maintain very good family relations. But the differences were arised because of Mrs. Komala wanted to continue her higher studies, for which her husband and in –laws not encouraged. Mrs. Komala depressed and use to struggle regularly to permit her for higher studies. After a couple of days, she went back to her parents house and approached the FCC of PASS.

After carefully hearing the clients problem, the counsellors of FCC wrote a letter to the clients husband Mr. Ramesh Kumar. He rushed to the centre and met the counsellors immediately. He reported his family problem to the counsellors and stated that their family is a traditional Brahmin family and having many social restrictions. However, his wife wanted to continue her studies for which his parents won't allow. Due to this reason, the problems were raised between them. Even at the time of marriage, they told her to stop studies for which she readily accepted then. Now she is creating problem by raising issue of her further studies.

After sitting two or three sittings with all her family members, the counsellors emphasized the importance of education in the society. After two days, the counsellors, discussed this case with the sub-committee members. The legal advisor, first advised the counsellors and the client's husband, then the counsellors advised to all the family members of clients. After three or four sittings, the client's husband Mr. Murali agree to continue her studies in vocational courses only. Komala also agreed this restriction and joined vocational course in Computer training under TRYSEM scheme. Now they are leading happy life.

Case—2

Nature of Problem: Spouse Extra-marital Relationship

The client Y. Jeeramma is a 48 years old. She got married at the age of 29 years with Mr. Kanakayya, aged about 54 years who has completed his B.A. and working as a clerk. He is drawing ₹ 4,000 per month. Jeeramma also studied upto B.Sc. B.Ed. and working as a teacher. She is getting ₹ 5,400 per month. They have one daughter and one son. They are studying Intermediate and IX classes. Their family is a nuclear family.

Jeeramma's husband has extra-marital relationship with her sister. Jeeramma wanted to solve her maladjustment in the family. Her sister was studying B.Com and staying in her house. At the same time, she has developing sexual relation with her brother-in-law who works outside. They have put up separate family. Now they have one daughter. Teeramma sought some type of justice to her family through the counselling centre.

Counselling made by the FCC of PASS

After hearing the client's problem, the counsellors of FCC wrote letters to client's husband and her sister. They came to the centre and meet the counsellors immediately. They are also reported their family problems. The counsellors were hearing their family history, family situations. After conducting two counselling sessions with both wife and husband, the counsellors have discussed with her sister about their family problems and the client was not interested to live with her sister. After few days, the counsellors discussed this case with sub-committee members. The legal adviser first advised the counsellors and the client's husband and stated that, legally the client's sister is not a wife and also she is a conquebin. So the counsellors advised the same to the client's sister. The counsellor provided the employment to her and separated from the client's husband. Now she is living with her kid separately. Now the client's husband is giving ₹ 400 per month to second family for maintenance and now all are leading happy life.

Case—3

Nature of Problem: Pre-marital Counselling

The client Miss. N. Venkayamma is a 24 years old. She came from Prakasam district. She completed her B.Sc and studying AMIE. Her family is a nuclear family with her father, mother and borther. Her father is a cultivator, mother is a house wife. Venkayamma was fell-in-love with Nagaraju who is M.B.B.S. (House Surgeon). Nagaraju belongs to Christian community and the client Venkayamma came from Kamma community. But their love has been continuing for 8 years. Nagaraju has carried out his studies with the help of Venkayamma. She provided the economic support to him.

Recently Venkayamma's parents made a marriage proposal to her. But she rejected the marriage proposal. At that time she told her parents about her love. Subsequently her parents went to Raju's house and ask him about their love and requested to marry her. Already he got betrothal with his classmate Sabitha. But Venkayama did not change her attitude mentally and left the house due to this reasons and depressed mentally and reach the FCC through Mahila Sakthi.

Counselling made by the FCC

After hearing her problems, the counsellors were referred her to short stay home which is run by PASS. She rejected to give her parents address. After one month she revealed her parents address. The counsellors use to counsel her for one hour a day. After some time she changed her attitude towards Nagaraju. After receiving the letter from the counsellors her parents are rushed to the centre and met the counsellors. They are also told their problems to the counsellors. The client was learning vocational training at SSH and she rejected to go to her parents. After one month she went to her parents to her native place. Now she agree to marry any other person to be arranged by their parents.

Case—4

Nature of Problem: Maladjustment with Spouse

The client G.S. Prasad aged about 35 years old, married Mrs. Padmaja before five years. She is 25 years old and they have one and half year boy.

Wife belongs to well-to-do family and passed B.Com. Client hail from middle class family and working as a cashier at Andhra Bank at Chandragiri and drawing ₹ 7000 per month. Client has parents and siblings. All are living jointly at Tirupati in their own house. Father was a retired employee. His income also extends for family expenses. The client Mr. Prasad wall ill-treated by his spouse and in-laws. Due to this reason the differences are raised between wife and husband. So his spouse was reached to their parents house. After 10 days she came to the in-laws house without mediation.

After 3 months the problems are again arised between the client's mother and his wife, even for simple things. Due to this reason Prasad's mother was committed suicide. With the force of his relatives he sent his wife to her parents house.

After 10 months the client's wife Padmaja registered dowry harassment case on her husband at Mahila Police Station. Due to this the client approached the family counselling centre through DSP for salvation of his problem.

Counselling made by the FCC

At the outset the counsellors called Mrs. Padmaja through phone. Immediately spouse has attended the centre with the help of her brother and relatives. She reported the counsellors that how differences were arised since their marriage. After two sittings counsellors discussed with SI, CI and DSP for settlement of the case through our counselling centre.

Subsequently spouse wanted to go with her husband with the help of counsellors. The counsellors asked them why they have registered the dowry harassment case. She admitted with influence of others she registered like that ultimately they have put up separate family and leading happy life.

Case—5

Nature of Problem: Maladjustment with Spouse Due to Alcoholism/Drug Addiction

The client Govindamma is 32 years old. She got married to a person by name Rajendra Naidu who studied upto intermediate and an unemployee. The client passed D. Pharmacy and B.A. Litt. Now she is working in RASS in IGP as a field supervisor cum-accountant and she gets ₹ 1,800 per month. They have 8 years daughter and 6 years male children and their daughter was adopted by her widow sister having no children to her.

Rajendra Naidu addicted to alcohol and collects the money of house rents and spent all the amount to alcohol and gambling.

Before marriage also he was like that. She came to know about all his bad habits after three months of their marriage. Client has father, brother, sister and two married siblings.

Her family maintenance depends on her salary only which is not sufficient to maintain their family. Husband used harsh words and quarrels when she asked about his bad habits and the maintenance of family expenses.

She was harassed by her husband several times for money because of his habits of gambling and alcohol. She beared all his harassment for 9 years. He was the only son of his parents. Client has no mother-in-law and father-in-law. Father-in-law was not legally married a women and used to keep somebody who have no children. Father-in-law is working as a driver in APSRTC. Rajendra looked after by his uncle who is a owner of the borewell cart at the time of marriage. So more times Rajendra and his friends used to take alcohol at their house. When she objected to take alcohol at house, differences were started between wife and husband. She left the home and reached the FCC with her male child. With all these reasons the client approached the FCC for reasonable help.

Counselling made by the FCC

Immediately both of them were referred to short stay home run by PASS. Subsequently the counsellor sent a notice to the husband. Husband and relatives attended the centre to get back his wife and child.

Husband was admitted about all his bad habits. After having three more sittings with husband he agreed to give up the drinking habit of alcohol and gambling. This is through the counsellings, the husband realized and the client accepted to go back with her husband. Counselling was successful and both of them are leading a happy married life.

Case—6

Problem: Mental Illness Due to Economic Crises

D. Vallidevi studied upto B.A. now she is 30 years old. Her father was financially sound. He is running a business with partners in Tirumala. They cheated him and he lost every thing (gold, money, and even own house) in business. He left Tirupati and went away. Valli Devis mother is a housewife. Due this the client got depressed. She was always thinking that her friends got married and settled happily. She fell in love who is residing in front of her house. He is a police man. When his marriage was settled with others she went and expressed her love towards him, he rejected her. Since, then she got depressed and succumbed for mental illness. Her mother and brother came to the counselling centre to refer her. FCC counselled her and referred to the short stay home.

Counsels made: After hearing the client's problem, and practically seeing her, the counsellors offered to counsel individually. But she was not convinced. She was not in a position to listen the counsellors words. The counsellors referred her to the short stay home, which is run by PASS. One day evening the client succumbed for fits. The counsellors and the superintendent of short stay home took her to the doctor and provided the medical treatment. After two days the counsellors discussed the clients problem in sub-committee meeting with sub-committee members. The psychologist came and saw the client's condition and started the treatment to the client for 3 months. After 3 months, she became normal. Then she relieved from short stay home. After two months she got married with another person, who is working in RTC as a mechanic and she is also working as Receptionist at private nursing home. Now she is leading a happy life with her husband.

REFERENCES

1. Albari, K.M., *Women a Vulnerable Lot*, Mumbai, 1985.
2. Caroline, O.N., Moser & Fiona C. Clart (Ed.), *Victims, Perpetrators or Actor – Gender Armed Conflict and Political Violence,* Kali for Women, New Delhi, 2001.
3. Government of India, Dept. of Social Welfare, *Report of the Committee on Status of Women in India towards Equality*, New Delhi, 1974.
4. Martin D. Schwartz (Ed). *Researching Sexual Violence against Women—Methodological and Personal Perspectives,* Sage Publications, New Delhi, 1997.
5. Malladi Subbamma, *Atrocities on Women*, Malladi Publications, Hyderabad, 1987.
6. Manish Bahl, *Violence on Women by Men*, Cyber Tech Publications, New Delhi, 2001.
7. Philip Burnard, *Counselling Skills Training* (A Source Book of Activities), Viva Booka Pvt. Ltd., New Delhi, 2002.
8. Udai Veer, *Crimes Against Women*, Anmol Publications Pvt. Ltd., New Delhi, 2002.

CHAPTER 15

Atrocities on Women Wife Battering *Break the Silence*

Dr. B. Suguna Reddy
Dr. G. Sandhya Rani

Wife Battering—Concept and Meaning

Beating of the wife or wife battering is perhaps the most heinous and pervasive ag—old method of subjugating women to the males in marital life. Despite the paucity of research in this area of study, we can through our day-to-day observation easily acknowledge the fact that a high percentage of women are being battered by men in every country of the world. India, with its rigid patriarchal structure of family and society and the hold of feudal values is no exception, but a glaring example of such violence. Freeman (1979) and maidment (1978) both agree that the problems of violence against women is a societal one, arising out of family system in which the husband's over powering authority over their wives create a particular 'marriage power relationship' and the subordinate status to wives and mothers (Dobash and Dobash 1980). However, patriarchy can be adduced as a potent reason and in communities where male domination is strong, wife battering is likely to be more frequent (Jean Renovire 1979) for centuries.

The laws of Manu as regards the role and behaviour of women have been rigidly adhered to in the Hindu society, who propounded a theory as perpetual slavery for women. A woman is to be under her father's guardianship in child-hood, husband in youth and son in old age. Obedience and subservience to the male was prescribed as her supreme virtue along with 'chastity' or 'Pavitrata'. In such a set up beating of the wife can easily be understood as a way of life. She can be beaten if she disgress with her master, if she does not produce male children, if she does not readily submit to sex, if she spends more on the household, then she is entitled to by her.

It is bewildering to note that hardly there has been any serious research on this most commonly prevalent form of marital violence. It is almost always shrouded and hidden by the 'myth' of family privacy while wife beating is clearly observable among the low-caste and low-income group, but in so-called high class and middle income group it is almost always concealed. Even the 'victims' of such violence do not come out and make themselves bold to speak about it, because it is so humiliating, distreassing and disrespectable. The women's organizations (Action group) have put up many forms of violence on their agenda such as dowry-deaths, sati, desertion, eve-teasing, rape and so on but appallingly this form of marital violence has not been taken up as an exclusive issue for action. Neither has the media give it much importance. But the fact remains that this acts as a 'slow poison', ultimately driving women in hollow shells or in some cases in suicide. Wife battering has been therefore often taken as a physical assault on the wife and undoubtedly leading to mental battering which is subtle and slow, and yet devastating in its after effects. It may be said to be a constant humiliation by the husband who is set in ridiculing his wife in public or proving her wrong to reinforce his own authority. Insults and pestering criticism can reach intolerable heights and when it goes on and on. The woman is as bemused by it as after physical battering and eventually loses her confidence in her self and her ability to cope.

Accordingly the present chapter envisages to delineate some unique cases of wife battering in Tirupati urban and rural setting and deduce the reasons therefor. The cases are not present with real names to protect the women's individual identity. The sample is cross-caste, cross-religious and cross-economic status confirming the fact that this sort of marital violence on women cuts across education, caste, religion and economic barriers. The information is based on two sources of wife-battering in high caste high income and educated families and low caste low income groups and uneducated families.

Some Case Studies

'A' woman highly affluent by inheritance and medical surgeon by profession was married to a surgeon with exceptional proficiency. Of course money is no detriment in their family relationship. The entire problem is one of 'personality clash' or 'clash of ego' which hindered their harmonious living. The wife is beaten on trivial grounds like non-compliance to sex or for the vehement disagreement in views. The wife is non-plussed finding it hard to make any decision. An intricate marital predicament indeed.

'B' a bewitching lady hailing from a rich and respectable Muslim family given in marriage to a sadist intellectual endowed with high academic excevence. In view of wide difference in age he has been cruel to her and batters her on suspicion and alleged infidility. He does not deter from violence despite her pleadings to the contrary.

'C' an accomplished housewife has been battered ever since she got married for not getting dowry. She has no support from any quarter. The husband ridiculously beats her in the presence of every one. However, they have two children. The wife is constrained to submit herself to this kind of violent situation condoning the ruthless acts of the husband finding excuse for his behaviour.

'D' is a housewife belonging to business community, is subjected to mental battering and physical assault. The husband being a chronic alcoholic assumes himself as highly superior to his wife and mercilessly beats her at the instigation of his mother and brother. The helpless wife tends to believe in the concept of 'fate' and thinks it is only her fault if things go wrong.

'E' a housewife turned working woman, works in the same establishment where her husband works. In course of time he feels jealous of her and feels she is becoming indifferent after getting the job and started beating her up, probably to show her a proper place.

'F' a modest housewife and the husband an engineer, was beaten by her husband too often for not obviously yielding to perverse sexual acts. The helpless woman commented in a matter of fact manner and be moaned that she is always beaten up. What would be the possible way out is any body's guess.

'G' is a working woman hailing from a low-income background and backward caste. Her husband is an ordinary government employee while she is a member of the teaching faculty. Naturally the clash is due to the 'low-self-esteem' of the husband in himself and morbid jealousy on his part of his wife's present position and status. No doubt they are living together, however, the wife is subjected both mental and physical torture at every opportune moment. What a strange complex.

'H' a working woman, soon after her marriage suspected the abnormality of the situation and in course of time to her utter dismay found that her husband was having illicit relations with her own younger sister. She dared to object but of no avail and therefore she was inflicted to intensive mental torture. There was constant altercation between her husband and herself which culminated at times in physical assault. Ultimately she obtained decree of divorce in the court. Now she strongly opines that the prime need of the hour is to oppose this form for male chauvinism.

'I' hails from a bureaucratic and high income background is married to well established businessman and a doubting Thomas. She lived with her husband for 5 years and faced man a mental and physical battering on trifling matters. She was forced in to sex resulting in the birth of a female baby. She was abused and even burnt by glowing cigarettes by her husband. She has ultimately separated and now living with her parents along with her daughter.

Findings : An observation of the above cases amply reveal the following factors.

Wife beating follows almost always when the wife dares to disagree. The issues of disagreement may be vital ones such as infidelity of the husbands, intellectual issues, sexual perversity or some petty issues of household management. Low self-esteem on the part of the husband and jealousy are important reasons. The wives in ability or refusal to act as an instrument of satisfaction of the husband's ambition also lead to violent situations. In some cases total economic dependency of the wife forms part of violence against the wife.

The second part of the study is based on informal conversation, the reasons that came up for wife beating are :

- To get money from the working wife. Though husbands earn more than their wives they think they have legitimate right on the earnings of their wives;
- Most of the communities are alcoholic and this may be major reason behind beating of the wife;
- While the husband might be having illicit relationship with another woman he beats his wife on assumed or real charges of adultery;
- Some times it is just habitual to project that the husband has full control over his wife;
- Some women openly admit that their husbands force them into prostitution or else they are badly beaten up.

On the basis of the findings an attempt is made to get down to the roots of such violence on women:

Firstly, violence against women is very much gender specific where men are dominant and women are subservient. The forms of control exercised over women cover mainly three areas namely, sexuality, fertility and labour. Secondly, women become instruments through which systematic inequality is maintained. This is achieved through rules of legitimacy of off spring through controlling access to women and in general through the establishment of possessional rights over women. Such rights include promise of protection in return for submission or for exclusive use. This is further maintained over time be socialization process that embeds women within the familial structure and he irarchic gender relations such that they have no independent status. The situation of wife beating arises out of a patriarchal family system in which the husband's authority over their wives create a 'particular marriage power relationship' and a subordinate status to wives and mothers (Dobash and Dobash 1980).

Economic Factor

The economic dependency of women contines to be fundamental feature of any society, especially with regard to middle class and upper class families. Attempts by women to have violent relationships or to find viable alternatives to them to be constrained by this basic inequality. They are subject to primary poverty irrespective of family income level (Major, Homer, Anne Leonard and Pat Tayhar 1985). Financial hardship, burden of responsibilities and the prospect of deeper poverty preserve a violent relationship to a great extent. Kalmus and Straus maintain that economic dependency of the husband is the reason for violent beating of the wife. Evidences show that the husbands power of the purse is an important factor. However, the study of low-caste and low-income groups add a new dimension to theses facts, which is that despite economic independence, women are subject to beating. The husband demands more than a share of the wives earning. In well to do families also the income of the wife is more than the husband, creates problems of ego leading to mental battering if not physical beating. Low-income creates strong feelings of 'inadequacy and low-esteem' resulting in violent behaviour of the spouses.

Psychological Factor

The problem of male ego is an important factor. Richard Yelles (1978) hypothesized that where women is more educated and better placed than her husband, the husband may feel frustrated that he is not providing his wife with the kind of life she expects or deserves., Jealousy on the part of the husband towards the wife is an important factor in battering of the wife. This may be of a sexual in nature and may reflect about his own potency on the part of the male.

Now, the question arises as to why do not women (wives) retaliate ? In answer we have to fall back to socialization process through which women have been conditioned into playing their submission role. Thus the wife goes on condoning violent acts of the husband finding excuse for his behaviour. The women also tend to believe that the 'onus' of making a good marriage primarily rests on them and it is their fault if things go wrong.

Interventions

The following are some of the interventions:

- Generating of awareness is one important method. Forums against wife battering should be formed at all levels and there should be mobilization of opinion to oppose this form of violence;
- At the institutional level, provision of 'Women and shelter Homes' is of utmost importance'
- Another wayout could be provision for flexible and legal system for identifying the crime and making it possible to report wife-battering and giving protection to battered wives;
- Women's action groups and media to give this issue the needed priority as compared to other forms of violence against women;
- It is a timely need that the activists make it a prime-issue on their agenda;
- It is high time an intensive research to be initiated to unearth and identify the deep rooted reasons to combat this most pervasive and common manifestation of violence in marital life which cuts across class, caste, religion, race and even defies importance of education and economic independence.

Conclusion

In conclusion it may be admitted that the basic need is to provide an alternative to the theory of patriarchy and gender discrimination. We can safely agree with the feminists who have identified gender discrimination being the root cause of such forms of violence for gender domination. In a society which allows pervasive discrimination of women both in the home and the work place, women could be seen by their husbands and co-habitants to be 'appropriate victims of violence in the home'. Thus the remedies lie in devising a different process of socialization for both men and women equally, to envisage a system of parallel relationship between male and female in the family and marital relationships.

REFERENCES

1. Bela Rani Sharma, *Women: Marriage, Family Violence and Divorce*, 1997.
2. Chakraborty, *Atrocities on Indian Women*, APH Publishing Corporation, New Delhi, 1999.
3. Mello D. Flavia, *Domestic Violence*, SNDT Women's Centre Publication, Bombay, 1984.
4. Niroj Sinha, *Women and Violence*, Vikas Publishing House, New Delhi, 1990.
5. Sushma Sood, *Violence against Women*, Arihant Publishers, Jaipur, 1990.

CHAPTER

16

Causes of Domestic Violence Strategies and Interventions with Reference to India

Dr. G. Sandhya Rani

Introduction

There is no one single factor to account for violence perpetrated against women. Increasingly, research has focussed on the inter-relatedness of various factors that should improve our understanding of the problem within different cultural contexts.

Several complex and interconnected institutionalized social and cultural factors have kept women particularly vulnerable to the violence directed at them, all of them manifestations of historically unequal power relations between men and women. Factors contributing to these unequal power relations include: socio-economic forces, the family institution where power relations are enforced, fear of and control over female sexuality, belief in the inherent superiority of males, and legislation and cultural sanctions that have traditionally denied women and children an independent legal and social status.

Lack of economic resources underpins women's vulnerability to violence and their difficulty in extricating themselves from a violent relationship. The link between violence and lack of economic resources and dependence is circular. On the one hand, the threat and fear of violence keeps women from seeking employment, or at best, compels them to accept low paid home based exploitative labour. And on the other, without economic independence, women have no power to escape from an abusive relationship.

The reverse of this argument also holds true in some countries, that is, women's increasing economic activity and independence is viewed as a threat which leads to increased male violence. This is particularly true when the male partner is unemployed, and feels his power undermined in the household.

Studies have also linked a rise in violence to the destabilization of economic patterns in society. Macro-economic policies such as structural adjustment programmes, globalization, and the growing inequalities they have created, have been linked to increasing levels of violence in several regions, including Latin America, Africa and Asia. The transition period in the countries of Central and Eastern Europe and the former Soviet Union with increases in poverty, unemployment, hardship, income inequality, stress and alcohol abuse has led to increased violence in society in general, including violence against women. These factors also act indirectly to raise women's vulnerability, more alcohol and drug abuse, the breakdown of social support networks, and the economic dependence of women on their partners.

Dowry-related Violence

Even though India has legally abolished the institution of dowry, dowry-related violence is actually on the rise. More than 5000 women are killed annually by their husbands and in-laws, who burn them in accidental kitchen fires if their ongoing demands for dowry before if their ongoing demands for dowry before and after marriage are not met. An average of five women a day are burned, and many more cases go unreported.

Deaths by kitchen fires also on the rise, for example, in certain regions of Pakistan. The Human Rights Commission of Pakistan reports that at least four women are burned to death daily by husbands and family members as a result of domestic disputes.

Acid Attacks

Sulphuric acid has emerged as a cheap and easily accessible weapon to disfigure and sometimes kill women and girls for reasons as varied as family feuds, inability to meet the dowry demands, and rejection of marriage proposals. In Bangladesh, it is estimated that there are over 200 acid attacks each year.

Killing in the Name of Honour

In several countries in the world including, but not limited to Bangladesh, Egypt, Jordan, Lebanon, Pakistan and Turkey, women are killed in order to uphold the 'honour' of the family. Any reason—alleged adultery, pre-marital relationships (with or without sexual relations), rape, falling in love with a person of whom the family disapproves—are all reason enough for a male member of the family to kill the woman concerned. In 1997, more than 300 women were victims of these so called 'honour' crimes in just one province of Pakistan. In Jordan, the official tolls is rising and in reality the numbers are higher because many such murders are recorded as suicides or accidents. Victim-survivors of attempted murders are forced to remain in protective custody, knowing that leaving custody would result in death at the hands of the family.

Early Marriages

Early marriage, with or without the consent of the girl, constitutes a

Table 16.1 : Factors that perpetuate Domestic Violence

Cultural	• Gender specific socialization • Cultural definition of appropriate sex roles • Expectations of roles within relationships • Belief in the inherent superiority of males • Values that give men proprietary rights over women and girls • Notion of the family as the private sphere and under male control • Customs of marriage (bride price/dowry) • Acceptability of violence as a means to resolve conflict
Economic	• Women's economic dependence on men • Limited access to cash and credit • Discriminatory laws regarding inheritance, property rights use of communal lands, and maintenance after divorce or widowhood • Limited access to employment in formal and informal sectors • Limited access to education and training for women
Legal	• Lesser legal status of women either by written law and/or by practice • Laws regarding divorce, child custody, maintenance and inheritance • Legal definitions of rape and domestic abuse • Low levels of legal literacy among women • Insensitive treatment of women and girls by police and judiciary
Political	• Under-representation of women in poser, politics, the media and the legal and medical professions • Domestic violence not taken seriously • Notions of family being private and beyond control of the state • Risk of challenge to status que/religious laws • Limited organization of women as a political force • Limited participation of women in organized political system

form of violence as it undermines the health and autonomy of millions of young girls. The legal minimum age of marriage is usually lower for females than for males. In many countries, the minimum legal age for marriage with parental consent is considerably lower than without it, more than 50 countries allow marriage at 16 or below with parental consent. Early marriage leads to childhood/teenage pregnancy and can expose the girl to HIV/AIDS and other sexually transmitted diseases. It is also associated with adverse health effects for her children, such as low birth weight. Furthermore, it has an adverse effect on the education and employment opportunities of girls.

Cultural ideologies both in industrialized and developing countries provide legitimacy for violence against women in certain circumstances. Religious and historical traditions in the past have sanctioned the chastising and beating of wives. The physical punishment of wives has been particularly sanctioned under the notion of entitlement and ownership of women. Male control of family wealth inevitably places decision making authority in male hands, leading to male dominance and proprietary rights over women and girls.

Consequences

Denial of Fundamental Rights

Perhaps the most crucial consequences of violence against women and girls is the denial of fundamental human rights to women and girls. International human rights instruments such as the Universal Declaration of Human Rights (UDHR), adopted in 1948, the Convention on the Elimination of All Forms of Discrimination Against women (CEDAW), adopted in 1979, and the Convention on the Rights of the Child (CRC), adopted in 1989, affirm the principles of fundamental rights and freedoms of every human being. Both CEDAW and the CRC are guided by a broad concept of human rights that stretches beyond civil and political rights to the core issues of economic survival, health, and education that affect the quality of daily life for most women and children. The two Conventions call for the right to protection from gender-based abuse and neglect.

The strength of these treaties rests on an international consensus, and the assumption that all practices that harm women and girls, no matter how deeply they are embedded in culture, must be eradicated. Legally binding under international law for governments that have ratified them, these treaties oblige governments not only to protect women from crimes of violence, but also to investigate violations when they occur and to bring the perpetrators to justice.

Health Consequences

Domestic violence against women leads to far-reaching physical and psychological consequences, some with fatal outcomes (Table 6.2). While physical injury represents only a part of the negative health impacts on women, it is among the more visible forms of violence. The United States Department of Justice has reported that 37 per cent of all women who

Table 16.2 : Health Consequences of Violence against Women

Non-fatal Outcomes

Physical Health Outcomes:

- Injury (from lacerations to fractures and internal organs injury)
- Unwanted pregnancy
- Gynaecological problems
- STDs including HIV/AIDS
- Miscarriage
- Pelvic inflammatory diseases
- Chronic pelvic pain
- Headaches
- Permanent disabilities
- Asthma
- Irritable bowel syndrome
- Self-injurious behaviours (smoking, unprotected sex)

Mental health outcomes:

- Depression
- Fear
- Anxiety
- Low self esteem
- Sexual dysfunction
- Eating problems
- Obsessive compulsive disorder
- Post traumatic stress disorder

Fatal outcomes

- Suicide
- Homicide
- Maternal mortality
- HIV/AIDS

sought medical care in hospital emergency rooms for violence related injuries were injured by a current or former spouse or partner. Assaults result in injuries ranging from bruises and fractures to chronic disabilities such as partial or total loss of hearing or vision, and burns may lead to disfigurement. The medical complications resulting from FGM can range from haemorrhage and sterility to severe psychological trauma. Studies in many countries have shown high levels of violence during pregnancy resulting in risk to the health of both the mother and the unborn foetus. In the worst cases, all of these examples of domestic violence can result in the death of the woman murdered by her current or ex-partner.

Sexual assaults and rape can lead to unwanted pregnancies, and the dangerous complications that follow from resorting to illegal abortions. Girls who have been sexually abused in their childhood are more likely to engage in risky behaviour such as early sexual intercourse and are at greater risk of unwanted and early pregnancies. Women in violent situations are less able to use contraception or negotiate safer sex, and therefore run a high risk of contracting sexually transmitted diseases and HIV/AIDS.

The impact of violence on women's mental health leads to severe and fatal consequences. Battered women have a high incidence of stress and stress-related illnesses such as post-traumatic stress syndrome, panic attacks, depression stress syndrome, panic attacks, depression, sleeping and eating disturbances, elevated blood pressure, alcoholism, drug abuse, and low self-esteem. For some women, fatally depressed and demeaned by their abuser, there seems to be no escape from a violence relationship except suicide.

Table 16.3 : A glance at domestic violence against women

Industrialized countries
Canada
• 29% of women (a nationally representative sample of 12,300 women) reported being physically assaulted by a current or former partner since the age of 16.
Japan
• 59% of 796 women surveyed in 1993 reported being physically abused by their partner.
New Zealand
• 20% of 314 women surveyed reported being hit or physically abused by a male partner
Switzerland
• 20% of 1500 women reported being physically assaulted according to a 1997 survey.

...(Contd.)

United Kingdom

- 25% of women (a random sample of women from one district) had been punched or slapped by a partner or ex-partner in their lifetime.

United States

- 28% of women (a nationally representative sample of women) reported at least one episode of physical violence from their partner.

Asia and the Pacific

Cambodia

- 16% of women (a nationally representative sample of women) reported being physically abused by a spouse, 8% report being injured.

India

- Upto 45% of married men acknowledged physically abusing their wives, according to a 1996 survey of 6,902 men in the state of Uttar Pradesh

Korea

- 38% of wives reported being physically abused by their spouse, based on a survey of a random sample of women.

Thailand

- 20% of husbands (a representative sample of 619 husbands) acknowledged physically abusing their wives at least once in their marriage.

Middle East

Egypt

- 35% of women (a nationally representative sample of women) reported being beaten by their husband at some point in their marriage.

Israel

- 32% of women reported at least one episode of physical abuse by their partner and 30% report sexual coercion by their husbands in the previous year, according to a 1997 survey of 1826 Arab women.

Africa

Kenya

- 42% of 612 women surveyed in one district reported having been beaten by a partner, of those 58% reported that they were beaten often or sometimes.

Uganda

- 41% of women reported being beaten or physically harmed by a partner, 41% of men reported beating their partner (representative sample of women and their partners in two districts).

Zimbabwe

- 32% of 966 women in one province reported physical abuse by a family or household member since the age of 16, according to 1996 survey.

...(Contd.)

Latin America and the Caribbean

Chile

- 26% of women (representative sample of women from Santiago) reported at least one episode of violence by a partner, 11% reported at least one episode of severe violence and 15% of women reported at least one episode of less severe violence.

Colombia

- 19% of 6097 women surveyed have been physically assaulted by their partner in their lifetime.

Mexico

- 30% of 650 women surveyed in Guadalajara reported at least one episode of physical violence by a partner, 13% reported physical violence within the previous year, according to a 1997 report.

Nicaragua

- 52% of women (representative sample of women in Leon) reported being physically abused by a partner at least once, 27% reported physical abuse in the previous year, according to a 1996 report.

Central and Eastern Europe/CIS/Baltic States

Estonia

- 29% of women aged 18-24 fear domestic violence, and the share rises with age, affecting 52% of women 65 or older, according to a 1994 survey fo 2315 women.

Poland

- 60% of divorced women surveyed in 1993 by the Centre for the examination of Public opinion reported having been hit at least once by their ex-husbands, an additional 25% reported repeated violence.

Russia (St. Petersburg)

- 25% of girls (and 11% of boys) reported unwanted sexual contact, according to a survey of 174 boys and 172 girls in grade 10 (aged 14-17).

Tajikistan

- 23% of 550 women aged 18-40 reported physical abuse, according to a survey.

Domestic Violence

The incidents of domestic violence are higher among the lower Socio-Economic Classes (SECs). The Protection of Women from Domestic Violence Act 2005 came into force on October 26, 2006.

Impact on Children

Children who have witnessed domestic violence or have themselves been abused, exhibit health and behaviour problems, including problems with their weight, their eating and their sleep. They may have difficulty at school and find it hard to develop close and positive friendships. They may try to run away or even display suicidal tendencies. Another effect under this category is the potential impact of domestic violence on the future capacity of children to obtain adequate employment. Apart from the loss of human capital, there are direct costs on the school system as children from violent homes may perform badly and have to repeat grade. According to an IDB study in Nicaragua, 63 per cent of children from families in which women are subjected to domestic violence repeat a grade at school, and on average drop out at age 9, compared with age 12 for children of women who are not victims of severe abuse.

Social and Economic Effects

Economic multiplier effects include, for example, decreased female labour participation and reduced productivity at work, and lower earnings. In the United States, it has been reported that 30 per cent of abused women lost their jobs as a direct results of the abuse. A study in Santiago, Chile estimates that women who do not suffer physical violence earn an average of US $150 in other words, less than half the earnings of other women. The study also focuses on the macro-economic impact as a result of loss of women's earnings. Social multiplier effects include the inter-generational impact of violence on children, erosion of social capital, reduced quality of life and reduced participation in democratic processes. These effects are difficult to measure quantitatively, but their impact is substantial in terms of country's social and economic development.

Crimes against Women in India

Police records show high incidence of crimes against women in India. The National Crime Records Bureau reported in 1998 that the growth rate of crimes against women would be higher than the population growth rate by 2010. Earlier many cases were not registered with the police due to the social stigma attached to rape and molestation cases. Official statistics show that there has been a dramatic increase in the number of reported crimes against women.

Sexual Harassment

Half of the total number of crimes against women reported in 1990 related to molestation and harassment at the workplace. Eve-teasing is a euphemism used for sexual harassment or molestation of women by men. Many activists blame the rising incidents of sexual harassment against women on the influence of Western culture. In 1987, The Indecent Representation of Women (Prohibition) Act was passed to prohibit indecent representation of women through advertisements or in publications, writings, paintings, figures or in any other manner.

In 1997, in a landmark judgment, the Supreme Court of India took a strong stand against sexual harassment of women in the workplace. The court also laid down detailed guidelines for prevention and redressal of grievances. The National Commission for Women subsequently elaborated these guidelines into a code of conduct for employers.

Dowry

In 1961, the Government of India passed the Dowry Prohibition Act making the dowry demands in wedding arrangements illegal. However, many cases of dowry related domestic violence, suicides and murders have been reported. In the 1980s numerous such cases were reported.

In 1985 the Dowry Prohibition (maintenance of lists of presents to the bride and bridegrooms) rules were framed. According to these rules, a signed list of presents given at the time of the marriage to the bride and the bridegroom should be maintained. The list should contain a brief description of the each present, its approximate value, the name of whoever has given the present and his/her relationship to the person. However, such rules are hardly enforced.

A 1997 report claimed that at least 5000 women die each year because of dowry deaths, and at least a dozen die each day in kitchen fires thought to be intentional. The term for this is bride burning and is criticized within India itself. Amongst the urban educated, such dowry abuse has reduced considerably.

Child Marriage

Child marriage has been traditionally prevalent in India and continues to this day. Historically young girls would live with their parents till they reached puberty. In the past, the child widows were condemned to a life of great agony, shaving heads, living in isolation and shunned by the society. Although child marriage was outlawed in1860, it is still a common practice.

According to UNICEF's 'State of the World's Children—2009' report, 47 per cent of India's women aged 20-24 were married before the legal age of 18, with 56 per cent in rural areas. The report also showed that 40 per cent of the worlds child marriages occur in India.

Female Infanticides and Sex Selective Abortions

India has a highly masculine sex ratio, the chief reason being that many women die before reaching adulthood. Tribal societies in India have a less masculine sex ratio than all other caste groups. This, in spite of the fact that tribal communities have far lower levels of income, literacy and health facilities. It is therefore suggested by many experts, that the highly masculine sex ratio in India can be attributed to female infanticide and sex-selective abortions.

All medical tests that can be used to determine the sex of the child have been banned in India, due to incidents of these tests being used to get rid of unwanted female children before birth. Female infanticide (killing of girl infants) is still prevalent in some rural areas. The abuse of the dowry tradition has been one of the main reasons for sex-selective abortions and female infanticide in India.

Other Concerns

The average female life expectancy today in India is low compared to many countries, but it has shown gradual improvement over the years. In many families, especially rural ones, the girls and women face nutritional discrimination within the family and are anaemic and malnourished.

The maternal mortality in India is the second highest in the world. Only 42 per cent of births in the country are supervised by health professionals. Most women deliver with help from women in the family who often lack the skills and resources to save the mother's life if it is in danger. According to UNDP Human Development Report (1997), 88 per cent of pregnant women (age 15-49) were found to be suffering from anaemia.

Family Planning

The average woman in rural areas of India has little or no control over her reproductivity. Women, particularly women in rural areas, do not have access to safe and self-controlled methods of contraception. The public health system emphasizes permanent methods like sterilization, or long term methods like IUDs that do not need follow up. Sterilization accounts for more than 75 per cent of total contraception, with female sterilization accounting for almost 95 per cent of all sterilizations.

Strategies and Interventions: An Integration Approach

Domestic violence is a complex problem and there is no one strategy that will work in all situations. To begin with, violence may take place within very different societal contexts, and the degree to which it is sanctioned by a community will naturally influence the kind of strategy needed.

Considering the interconnections between the factors responsible for domestic violence gender dynamics of power, culture and economics strategies and interventions should be designed within a comprehensive and integrated framework.

When planning strategies and interventions, there are a variety of stakeholders that should be borne in mind. Partnerships with these stakeholders can operate on several levels at once.

- At the level of the family, the stakeholders include women, men, adolescents and children.
- Within the local community, partnerships have to be developed with traditional elders, religious leaders, community based groups, neighbourhood associations, men's groups (eg. village farmers, associations), local councils and village level bodies.
- Within civil society, the range of partners include professional groups, women's and men's groups, NGOs the private sector, the media, academia and trade unions.
- At the state level, strategies must be designed in partnership with the criminal justice system.
- At the international level, the stakeholders include international organizations (such as the United Nations agencies, the World Bank, and the regional development banks).

Domestic violence is a health, legal, economic, educational, developmental and human rights problem. Strategies should be designed to operate across a broad range of areas depending upon the context in which they are delivered. Key areas for intervention include:

- Advocacy and awareness raising
- Education for building a culture of non-violence
- Training
- Resource development
- Direct service provision to victim survivors and perpetrators
- Networking and community mobilization
- Direct intervention to help victim survivors rebuild their lives
- Legal reform
- Monitoring interventions and measures
- Data collection and analysis

- Early identification of 'at risk' families, communities, groups and individuals.

These areas are not mutually exclusive; interventions may touch upon several areas at once. Above all five underlying principles should guide all strategies and interventions attempting to address domestic violence:

- Prevention
- Protection
- Early intervention
- Rebuilding the lives of victim-survivors
- Accountability

Women because their life and dignity are at stake, women have emerged as the most significant agents of change in the struggle against gender based violence. While women's organizations have played a critical role, the collective strength and courage of individual women has been notable in fighting many forms violence. A systematic effort has to be made to listen to the voices of grassroots women and survivors of domestic violence, and to incorporate solutions they have to offer. Their perspective will provide valuable lessons in making programmes and services effective and targeted to their needs.

Women need to be empowered through education, employment opportunities, legal literacy, and right to inheritance. Human rights education and information regarding domestic violence should be provided to them because this is a matter of their absolute rights.

Community groups and government institutions should be trained to identify women, men, adolescent boys and girls, and children at risk of domestic violence and to refer them to confidential and accessible services. Where such services are not available, communities must be helped to establish local culturally appropriate mechanism to support women.

Men need to challenge other men to stop abusing women, and to change the norms that encourage this violence. This requires support for men to act as healthy role models to younger men, and the raising of boys in a non-violent climate to respect women.

Adolescent girls and boys, adolescent girls need all the protection and support that should be available to adult women. They need clear messages about their rights from society and the educational system. Educational programmes that equip girls with self-esteem and negotiation skills and enhance participation of girls in leadership roles should become part of the school curriculum.

Adolescent boys need positive role models and clear messages from the men in their families and society in general that violence against women is not acceptable and that they will be held accountable. Support services need to address associated behaviour patterns such as drug and alcohol problems, or the risky sexual behaviour in which adolescent girls and boys may indulge as a result of being victimized themselves.

Academia and Research Organizations should address the chronic lack of statistics on domestic violence that acts as a barrier to policy change on this issue. The lack of adequate data and documentation about violence against women, and domestic violence in particular, reinforces governments' silence. In the absence of concrete data, governments have been able to deny the fact of, and their responsibility to address, such violence.

In the area of research, there are several priorities. Reliable data on the magnitude, consequences, and the economic and health costs of gender based violence will help to place the issue on the policy makers' radar screen. Researchers need to identify best practices in prevention and treatment, and evaluate them for effectiveness and replicability.

Greater collaboration is required between research and academic institutes, women's organizations, NGOs, and service provides when conducting qualitative research to deepen understanding of the causes of domestic violence, and this physical and psychological impact on women. Such research needs to be fed back to the community so that it can lead to awareness and transformation.

Women's Police Stations

Special women's police stations, staffed with multi-disciplinary female teams equipped to respond to the different needs of victim survivors, have been set up in several countries as an attempt to make police stations more accessible to women. The first such station was established in Sao Paulo, Brazil in 1985 in response to women's complaints that they could not report violations in regular police stations because they were treated with disrespect and disbelief. Brazil's success encouraged Argentina, Colombia, Costa Rica, Peru, Uruguay and Venezuela to set up their own specialized units.

Malaysia, Spain, Pakistan, and India, too, have introduced their own versions. In India, each station has female civilian workers attached, who provide advice and support, referring women to support networks and suggesting other options. Because these stations are designed to provide comprehensive support to women, including social, legal, psychological housing, health and day-care services, they respond to the many levels of support that a victim of domestic violence needs.

However, a recent study in India points to several problems with these stations, the most notable being that women are discouraged from registering complaints at other police stations. As a result, victim survivors have to travel great distance to register their complaints at the special women's police stations, and are no longer assured of protection from the regular police stations in their neighbourhood.

Legislation on Domestic Violence

In the 1990s, several factors contributed to significant changes in domestic violence legislation in many countries. Women's successful campaigning raised the profile of the issue of violence against women, and several United Nations conferences (Vienna, 1993; Cairo, 1994; and Beijing, 1995) recognized women's rights as an inalienable part of universal human rights. As a result of the new awareness generated, laws on domestic violence were adopted in many countries.

To date, around 44 countries have adopted specific legislation on domestic violence, of which 13 are in Latin America, Argentina, Bolivia, Chile, Colombia, Costa Rica, Ecuador, Salvador, Mexico, Nicaragua., Peru, Puerto Rico, Uruguay and Venezuela. The signing of the inter-American Convention on the Prevention, Punishment and Eradication of Violence Against Women in 1994 provided the momentum to enact such legislation.

The South African Domestic Violence Act of 1998 contains a particularly innovative feature granting of a temporary protection order in cases where the court is satisfied that the actions of the aggressor pose imminent harm to the complainant. This ruling allows protection of the health, safety, and well-being of the applicant and includes provision for the aggressor to be evicted from the matrimonial home while continuing to provide monetary relief to the applicant.

Protection of Women from Domestic Violence Act, 2005

The Protection of Women from Domestic Violence Act 2005 was brought into force by the Indian Government from October 26, 2006. The act was passed by the Parliament in August 2005 and assented to by the President on 13 September, 2005. As of November 2007, it has been ratified by four of twenty eight state governments in India, namely Andhra Pradesh, Tamil Nadu, Uttar Pradesh and Orissa. Of about 8,000 criminal cases registered all over India under this act, Rajasthan had 3440 cases, Kerala had 1,028 cases while Punjab had 172 cases registered.

Definition and Scope of the Act

Domestic Violence (1) For the purposes of this Act, any conduct of the respondent shall constitute domestic violence if he—(*a*) habitually assaults or makes the life of the aggrieved person miserable by cruelty of conduct even if such conduct does not amount to physical ill treatment, or (*b*) forces the aggrieved person to lead an immoral life, or (*c*) otherwise injuries or harms the aggrieved person (2) Nothing contained in clause (c) of sub-section (1) shall amount to domestic violence if the pursuit of course of conduct by the respondent was reasonable for his own protection or for the protection of his or another's property.

Scope

Primarily meant to provide protection to the wife or female live in partner from domestic violence at the hands of the husband or male live in partner or his relatives, the law also extends its protection to women who are sisters, widows or mothers. Domestic violence under the act includes actual abuse or the threat of abuse whether physical, sexual, verbal, emotional or economic. Harassment by way of unlawful dowry demands to the woman or her relatives would also be covered under this definition.

The salient features of the Protection from Domestic Violence Act, 2005 are as follows:

- The Act seeks to cover those women who are or have been in a relationship with the abuser where both parties have lived together in a shared household and are related by consanguinity, marriage or a relationship in the nature of marriage, or adoption, in addition relationship with family members living together as a joint family are also included. Even those women who are sisters, widows, mothers, single women, or living with the abuser are entitled to get legal protection under the proposed Act.
- Domestic violence includes actual abuse or the threat of abuse that is physical, sexual, verbal, emotional and economic. Harassment by way of unlawful dowry demands to the woman or her relatives would also be covered under this definition.
- One of the most important features of the Act is the woman's right to secure housing. The Act provides for the woman's right to reside in the matrimonial or shared household, whether or not she has any title or rights in the household. This right is secured by a residence order, which is passed by a court. These residence orders cannot be passed against anyone who is a woman.

- The other relief envisaged under the Act is that of the power of the court to pass protection orders that prevent the abuser from aiding or committing an act of domestic violence or any other specified act, entering a work place or any other place frequented by the abused, attempting to communicate with the abused, isolating any assets used by both the parties and causing violence to the abused, her relatives and others who provide her assistance from the domestic violence.
- The draft Act provides for appointment of Protection Officers and NGOs to provide assistance to the woman w.r.t. medical examination, legal aid, safe shelter etc.
- The Act provides for breach of protection order or interim protection order by respondent as a cognizable and non-bailable offence punishable with imprisonment for a term which may extend to one year or with fine which may extend to twenty thousand rupees or with both. Similarly, non-compliance or discharge of duties by the Protection Officer is also sought to be made in offence under the Act with similar punishment.

While 'economic abuse' includes deprivation of all or any economic or financial resources to which the victim is entitled under any law or custom whether payable under an order of a court or otherwise or which the victim requires out of necessity including, but not limited to, household necessities for the aggrieved person and her children, if any, stridhan, property, jointly or separately owned by her, payment of rental related to the shared household and maintenance and disposal of household effects, any alienation of assets whether movable or immovable, valuables, shares, securities, bonds and the life or other property in which the victim has an interest or is entitled to use by virtue of the domestic relationship or which may be reasonably required by the victim or her children or her stridhan or any other property jointly or separately held by the victim and prohibition or restriction to continued access to resources or facilities which the victim is entitled to use or enjoy by virtue of the domestic relationship including access to the shared household, 'physical abuse' means any act or conduct which is of such a nature as to cause bodily pain, harm or danger to life, limb, or health or impair the health or development of the victim and includes assault, criminal intimidation and criminal force.

Criticism

Men's organizations such as Save Indian Family and Save Family Foundation have criticized the law since it is not gender neutral and abused men are not covered. Moreover, it might be abused by women and their families during family disputes. Renuka Chowdhury, the Indian Minister for Women and Child Development, agreed in an Hindustan Times article that "an equal gender law would be ideal. But there is simply too much physical evidence to prove that it is mainly the woman who suffers at the hands of man" in a CNN-IBN interview, she commented that "this act won't hit good hubbies. The former Attorney General of India Soli Sorabjee has also criticized the broad definition of verbal abuse in the act. According to President of India in one of her speech, she said "Another disquieting trend has been that women themselves have not been innocent of abusing women. At times women have played an unsavory, catalytic role in perpetrating violence whether against the daughter-in-law, the mother-in-law or female domestic helps. Instances exist whereby protective legal provisions for the benefit of women have been subjected to distortion and misuse to wreak petty vengeance and to settle scores. Some surveys have concluded that around 80 per cent of dowry complaints are false and were registered primarily to settle scores. It is unfortunate if laws meant to protect women get abused as instruments of oppression.

Conclusion

There is a growing recognition that countries cannot reach their full potential as long as women's potential to participate fully in their society is denied. Data on the social, economic and health costs of violence leave no doubt that violence against women undermines progress towards human and economic development. Women's participation has become key in all social development programmes, be they environmental, for poverty alleviation, or for good governance. By hampering the full involvement and participation of women, countries are eroding the human capital of half their populations. True indicators of a country's commitment to gender equality lie in its actions to eliminate violence against women in all its forms and in all areas of life.

It is clear that all sectors of society are deeply affected by and bear the consequence of violence against women. More studies need to be carried out in both developing and industrialized countries to estimate the costs of domestic violence in order to advocate for national policies to eradicate this largely preventable crime.

Abuses are said to happening. If abused it is waste of court time. Abusers must pay for the wastage. It is such a good Act, it must used wherever it is genuinely needed. This is one way our society can be instigated to move towards a level of sophistication where pleasure for the most (the most possible) and pain for the least (the least possible, almost nil, or as close to it as possible) can be achieved. There are many other areas of course that need changes for better, in our society and other societies. But this Act (PWADV) in India is most needed. I see a lot of couples that go through marriages of angst. A lot of couples need to separate or divorce. A lot can be helped to maintain their marriage and change their style of interaction. To recognize early enough which couples can work it out and stay together and which need to go two ways, is badly needed. Otherwise, it is waste of time where the couple continue in their misery of being abused or of having to abuse (for lack of knowledge of any better way of dealing with it). Stern laws and brisk, predictable clear cut intervention by societal agents including the courts is going to help many souls yearning for peace.

REFERENCES

1. *The Tribune*, Chandrigarh, India–Punjab. (http://www.tribuneindia.com/ 2007/ 20071123/punjab1.htm#8)
2. *Save Family Foundation* (http://www.savefamily.org).
3. ibnlive.com (http://www.ibnlive.com/news/act-wont-hit-good-hubbies-renuka/ 26051-3.html)
4. timesofindia.indiatimes.com (http://timesofindia.indiatimes.com/article show/ msid-322617,curpg1.cms)
5. *Protection of Women from Domestic Violence* Rules, 2005. (http://ncw. Nic.in/ DomesticViolenceBill2005.pdf) implementing rules issued by the Indian Central Government.
6. *Tata Sky Exposes Cruel Wives*! Good Job (http://www.wethemen.us/ articles/ blogs/902-tata-sky-exposes-cruel-wives-good-job.html)

CHAPTER 17

Violence against Women Causes and Consequences

Dr. B. Suguna Reddy
Dr. G. Sandhya Rani

Introduction

Violence against women is not a new or recent phenomenon. Women have been the victims of violence all through the ages in all societies, cultures, regions and religious communities in the world. Women have been vulnerable to acts of violence in the family, community and the state. Violence against women is an obstacle to the achievement of equality, development and peace. Violence is a part of a historical process and is not natural or born of biological determinism. Violence against women is the manifestation of historically unequal power relations between males and females.

The Constitution of India guarantees equality of opportunity and status to men and women. It directs that women shall not only have equal rights and privileges with men but also that the state shall make provisions both general and special for the welfare of women. Despite these constitutional guarantees, women have been subjected to deprivation, brutality and extortion.

Definition of Violence Against Women

The subject of violence against women is related to offensive behaviour against women be it against their body or against their sensibility.

According to the UNO, violence against women consists of any act of gender-based violence that results in or is likely to result in physical, sexual or psychological harm or suffering to women including threats of such acts, coercion or arbitrary deprivation of liberty whether occurring in public or private life.

Under the Indian Penal Code (IPC) and special laws, the acts of violence against women are defined as crimes against women in which only women are the victims and which is directed specially against women.

Violence Against Women Through the Ages

In the Vedic period women enjoyed equal status. Gradually, violence against them began to be practised. The educational, economic, social, political and cultural opportunities were gradually closed. Even their personal freedom in respect of movement, diet, dress, marriage etc., came to be curtailed. Every effort was made to make them weak and docile. Women became commodities which could be sold and purchased which could be tailored to perform different functions. Thus violence against women came to have a social sanction.

Manu's laws insisted that a woman must consider her husband as a God. She should be kept under the control of the father before marriage, after marriage the happiness of a women resolve round her virtue and chastity as a daughter, a wife and a widow. Violence against women further increases when the young girls began to be forced to serve as Devadasis in the temples.

During the mediaeval period purdah system was insisted on women which was a violence against women. Sati, child marriage, female infanticide and polygamy took strong roots in the society. Rapes and forced marriages became common.

The British Government by and large remained indifferent to the violence against women. After independence violence has grown in all its dimensions. A few more forms of violence like female foeticide have developed because of the progress in science and technology. Dowry system has been prevailed in the society for a long time.

Today, violence against women in India has assumed an alarming proportion. According to survey and research studies, there are about thirty specific forms of violence being committed against women from the pre-natal stage to their deaths.

The following table depicts the various forms of violence that takes place in the different stages of a girl child/woman.

Various forms of Violence against Women

Life Phases	Type of Violence
Pre – birth	• Sex selective abortions • Coerced Pregnancy (for example mass rape in war, during riots, caste rapes etc.)
Infancy	• Female infanticide • Emotional and physical abuse of females • Different access to food and medical care for girl infants (death from malnutrition)
Girlhood	• Child marriages • Genital mutilation • Sexual abuse by family members and strangers • Child prostitution
Adolescence	• Courtship violence (if couple are from different castes, religions or strata, the male and at times even the female faces death, beating and ostracization) • Sexual abuse in work place • Rape • Sexual harassment • Forced prostitution • Eve teasing • Exploitation & Abduction • Kidnapping
Productive/ Marital Period	• Dowry harassment and murder • Bride burning • Partner homicide • Psychological abuse • Wife battering • Sexual abuse in work place • Sexual harassment • Rape • Pregnancies at small intervals
Elderly	• Abuse of widows (mother forced by sons to take the blame for dowry murder) • Cursing widow

Women are vulnerable to violence . Because of their female sexuality they have fallen victims to rape, female genital mutilation, domestic violence and dowry deaths. They are subject to violence not only in the family (battering, sexual abuse of female children, dowry related violence, deprivation of food, marital rape, female genital mutilation) but also in the community (rape, gang rape, sexual abuse, sexual harassment, trafficking in women) and the state as well (women in detention and rape during times of armed conflict). A number of incidents are reported in the press regarding the offences against women especially rape, molestation, kidnapping, family violence, dowry harassment, dowry deaths, wife beating, eve-teasing, etc. there has been a constant increase in the violence against women and hardly a day passes without reports in the newspaper or a magazine.

Causes

The roots of female subordination lies in the historical power relations within the society, the institutions of state and civil society. Among the historical power relations responsible for violence against women are the economic an social factors which exploit female labour and the female body. Economically disadvantaged women are vulnerable to sexual harassment, trafficking and sexual slavery.

In the context of the historical unequal power relations between men and women, women must confront the problem that men control the knowledge system of the world. Whether it be in the field of science, culture, religion or language, men control the accompanying discourse. Women have been excluded from the enterprise of creating symbolic systems or interpreting historical experience. It is this lack of control ever knowledge systems which allows them not only to be victims of violence, but to be part of a discourse which often legitimate or trivialises violence against women.

The institution of family is an area where historical power relations are often played out. On the one hand, family is the source of positive nurturing and caring values where individuals bond through mutual respect, love and affection. On the other hand, it is a social institution where labour is exploited, where male sexual power is violently expressed and where a certain type of socialization disempowers women.

Modern technology is another factor impinging on the question of violence against women. The area which is particularly relevant to the problem of violence against women in the context of technology is the issue of reproductive technology. Though reproductive technology has allowed women greater freedom and greater choice with regard to the function of child birth, it has also created innumerable health problems for women. These health problems have resulted in female deaths.

In addition to historical power relations, the causes of violence are linked to the question of female sexuality. Violence is often used as an instrument to control female sexual behaviour. In many traditions, concept of honour is linked to a women's sexuality. Violence is often justified by the argument that honour has been violated by a women's sexual behaviour. If attitudes towards female sexuality are often the cause of violence, it is important for society to protect the women from the violence of the other. This protection often entails restrictions being placed on women, whether in the form of dress codes or the freedom of movement. Many authors who have analysed the subordination of women argue that fear of rape and male sexual assault remain the most important aspects of life for women in all societies.

Besides unequal power relations and sexuality, the prevalence of ideologies which justify the subordinate position of women is another cause of violence directed against women. In both developed and developing countries, there have been cultural sanctions in the past for husbands chasting or beating their wives in certain circumstances.

Elements of national and international media may also be blamed for causing attitudes which give rise to violence against women. Pornography is perhaps the extreme manifestation of media violence against women. Although the question involves important issues concerning the right to freedom of expression, the portrayal of violence against women in pornographic literature and film, where women are shown bound, tortured, battered, humiliated and degraded is a major problem for those confronting violence against women. Pornography is both a symptom and a cause of violence against women.

Doctrines of privacy and the concept of the sanctity of the family are other causes for violence against women to persist in the society. In the past, the state and the Law intervened with regard to violence in the home only when violence became a public nuisance. Otherwise, the doctrine of privacy allowed for violence to continue unabated. In recent times, the approach to law has changed. States are increasingly reaching into the privacy of the home.

Certain customary practices along with some aspects of tradition are often the cause of violence against women. According to the World Health Organisation (WHO) more than 80 million women have undergone female genital mutilation in Africa alone. Further 2 million women are estimated to be at risk each year. Besides female genital mutilations, there are a whole host of practices which violate female dignity. Foot and hands binding, virginity tests, dowry deaths, dowry harassments, Sati, son preference etc., are among the many practices which violate a women's human rights. Blind adherence to these practices and state inaction with regard to these customs and traditions have allowed for large scale violence against women.

Consequences

The consequences of violence directed against women are difficult to ascertain because the crimes are often invisible and there is very less data on the subject matter. However, it is very clear that fear is perhaps the greatest consequences. Fear of violence prevents many women from living independent lives. Fear curtails their movements so that women in many parts of the world do not venture out alone. Fear of violence requires that they seek out male protection to prevent violence being directed at them. This protection can result in a situation of vulnerability and dependence which is not conducive to women's empowerment.

Table 17.1 : Incidence of Violence Against Women and their Percentage Distribution During 1990–94

Crime Head	1990	1991	1992	1993	1994
Torture	13,450 (19.6)	15,949 (21.3)	19,750 (25.0)	22,064 (26.3)	25,946 (26.1)
Molestation	20,194 (29.5)	20,611 (27.8)	20,385 (25.8)	20,985 (25.0)	24,117 (24.4)
Kidnapping & Abduction	11,699 (17.2)	12,300 (16.6)	12,077 (15.3)	11,837 (14.1)	12,998 (13.1)
Rape	9,518 (13.9)	9,793 (13.2)	11,112 (14.0)	12,242 (13.4)	12,351 (12.5)
Sexual Harassment	8,620 (12.6)	10,283 (13.9)	10,751 (13.6)	12,009 (14.3)	10,496 (10.6)
Dowry Deaths	4,836 (7.2)	5,157 (7.0)	4,962 (6.3)	5,817 (6.9)	4,935 (5.0)
*Immoral Traffic Prevention Act					7,547 (7.6)
*Others (Includes importation of girls. Prevention of Sati and indecent representation of women)					558 (0.6)
Total	**68,317 (100.0)**	**74,093 (100.0)**	**79,037 (100.0)**	**83,954 (100.0)**	**98,948 (100.0)**

Source : Crimes in India 1994.

In recent years a number of studies have been conducted on the harmful physical and emotional impact of violence on women. Forms of abuse result in physical injury to the body of the victim. In addition, there are psychological effects. Abused women are subject to depression and personality disorders. They manifest high levels of anxiety and somatic disorders. These psychological effects will have a negative effect on women. Violence in the family, in particular has serious consequences for both the women and the children.

The following tables present incidence of violence committed against women in India during the period 1990-94 along with percentage distribution of crimes in the total number of crimes for each year.

Table 17.2 : States/UTs in India with Highest Crime Rates during the Years 1991-94

State / UT	1991	1992	1993	1994
All India	8.7	9.1	9.5	11.0
Pondicherry	95.0	91.6	63.6	48.6
Madhya Pradesh	19.8	18.3	16.4	19.1
Delhi	38.2	37.3	34.1	16.8
Maharashtra	14.0	14.7	10.8	16.1
Rajasthan	12.9	15.7	15.5	15.8

Table 17.3 : Torture

Year	Annual Growth (in Percentage)	Violence Rate
1991	18.6	1.9
1992	23.8	2.3
1993	11.7	2.5
1994	17.6	2.9

Table 17.4 : Rape

Year	Annual growth (in Percentage)				
	16 years	16 – 30 years	30 years & above	All age groups	Violence Rate
1991	9.2	10.8	14.5	3.5	1.2
1992	16.5	30.2	22.9	12.6	1.3
1993	9.0	5.4	10.5	4.2	1.3
1994	17.2	5.7	0.3	8.1	1.4

Table 17.5 : Sexual Harassment / Eve-Teasing

Year	Annual Growth (in Percentage)	Violence Rate
1991	19.3	1.2
1992	4.6	1.2
1993	11.7	1.4
1994	12.6	1.2

Table 17.6 : Kidnapping and Abduction

Year	Annual Growth (in Percentage)	Violence Rate
1991	5.1	1.4
1992	1.8	1.4
1993	2.0	1.3
1994	9.8	1.4

Table 17.7 : Dowry Deaths

Year	Annual Growth (in Percentage)	Violence Rate
1991	6.6	0.6
1992	3.8	0.6
1993	17.2	0.7
1994	15.2	0.5

Interventionists Strategies

In our patriarchal society the secondary status and role of women is mainly responsible for the physical, mental and social violence committed against them. To contain ever-escalating incidence of violence against women, vigorous efforts are necessary to enforce existing legislations and to sensitize law enforcing machinery about the gravity of the problem. The judicial and police should be trained with regard to the issues concerning violence against women. Educational curricula should be reformed so as to instill values which will prevent violence against women. Cells to monitor the violence against women should be formed at all circle levels in the district. These cells must be sufficiently empowered to take necessary legal action against the perpetuators of crime as they are reported. They can further co-ordinate with the voluntary organisations in checking the crime by taking necessary preventive measures. They can conduct periodical surveyes and educate the masses on the need for protection of women against all forms of crimes.

The media can play an effective role be not only reporting such crimes, but informing the police for necessary action. Any laxity on the part of police must be brought to public limelight. Further the media can publish articles by focusing the existing loopholes in the system and bringout necessary changes and reforms by way of suggestions.

The Government with the assistance of voluntary organisations and other bodies should organise seminars, symposia and discussions periodically and educate the public on various aspects of violence against women.

REFERENCES

1. Freeman, M.D.A., *Violence in the Home*, Saxon House, London, 1991.
2. Ghose, S.K., *Indian Women through the Ages*, Arihant Publishers, Jaipur, 1989.
3. Jean Renvoire, *Web of Violence*, Routedge Gan and Paul, London, 1978.
4. Leelama Devasia and Devasia, *Girl Child in India*, Ashish Publishing House, New Delhi, 1991.
5. Niroj Sinha, *Women and Violence*, Vikas Publishing House, Delhi, 1989.
6. Paul Chowdary, *Women Welfare and Development*, Inter India Publications, New Delhi, 1992.

CHAPTER 18

Implementing the Beijing Platform for Action with Special Reference to Violence Against Women in India

Dr. B. Suguna Reddy
Dr. G. Sandhya Rani

Introduction

In September 1995 thousands of women and men around the world met at Beijing for the Fourth World Conference for women. Participants assessed how women's lives have changed over the past decade, and takes steps to keep issues of women high on the International agenda.

"In Beijing we will determine what can be done to eliminate gender discrimination and promote new partnerships between women and men into the 21st century", says Gertrudc Mongella Secretary-General of the Conference. The coming generation will be entrusted with advancing the achievements of the past two decades. The pursuit of gender equity is crucial, if the quality of life is to be truly enhanced. Since 1975 International Women's Year and the year of the first world conference on women, in Mexcio City there has been increasing awareness that what happens to women and their children has a profound impact on the well being of nations.

The United Nations Decade for women and the Third World Conference on Women, held in Nairobi in 1985, had as their theme: Equality, Development and Peace. In Beijing, they looked at the theme has fared in light of the changes the world has seen over the past decade.

Today, women are perceived less as passive beneficiaries of economic growth and social and political development and more as key players in their own right with knowledge, skills and energy. They are active and activists in thc family communities and nations determined to ensure a better world for their children.

Progress and Setbacks

At Beijing, delegates from United Nations member countries looked at recent trends affecting the status of women, with an eye on the future. They reviewed how women have fared in the areas of health, education, employment, family life, politics and human rights. Despite the progress made during the past 20 years, disparities between North and South, rural and urban, rich and poor, continue to concern women everywhere and declared a 'Platform for Action' for protection the rights of women.

A Platform for Action

While much of the Conference was dedicated to planning for the future, as reflected in the Platform for Action, delegates also be making a critical assessment of the past—of areas in which advances, or setbacks, have been made since 1985, when goals to the year 2000 were established at the Nairobi Conference. Known as the Nairobi Forward-looking Strategies for the Advancement of Women to the Year 2000, those goals were an appeal for government strategies to address the impact on women of government policies in areas such as employment, education, industrial investment, housing, transportation and the environment.

The Platform was intended to speed up the process of making the Forward-looking Strategies a reality, by proposing actions to be taken by policy makers and by women and men at the grassroots. The proposed actions will have realistic and quantifiable targets; the average women could either undertake them herself or ask her political leaders to do so. They will focus on ten critical areas of concern: power-sharing; commitment to women's right: poverty; education and health; violence against women; the effects of armed or other kinds of conflict; economic participation; insufficient mechanisms to promote women's advancement; mass media; and environment and development.

The goals of the Forward looking Strategies, which intended to be implemented by the year 2000, are deliberately ambitious. In the legal domain, they include equal rights for women, the abolition of slavery and prostitutution, establishing a legal minimum age for marriage and punishing female infanticide. At the social policy level, the strategies call for access by all women to maternity leave, maternal healthcare, family planning, nutrition and education, as well as for increased national health budgets. The percentage of women in politics and management is to be increased.

Stronger Focus on Human Rights

Violence, rape, torture, humiliation, anger and anguish are all too familiar to women around the world. But as Ms. Mongella observes, the silence of the world community in the face of women's rights violations has been almost deafening. She feels it is crucial that the Conference help people see that women's human rights are the same, and have the same value as men's human rights.

One of the major achievements of the past 10 years has been the support by a growing number of countries for the Convention on the Elimination of All Forms of Discrimination Against Women, which legally binds them to achieve equal rights for women in all fields—political, economic, social, cultural and civil. First adopted in 1979, it has now been accepted by 133 countries. However, many of those countries have placed reservations on key provisions that they view as conflicting with their religious or cultural practices, especially with regard an area notorious for discrimination against women.

Women's human rights have also gained increasing recognition in recent years as the focus of women activists has expanded from economic development and equality to encompass more immediate and personal threats against women's well-being. Violence against women, for example, is receiving urgent attention, in part because the Nairobi Forward-looking Strategies helped people to see the close connection between violence at the personal and international levels. Today many women's rights watch organizations are energetically engaged in getting women's human rights onto the international and national agenda.

That potential will again be unleashed at the Beijing Conference, which, coming after a series of major world conferences, will mark the culmination of more than two decades of work on human rights, population and social of major World Conferences, will mark the culmination of more than two decades of work on human rights, population and social development. It will draw on the momentum created by the first three women's conferences—a momentum that generated important new laws, increased funding for projects aimed at improving women's lives, led to the creation of numerous new women's networks and galvanized the women's movement in general. It led many countries to create national bodies and appoint individual mandated specifically to improve and monitor the status of women.

A New Beginning

But the Conference will also mark a new beginning in the long process of improving the status of women. Veterans of the three previous UN Conferences on women think the 1995 event will differ from its predecessors in significant ways. In 1975, 1980 and 1985, certain political issues influenced, even dominated, the discussions and decision. With recent developments, however, there is a new opportunity to focus more specially on gender issues.

NGO's will play a vital role at the Conference at a parallel NGO Forum. As with previous UN conferences, the Beijing Forum is being planned as an event open to all. It will take place at the Beijing Worker's Sports Service Centre, a site close to the Beijing International Convention Centre, where the World Conference will convene.

Violence against Women in India

Gender-based violence is not easy to track down owing its conspicuous invisibility. The National Crimes Record Bureau of 2002 reports an increase in the number of cases of crime against women. However their proportion to total number of cases of crime has marginally declined from 2.74 per cent in 2000 to 2.67 per cent in 2002.

Gender Sensitization

Sensitization of the police force is essential to counter violence against women (VAW). The Annual Conference of highest state level police officials includes a session on violence against women. All women police stations have been set up in as many as 14 states to facilitate the reporting of crime against women. Voluntary Action Bureaus and Family Counselling Centres in police stations seek to provide rehabilitative services. In Tamil Nadu, to encourage women to approach police stations without fear and instill a feeling of confidence in them, the appointment of one woman sub-inspector and two women police constables, in each of the existing police stations in the state, is being made mandatory, and a massive recruitment drive is currently under way. The judiciary and organization such as British Council and UNIFEM have supported programmes for gender sensitization. Gender sensitization has been incorporated into regular programmes of the National Judicial Academy.

Interventions

To effectively deal with the problem of violence against women, and to bridge the gap between public and the private sphere, there has been numerous governmental and non-governmental interventions. The government is working in two steps. In the first step, it is working towards the strengthening of the existing legislation through review and amendments, wherever required and developing institutional mechanisms i.e., National and State Commission for Women, women police cells in police stations and all women' police stations, etc. Its other course of action centres around running projects that provide support to vulnerable women, rehabilitation of victims of violence through schemes like Swadhar and setting up of helplines for women in distress. Family courts have been set up in some states to adjudicate cases relating to maintenance, custory and divorce. The Parivarik Mahila Lok Adalat (PMLA) evolved by the NCW is an alternative justice delivery system which is part of the Lok Adalats (People's Courts) for providing speedy justice to women. NCW has been organizing PMLAs since 1995 in association with NGOs to complement the judicial system.

An important initiative is the development of a community-based strategy of neighbourhood committees to create zero violence zones. This new approach to contra-violence concentrates on activating Mahalla Committees (neighbourhood groups) to tackle domestic violence. A significant experiment on similar lines is the Z scheme, a scheme that attempts to integrate enforcement machinery with people's effort. One of the key features of this scheme is the way it is encouraging different actors to participate in the programme. For instance the United Nation's Global Fund for women and the Stree Adhar Kendra in a project, which started in 1998, have worked together to highlight and combat violence in Pune and Maharashtra. Two counselling centres have been set up in Pune and Mumbai which seek to strengthen the interaction of social workers with rural women.

The emergence of community level responses to VAW initiated and sustained by grassroots collective is especially heartening. For example, Nari Adalat and Mahila Panch have emerged out of the collectives formed under the Mahila Samakhya programme in select districts of Uttar Pradesh of Gujarat. They function outside the formal legal system and use community pressure and informal social control and mechanisms to punish perpetrators of violence and restore women's rights within the family. Cases of domestic violence, rape, child sexual abuse, and harassment are handled. Some other examples of such collectives are Sahara Sanga, the support groups in Tehri Garhwal district of Uttaranchal and Shalishi, which is the traditional system of dispute resolution prevalent particularly in West Bengal. Additional examples of organized advocacy efforts include community policing initiatives such as Mahila Suraksha Samiti and Women state Committee in Gujarat which operate at the district and the state level, to promote prevention, pressurize state bodies and mobilize public awareness programmes.

The Department of Women and Child Development in 2001-02 launched Swadhar, a scheme for holistic rehabilitation of women in difficult circumstances. The target group includes destitute women, widows deserted by their families, women released from prison, trafficked girls or women rescued from brothels, victims of sexual crimes etc.

Law and Legal Decisions

In December 2002, the Union Cabinet paved the way for a new legislation that seeks to protect women from domestic violence. Presently the Domestic Violence Bill is under scrutiny by the Government. The law will enable women to negotiate non-abusive matrimonial or other domestic relationships and will provide a civil remedy to women who are victims of violence of any kind occurring in the family. Recent years have been witness to some landmark interpretations and directives related to sexual harassment at work place, maintenance rights of women, divorce, guardianship and benefits of work. For instance, in a landmark case of rape of a minor (Gumit Singh *Vs* State of Punjab, 1996) the Supreme Court held that the failure of the investigation properly and arrest of the accused could not be the grounds for discrediting the victim. The court pointed out that in case of sexual offences, concerns of the victim and of the family about questions of honour could delay the registration of the formal complaint. It further stated that the trial court should not be a silent spectator during the cross examination of the witness, it must ensure that the cross-examinations do not become means of humiliation and harassment for the victim.

Sexual Harassment of Women

The Supreme Court in the Vishakha *Vs* State of Rajasthan case in August 1997 considered provisions in CEDAW to address sexual harassment at the workplace. It laid down guidelines on sexual harassment at the workplace by holding that actual molestation or even physical contact is not required for it to be construed as sexual harassment, if the background of the entire case establishes the genuineness of the complaint. The significance of the Supreme court ruling was that CEDAW, though not directly part of domestic law, could be used by the Indian courts to shape national laws.

The Supreme Court of India has passed an order in April 2004 according to which the complaints committee as envisaged by the Supreme court in Vishakha judgment will be deemed to be an inquiry authority for the purposes of Central Civil Services (conduct) Rules, 1964 and the report of the complaints committees shall be deemed to be an inquiry report. Taking into account the Supreme Court's judgment in the Vishakha case, the Government of India is actively considering enactment of a law for prevention and redressal of sexual harassment of women at the work place. Rape laws are under scrutiny following the report of the Justice Malimath Committee (2003).

Progressive legislation in the context of personal laws has endeavoured to make Indian family law more gender just. Positive developments include the passing of the :

- Indian Divorce (Amendment) Act, 2001: amended to remove gender inequality and to do away with procedural delays in obtaining divorce;
- Marriage Laws (Amendment) Act 2001: enabling the applicants to apply for maintenance and education of minor children to be disposed of within 60 days from the date of service of the notice to the respondent;
- Marriage Laws (Amendment) Act 2003: aggrieved wife may file petition in the district court within local limits of whose jurisdiction she may be residing;
- Indian Succession (Amendment) act, 2001: enables a Christian widow to get a share in the husband's property even in the absence of a will.

The Hindu Succession Act is also being amended to grant coparcenary rights to women.

Legal Awareness

The National Commission for Women had initiated in 1996, a country-wide legal awareness programme to impart practical knowledge about basic legal rights and remedies provided under various laws. During the year 2003-04, the Commission modified the programme to make it more participative, and provide an opportunity to the participants to come together to form SHGs to avail the advantages of development schemes and to enable them to fight for their legal rights as a group. The Commission inspects jails, remand homes, women institutions and other places of custody where women are kept as prisoners. The Commission has regularly visited the various jails and have suggested that women jails instead of male jailors. Other suggestions made are that ambulance facility should be provided. The Commission also points out that women courts should be established for expediting existing cases for women who are in jails, without establishment of any crimes against them. It has also recommended that State Commissions for Women (SCW) be asked to hold Parivarik Mahila Lok Adalat with the cooperation of local legal aid cell, district judge, district court, NGOs and the National Commission for Women.

Consultations and Domestic Violence Bill Draft

UNIFEM has supported Lawyers Collective Rights Initiative (LCWRI) in facilitating two national consultations in Delhi and Mumbai to provide a platform for lawyers and activists from across the country to provide inputs to the Draft Domestic Violence Bill drafted by the Lawyers Collective. At the end of the day long consultation, a delegation of representatives from women's groups and State Women's Commissions called on the Minister for Human Resource Development, Mr Arjun Singh regarding the urgent need to enact a law on domestic violence. The redrafted bill drawing on suggestions and feedback of the various partners was submitted to the Ministry of Human Resource Development for consideration and inclusion. The Department of Women and Child has accepted the suggestions made by the LCWRI and the proposed bill is now with the Law Ministry awaiting introduction in Parliament.

Trafficking

The Government of India in 2000 has signed the UN convention against Transnationational Organised Crime (UNTOC), which includes the protocol to prevent, suppress and punish trafficking in persons, especially women and children.

In 1998 the Department of Women and Child Development drew up a Plan of Action and constituted a Central Advisory Committee to combat trafficking, rescue and rehabilitate victims of trafficking and commercial sexual exploitation and activate legal and law enforcement systems to strengthen the implementation of the ITPA (Immoral Trafficking Prevention Act). State Advisory Committees on Trafficking have been set up and guidelines issued for effective implementation of the Plan of Action. The existing legal framework for tackling trafficking, including the Immoral Trafficking (Prevention) Act, is presently being reviewed. Community awareness and community involvement awareness and community involvement being essential for prevention of trafficking, the involvement of Panchayati Raj Institutions in anti-trafficking work has produced good results in some states. The Government is spearheading active advocacy against trafficking in partnership with NGOs and has formulated a detailed media campaign using TV, radio and print.

The Government has formulated a model grant-in-aid scheme for assistance to NGOs to combat trafficking in source areas, traditional areas and disturbed areas through prevention, rescue and rehabilitation.

Emphasis is placed on awareness generation, networking amongst stakeholders, counselling non-formal education and vocational training for prevention of trafficking.

Table 18.1 : Special measures against Trafficking taken by State Governments

State Govts.	Special Measures
Andhra Pradesh	Establishment of a State policy for trafficking of women and children,Creation of a Relief Fund for providing relief to trafficked persons;Special rehabilitation measures for Devadas
Bihar	Establishment of a State Action Plan for the welfare and rehabilitation of trafficked women and child
Goa	Enactment of Goa Children's Act, 2003
Gujarat	Recognition of homes run by NGOs as protection homes under the ITPA
Haryana	Creation of Juvenile Justice Fund, Juvenile Welfare Board and Juvenile courts
Karnataka	Launching of Devadasis rehabilitation scheme
Madhya Pradesh	Launching of Jabali Scheme to focus on welfare and development of trafficked women and children
Maharashtra	Running of 150 family counselling centres by Maharashtra State Social Welfare Advisory Board Creation of a Monitoring Committee under the chairmanship of a retired judge to monitor working of children's homes, arrangements for economic empowerment and rehabilitation of devadasis.
Tamil Nadu.	Creation of Anti Vice Squad exclusively to deal with trafficking Creation of District Advisory Committees and Village level watch dog committees Creation of Social Defence Welfare Fund for rehabilitation of women and children. Comprehensive mapping of trafficking in terms of source, transit and destination points. Exposure of women police officials basic counselling courses. Creation of a crisis intervention centre to prevent child abuse
West Bengal	Establishment of homes for HIV infected persons

NHRC, in association with the Department of Women and Child Development, UNIFEM and the Institute for Social Sciences (ISS) completed a survey in 2004, on trafficking, which throws light on the causal and behavioural aspects of all agents in trafficking.

Project Prahari: An initiative in Community Policing

In village after village in Assam, a unique community policing initiative is changing the face of society and encouraging community participation for sustainable development.

From a small beginning in a remote backward village in militancy affected Kokrajahar district of Assam, Project Prahari, an acronym for people for progress is now a state level initiative. The aim of the project is to infuse a sense of empowerment in the people to resolve conflict situations affecting their daily lives by means of community participation, decision-making and mobilizing local resources to achieve sustainable development.

Thrust areas range from income generation ventures for women and youth, infrastructure development, education, health and hygiene and adaptation of technology to local needs. Community management groups with representation of all groups and majority participation of women are constituted in each village. This group draws up on action plan tuned to the needs of the community. The police act as change agents facilitating networking and tie-ups with developmental agencies.

The success of the project is evident in each of the 48 villages where it has been implemented. The village communities have built roads, bridges, irrigation canals, repaired dilapidated schools and started income generation ventures. Crime in the area has decreased dacoits have been rehabilitated and unemployed youth have channelised their energies into making better lives for themselves and their communities.

Women Police

Women police now form a part of the police force of all states and Union Territories except Daman & Diu. Some state/cities have experimented with setting up police stations managed and run exclusively women police personnel. They are utilized mostly in performing specialized tasks of dealing with women and children. In this context, the National Police Commission (NPC) has stated that women police have not be given an equal share in various areas of police work and directly involved in police investigations.

Facts and Figures

On 1.1.2001, the total strength of women police in States/union territories have 26,018. Two of them were holding the post of IGP, 7 of Dy. IGP, 29

Table 18.2. Statement of Budget Estimates—Ministry of Home Affairs

S;/Mp/	Police head	Major	1997-98 Budget			1997-98 Revised			1998-99 Budget		
			Plan	Non-Plan	Total	Plan	Non-Plan	Total	Plan	Non-Plan	Total
1	2	3	4	5	6	7	8	9	10	11	12
		Revenue	13.50	3960.00	3973.50	17.38	5194.14	5211.52	18.50	5419.58	5438.08
		Capital	96.75	416.00	512.75	83.12	353.86	436.98	91.75	401.07	492.82
		Total	110.25	4376.00	4486.25	100.50	5548.00	5458.50	110.25	5820.65	5930.90
	Police										
1.	Central Reserve Police	2055	0.90	1081.00	1081.90	0.90	1252.93	1253.83	0.90	1355.29	1356.19
2.	National Security Guard	2055	—	68.00	68.00	—	70.23	70.23	—	76.74	76.74
3.	Border Security Force	2055	0.90	1221.64	1222.54	0.90	1492.42	1495.32	0.90	1645.76	1646.66
4.	Indo-Tibetan Border Force	2055	0.20	208.50	208.70	0.20	262.45	262.65	0.20	284.77	284.97
5.	Central Industrial Security Force	2055	—	399.86	399.86	—	544.66	544.66	—	580.96	580.96
6.	Assam Rifles	2055	0.20	339.00	339.20	0.20	476.09	476.29	0.20	520.18	520.38
7.	Education, Training and Research	2055	2.80	10.15	12.95	2.80	12.08	14.88	2.80	12.80	15.60
8.	Criminal Investigation and Vigilance	2055	4.50	7.70	12.20	4.50	9.02	13.52	4.50	9.75	14.25

...(Contd.)

1	2	3	4	5	6	7	8	9	10	11	12
9.	Inter-State Police Wireless Scheme	2055	1.00	13.00	14.00	1.00	18.07	19.07	1.00	18.01	19.01
10.	Special Police	2055	—	47.00	47.00	—	115.29	115.29	—	123.51	123.51
11.	Modernisation of Police Force	3601	—	25.00	25.00	—	33.75	33.75	—	25.00	25.00
		7601	—	25.00	25.00	—	23.75	23.75	—	25.00	25.00
		Total	—	50.00	50.00	—	57.50	57.50	—	50.00	50.00
12.	Crime Criminal Information System	3601	—	2.00	2.00	—	0.90	0.90	—	0.08	0.08
13.	Delhi Police	2055	3.00	414.00	417.00	6.88	510.50	517.38	8.00	561.48	569.48
14.	Other Schemes										
14.01	Other Items	2055	—	17.10	17.10	—	20.59	20.59	—	29.94	29.94
14.02	Reimbursement to States for deployment of Battalions	3601	—	16.00	16.00	—	13.00	13.00	—	13.00	13.00
14.03	India Reserve Battalions	3601	—	15.00	15.00	—	14.00	14.00	—	14.00	14.00
		7601	—	20.00	20.00	—	19.00	19.00	—	20.00	20.00
14.04	Special Assistance to States	3601	—	60.00	60.00	—	331.11	331.11	—	125.00	125.00
	Housing										
15.	Construction of Residential Accommodation for Police										

...(Contd.)

1	2	3	4	5	6	7	8	9	10	11	12
15.01	Central Police Organisation	4055	50.00	34.00	84.00	51.55	31.67	83.22	50.00	48.25	98.25
15.02	Delhi Police	4055	30.75	—	30.75	19.58	—	19.58	30.75	—	30.75
	Total Construction of Residential Accommodation for Police	—	80.75	34.00	114.75	71.13	31.67	102.80	80.75	48.25	129.00
	Public Works										
16.	Construction of Buildings for Police										
16.01	Central Police Organization	4055	—	137.00	137.00	—	130.79	130.79	—	152.24	152.24
16.02	Delhi Police	4055	8.00	—	8.00	9.82	—	9.82	8.00	—	8.00
	Total Public Works		8.00	137.00	145.00	9.82	130.79	140.61	8.00	152.24	160.24
	Road and Bridges										
	Indo-Bangladesh Border Works										
17.	Erection of barbed wire fencing	4055	—	20.30	20.30	—	12.20	12.20	—	16.35	16.35
18.	Construction of Roads	4055	—	96.70	96.70	—	77.11	77.11	—	78.65	78.65
	Total Indo-Bangladesh Border works		—	117.00	117.00	—	89.31	89.31	—	95.00	95.00
19.	Indo-Pak Border works	4055	—	83.00	83.00	—	59.34	59.34	—	60.57	60.57

...(Contd.)

1	2	3	4	5	6	7	8	9	10	11	12
20.	Delhi Police – Installation of traffic signals etc.	4055	8.00	—	8.00	2.17	—	2.17	3.00	—	3.00
21.	Miscellaneous items	2055	—	15.05	15.05	—	15.05	15.05	—	23.31	23.31
		4055	—	—	—	—	—	—	—	0.01	0.01
		Total	—	15.05	15.05	—	15.05	15.05	—	23.32	23.32
	Grand Total		**110.25**	**4376.00**	**4186.25**	**100.50**	**5548.00**	**5648.50**	**110.25**	**5820.65**	**5930.90**

	C. Plan Outlay	**Head of**	**1997-98 Budget**			**1997-98 Revised**			**1998-99 Budget**		
		Dev.	**Budget support**	**IEBR**	**Total**	**Budget support**	**IEBR**	**Total**	**Budget support**	**IEBR**	**Total**
1.	Police	32055	110.25	—	10.25	100.50	-	100.5-	110.25	—	110.25

of SP and 79 were functioning as ASP/Dy.SP. There are as many as 255 Inspectors, 2649 Head constables and 20,877 constables. Though the strength of women police has increased to 26,018 even now they constitute only 1.79 per cent of the total police strength in states/UTs.

Table 18.3 : Growth of women police in a decade is hereunder

Year	Police strength in States / UTs	
	Total	Women
1991	1152586	13654
1992	1165872	13334
1993	1234674	14107
1994	1306268	14467
1995	1340983	16209
1996	1351047	18174
1997	1346940	18690
1998	1374608	20428
1999	1413602	21319
2000	1479024	24713

Specialized training courses are conducted on different subjects. These courses include:

- Dealing with problems of terrorism
- Computer applications
- Vigilance and Anti corruption
- Dealing with special crimes like those against women and children
- Human rights
- Radio wireless
- Cyber crimes
- Intelligence
- Commando training etc.

The state governments have not been made to spare adequate resources to bring about the desired improvements in the state of police training. The percentage of expenditure incurred on police training to total police expenditure ranged between 1.09 to 1.41 during last decade.

Police Budget

Table 18.4 : Police Expenditure in States

Year	₹ In crores
1990-91	4045.8
1991-92	4543.66
1992-93	NA
1993-94	6098.79
1994-95	6766.27
1995-96	7198.00
1996-97	7111.15
1997-98	9899.20
1998-99	12511.73
1999-00	14922.22
2000-01	15538.47

There is no special budgetary provision for women police in our Union or State Budgets though the number of women police is gradually increasing and no funds earmarked for controlling violence against women in the Budget estimates of Ministry of Home Affairs.

Conclusions

The Fourth World Conference of women was convened in Beijing in September, 1995 and formulated a platform for Action for elevating the around states of women in the world. India accepted the platform for action without any reservation. Accordingly the Government of India has designed a National Policy on women. The policy framework within which efforts are being made to ensure gender equality has been spelt out by the National policy for the empowerment of women and the X Five year plan. India's commitment to gender equality is further evidenced by the fact that it is a signatory to convention on the elimination of all forms of discrimination against women (CEDAW). To control violence against women the Central as well as the state governments of started the programmes of sensitization of the police and also initiated the development of a community-based strategy of neighbourhood committees to create zero based violence zones. NGO have also started working on this issue. Apart from all these the financial allocation in different budgets to protect women against violence or to strengthen the police force and law and order situation were not clear towards the set objectives. The funds allocated towards women's safety and security through the government plans was also not given clearly in any plan. Therefore, there is an immediate need to earmark funds to strengthen the police force, recruit more number of women police at different cadres and train them in activities to control violence against women. Apart from this counselling centres should be established and run by the police with the participation of counsellors from various fields like educationists extensionists, lawyers, psychologists, doctors and representatives from NGOs and women activists.

A multi layered strategy that addresses the structural causes of violence against women, while providing immediate services to victim-survivors ensures sustainability and is the only strategy that has the potential to eliminate this scourge.

REFERENCES

1. Platform of Action, *IV World Conference of Women*, Beijing, 1995.
2. *The Millennium Development Goals*, United Nations Division for the Advancement of Women (DAW), 2005.
3. Beijing Platform Action, *Ten Years After, India* country Report, Department of Women and Child Development, Ministry of Human Resource Development, Government of India 2005.
4. *Laws against Domestic Violence*, India Together.

SECTION–III

WOMEN'S DEVELOPMENT AND EMPOWERMENT

CHAPTER

19

Dr. B.R. Ambedkar's Views on Women's Empowerment

Dr. G. Sandhya Rani

Introduction

'Manusmrti' the ancient Hindu Code-book, the status granted to women is quite visible and she was put to the lowest rug of humanity as she was treated at par with the animals and slave by the proprietors of Hindu Dharma. Such was the placement earmarked to our mothers, sisters and even great grand mothers that the heads of humanity bend upon down with shame! That is why Dr. Ambedkar was of the firm opinion that until or unless, by applying dynamite, the Hindu Dharma-shastras are not blown up, nothing is going to happen. In the name sanskaras, the Hindu women are tied up with the bondage of superstitions, which they carry till their death. They are also responsible for inculcating these wrong notions learnt by them through baseless traditions and preaching of the Shastras in the budding minds of their offspring.

She has been used just like a machine for procreation. It has also been mentioned in Hindu Shastras that the woman is the bond slave of her father when she was young, to her husband when she is middle aged and to her son when she is a mother. Of course, all the epigrams, aphorisms, proverbs, platitudes and truisms bear necked truth about the stature of women in India.

He also suggests strategies for emancipation from oppression. He found their emancipation in Buddhist values, which promotes equality, self-respect and education. Ambedkar believes that Buddha treated women with respect and love, and never tried to degrade them like

Manu did. He taught women Buddha Dharma and religious philosophy. Ambedkar cites women like Vishakha, Amrapali of Visali, Gautami, Rani Mallika, queen of Prasenajith who approached Buddha, as evidences of Buddha's treatment of women as equals. (Paul, 1993:383-84) It was mainly the Hindu culture and social customs, which stood in the headway of women's empowerment.

Like Ambedkar, The National Policy for the Empowerment of Women 2001, also admits, "The underlying causes of gender inequality are related to social and economic structure... and practices. Consequently, the access of women, particularly those belonging to weaker sections including Scheduled Castes/Tribes, Other Backward Classes and Minorities ... to education, health, and productive resources, among others is inadequate. Therefore, they remain largely marginalised, poor and socially excluded". (Govt. of India, 2001: 2) Moreover, feminist scholars also realized the importance of caste in contemporary India. Many feminist scholars, especially after the Women Reservation Bill debate, agree that one cannot analyze Indian society without taking note of caste. Though patriarchy is pervasive in India, it varies in degree depending on the religion, region, caste, community and social group, maintained and perpetuated through endogamy.

In Maharashtra the renowned social reformer Jyotirao Phule, the founder of Satya Shodhak Samaj, started a school for untouchables as early as 1848. He started a school for girls in Pune. Sayajirao Gaekwad, the ruler of Baroda, Gopal Baba Walangkar, Col. Olcott, were some of the others who worked towards the abolition of untouchability and started educational institutions for untouchables in the second half of the Nineteenth century. Women's education was given ample stress in these schools. The main inspiration to raise the women question in India during this period was from the 'First wave feminism', which was characterized by the demand that women should enjoy the same legal and political rights as men. Its expression can be traced in many feminist works. Christine de Pisan's Book of the City of Ladies, published in Italy in 1405, foreshadowed many of the ideas of modern Feminism recording the deeds of famous women of the past, and advocating women's rights to education and political influence (Heywood, 1992:239).

Mary Astell (1666-1731) argued that since women also are rational beings, they should be educated equally; they should be enabled to live independently, if they wish, rather than being enforced by economic necessity to become the property of man through marriage. Mary Wollstonecraft's (1759-97) Vindication of the rights of Women claimed that women also are entitled to enjoy the same rights—right to education, employment, property and protection of civil law—as men do. She also presented the domestic sphere as a model of community and social order. During the Nineteenth century women's demand on the right to vote was articulated by feminists such as Elizabeth Candy Stanton (1815-1902), Susan Anthony (1820-1906) in United States, and Harriet Taylor (1807-58) and John Stuart Mill (1806-73) in Britain. Women's rights movements emerged in many countries such as American Women Suffrage Association, Women's Social and Political Union in U.K, and such others. It was when its waves reached India to form a new social awakening; Dr. Bhimrao Ramji Ambedkar was born at Mhow, in the erstwhile Central Province of the British India on 14th April 1891.

The numerical sexual disparity in marriage, he observes as "the problem of caste, then, ultimately resolves itself into one of repairing the disparity between the marriageable units of the two sexes within it". When woman and man became a surplus woman (widow), and a surplus man (widower) due to spouse's death, their existence was seen as a menace. To regulate them, the methods practiced in the mechanism of caste presents three singular uxorial customs, namely: "(*i*) Sati or the burning of the widow on the funeral pyre of her deceased husband; (*ii*) Enforced widowhood by which a widow is not allowed to remarry; (*iii*) Girl marriage". (Ambedkar, 1987:12-13). Since man has traditional domination over woman, his wishes have always been consulted. On the contrary, woman has been an easy prey to all kinds of iniquitous injunctions, religious, social or economic that is made by man. According to Ambedkar, the society must be based on reason, and not on atrocious traditions of caste system. Therefore, in the Annihilation of Caste he suggests as a means the annihilation of caste maintained through Shastras, "Make every man and woman free from the thralldom of the Shastras cleanse their minds of the pernicious notions founded on the Shastras and he or she will interdine and intermarry". He found education, intercaste marriage and interdine as methods, which may eliminate castes and patriarchy, maintained through endogamy.

After returning to India he devoted his life fully to work for the depressed classes including women. He was firmly committed to the ideals of equality, liberty and fraternity. In 1923, he started practising law at the Mumbai High Court. In Ambedkar's movement launched from 1920 onwards, women actively participated and acquired the confidence to voice their issues on various platforms. Venubai Bhatkar and Renubai Shambharakar are worth mentioning. In 1924, Bahishkrit Hitakarni Sabha was formed to work for the socio-political equality of depressed people and promoting their economic interests. Women started participating in satyagrahas and also launched women's associations for untouchable women for spreading education and awareness among them. In the Mahad Satyagraha for temple entry in 1927, even caste Hindus participated. Shandabai Shinde was one such participant. In the Satyagraha it was decided to burn the Manusmriti, which humiliated women, and shudras. In the demonstration after the bonfire of the Manusmriti more than fifty women participated. Ambedkar addressed the meeting thereafter and advised women to change their style of wearing saree, wear lightweight ornaments, not to eat meat of dead animals. It was upper caste women like Tipnis who taught them proper way of wearing sarees.

In January 1928, a women's association was founded in Bombay with Ramabai, Ambedkar's wife, as its president. Along with the Depressed Classes Conference in Nagpur in 1930, women also had their separate conference. In the Kalram Temple Entry Satyagraha at Nasik in 1930 five hundred women participated and many of them were arrested along with men and ill-treated in jails. To face tortures along with their men, women also organized their Samata Sainik Dal. When Ambedkar returned to India after attending the round table conference in 1932, hundreds of women were present for the committee meetings. At various places depressed classes women's conferences were held and they began to present their demands assertively. The encouragement of Ambedkar empowered women to speak out boldly their feelings. As Radhabai Vadale said in a press conference in 1931, "We should get the right to enter the Hindu temples, to fill water at their water resources. We call these social rights. We should also get the political right to rule, sitting near the seat of the Viceroy. We don't care even if we are given a severe sentence. We will fill all the jails in the country. Why should we be scared of lathi-charge or firing? On the battlefield does a warrior care for his life? It is better to die a hundred times than live a life full of humiliation. We will sacrifice our lives but we will win our rights." The credit for this self-respect and firm determination of women goes to Ambedkar.

All India Untouchable Women's Conference was held in Mumbai. (Limaye, 1999:57-61) In the movement, his strategy was similar to Gandhian method though he had disagreements on many things with Gandhi. To him the emphasis was on reconstruction of the Hindu society on the basis of equality rather than the social reforms initiated by Brahma Samaj or Arya Samaj because their attempts were limited only to the upper strata of the society.

Running newspapers, women's hostels, boarding schools participating in Sathyagrahas were some of the activities of woman for acquiring the personality development to secure efficient administrative and leadership capacity as men have. Gaining inspiration and encouragement from Ambedkar, many women wrote on topics like Planning, Buddhist philosophy and such other topics. Women also wrote plays, autobiographies, and participated in Satyagrahas. Tulsabai Bansode started a newspaper Chokhamela. This showed how Ambedkar created awareness among poor, illiterate women and inspired them to fight against the unjust social practices like child marriages and devdasi system.

Since Ambedkar was well convinced about the status of women, as the Chairman of the Drafting Committee, he tried an adequate inclusion of women's rights in the political vocabulary and constitution of India. Therefore, by considering women's equality both in formal and substantial senses he included special provisions for women while all other general provisions are applicable to them, as to men. Hence, there are Articles like 15(3), 51(A), and so on. His key work in the preparation of Indian Constitution made it to be known as a New Charter of Human Rights. He looked upon law as the instrument of creating a sane social order in which the development of individual should be in harmony with the growth of society. He incorporated the values of liberty, equality and fraternity in the Indian Constitution.

Ambedkar's defense for women as the Law Minister of free India appeared in the form of the Hindu Code Bill in Parliament on 11th April 1947, which invited strong opposition from the Hindu orthodoxy in post-independent India. The Bill provided for several basic rights to women.

It sought to abolish different marriage systems prevalent among Hindus and to establish monogamy as the only legal system. It aimed at conferment of right to property and adoption of women. It provided for restitution of conjugal rights and judicial separation. It attempted to unify the Hindu code in tune with progressive and modern thought. (Mathew, 1991:73-73; Ahir, 1990)

In 1948 when the Hindu Code Bill was introduced in parliament and debated on the floor of the house, the Opposition was strong against the Bill. Ambedkar tried his level best to defend the Bill by pointing out the drawbacks of Indian society and arguing that the ideals in the Bill are based on the Constitutional principles of equality, liberty and fraternity and that in the Indian society characterised by the caste system and the oppression of women since women are deprived of equality, a legal frame work is necessary for a social change in which women have equal rights with men. He also pointed out that the aim of the Bill was "to codify the rules of Hindu Law which are scattered in innumerable decisions of High Courts and of the Privy Council which form bewildering motley to the common man". (Arya, 2000:63).

Although most of the provisions proposed by Ambedkar were later passed during 1955-56 in four Bills on Hindu 'marriage', succession', 'minority and guardianship' and 'maintenance,' and later in 1976 some changes were made in Hindu Law, it still remains true that the basic rights of women have yet to be restored to them even after fifty years of the working of the Indian Constitution based on the principle of liberty, equality and justice to all Indian citizens.

This crusade of Ambedkar to emancipate women from injustice inspires the women leaders in Parliament to keep the issue alive until its enactment. This was the starting point for women to recognize their position and pursue rights movement by acquiring strength from 'second wave feminism' started in the early 1960s. Women are still fighting issues such as rape, dowry death, communalism, and fundamentalism, and sexual harassment, violence-domestic and social, poverty and so on.

Conclusion

Ambedkar suggests strategies for emancipation from oppression. He found their emancipation in Buddhist values, which promotes equality, self-respect and education. Ambedkar believes that Buddha treated women with respect and love, and never tried to degrade them like Manu did. He taught women Buddha Dharma and religious philosophy. He believed that the Hindu culture and social customs, which stood in the headway of women's empowerment.

He found education, intercaste marriage and interdine as methods, which may eliminate castes and patriarchy, maintained through endogamy. He was firmly committed to the ideals of equality, liberty and fraternity. In 1923, he started practising law at the Mumbai High Court. In Ambedkar's movement launched from 1920 onwards, women actively participated and acquired the confidence to voice their issues on various platforms. Women started participating in satyagrahas and also launched women's associations for untouchable women for spreading education and awareness among them.

All India Untouchable Women's Conference was held in Mumbai. (Limaye, 1999:57-61) In the movement, his strategy was similar to Gandhian method though he had disagreements on many things with Gandhi. To him the emphasis was on reconstruction of the Hindu society on the basis of equality rather than the social reforms initiated by Brahma Samaj or Arya Samaj because their attempts were limited only to the upper strata of the society.

REFERENCES

1. Ahir, D.C.: *The Legacy of Ambedkar*, Delhi, 1990
2. Ambedkar, B.R. *"Women and Counter Revolution"*, "Riddles of Hindu Women" in *Dr. Baba Saheb Ambedkar: Writings and Speeches*, Vol.3, Department of Education, Government of Maharashtra, 1987
3. Arya, Sudha, *Women Gender Equality and the State*, Deep and Deep Publications, New Delhi, 2000.
4. Castes in India: Their Mechanism Genesis and Development", "Castes in India" in *Dr. Baba Saheb Ambedkar: Speeches and Writings*, Vol. I Education Department, Government of Maharashtra, 1979
5. Chirakarode, Paul: *Ambedkar: Boudhika Vikshobhathinte Agnijwala*, Dalit Books, Thiruvalla, 1993.
6. Contributor K.B.USHA: U.G.C. Research Associate at the Department of Politics, University of Kerala. She has taken her Ph. D on Soviet Studies from the Jawaharlal Nehru University, New Delhi. Currently working on the topic 'Political Empowerment of Women – A Critical Study of the Indian Experience.'
7. Government of India: The National Policy for the Empowerment of Women 2001, Department of Women and Child Development, Ministry of Human Resource Development, New Delhi, 2001
8. Haksar, Nandita, *Demystification of Law for Women*, Lancer Press, New Delhi. 1986.
9. Heywood, Andrew: *Political Ideologies: An Introduction*, Macmillan Press, London. 1998.
10. Limaye, Champa: *Women: Power and Progress*, B.R.Publishing Corporation, New Delhi, 1999.
11. Mathew, Thomas: Ambedkar: Reform or Revolution, Segment Books, New Delhi, 1991.
12. The Rise and Fall of the Hindu Women", the Mahabodhi (Calcutta), 59.5-6. 137-151. 1950.

CHAPTER

20

Perceptions of Ambedkar Towards Women's Development

Dr. B. Suguna Reddy
Dr. G. Sandhya Rani

Introduction

The operation of caste, both at the systemic level and at the functioning of patriarchy, the growing caste/class divide in feminist political discourses made Ambedkar's views on women's oppression, social democracy, caste and Hindu social order and philosophy become significant to modern Indian feminist thinking. The contemporary social realities warrant close examination of the wide range of his topics, the width of his vision, the depth of his analysis, and the rationality of his outlook and the essential humanity of his suggestions for practical action. For the Indian Women's Movement, Ambedkar provides a powerful source of inspiration to formulate a feminist political agenda which simultaneously addresses the issues of class, caste and gender.

The operation of caste both at the systemic level and at the functioning of patriarchy, the growing caste/class divide in feminist political discourses makes Ambedkar's views on women's oppression, social democracy, caste and Hindu social order and philosophy, significant to modern Indian feminist thinking.

Hence, for Indian women's movement Ambedkar provides a powerful source of inspiration to formulate a feminist political agenda which simultaneously addresses the issues of class, caste and gender in the contemporary socio-political set up, which still keeps conservative and reactionary values in many respects, particularly on gender relations.

The Government of Maharashtra and Government of India have brought volumes of his published and unpublished works during the occasion of Ambedkar centenary celebrations. His works have been published in various regional languages also. Ambedkar saw women as the victims of the oppressive, caste-based and rigid hierarchical social system.

He believed that socio-cultural forces artificially construct gender relations, especially by Manusmriti and Hindu religion. As Simone De Beauvoir observed, "Women are made, they are not born", Ambedkar also raised the question, "Why Manu degraded her (woman)?" In his The Riddle of the Woman, The Woman and the Counter Revolution, The Rise and Fall of Hindu Women, Castes in India: Their Mechanism Genesis and Development and through the issues of his journals Mooknayak (1920) and Bahishkrit Bharat (1927), Ambedkar tries to show how the gender relations and differences are constructed by Hindu Brahminical order, which conditions women to conform a stereotype feminine behaviour, requiring them to be passive and submissive, suited only to a life of domestic and family responsibilities.

In the Women and Counter Revolution and The Riddle of Women Ambedkar portrays the way in which Manu treated women. He pointed out that the laws of Manu on the status of women are very important in moulding the Hindu attitude and perspective (Indian perspective) towards women, perpetuated and maintained through Hindu personal laws based on shastras, caste and endogamy, i.e. the base of Indian patriarchy. He attacked Manusmriti as a major source, which legitimizes the denial of freedom, self respect, right to education, property, divorce etc., to women by attributing a very lofty ideal to them. He observes in the law book of Manu that the killing of a woman is like the drinking of liquor, a minor offence. It was equated with killing of Sudra. Manu even advises a man not to sit in a lonely place with his own sister, daughter or even mother. Some of the other laws Manu prescribed are:

Day and night women must be kept in dependence by the males (of their families), and, if they attach themselves to sexual enjoyments, they must be kept under one's control. Her father protects her in childhood, her husband protects her in youth, and her sons protect her in old age; a woman is never fit for independence. Nothing must be done independently by a girl, by a young woman, or even by an aged one, even in her own house.

In the matter of property a wife was degraded by Manu just as a slave. He forbade women the study of Vedas, and performing Sanskaras uttering the Ved mantras because he projected women as unclear as untruth is. Manu instructs women: "Though destitute or virtuous or seeking pleasure elsewhere, or devoid of good qualities, yet a husband must be constantly worshipped as a god by a faithful wife. ...She must always be cheerful, clever in management of her household affairs, careful in cleaning her utensils, and economic in expenditure". Ambedkar cites evidences of higher status of women in the pre-Manu days. She was free and equal partner of man and had the right to education, divorce, remarriage and economic freedom. The story of public disputation between Janaka and Sulabha, Yajnavalkya and Maitrei, Yajnavalkya and Gargi, and Sankaracharya and Vidyadhari show that Indian women in the pre-Manu period could rise to the highest pinnacle of learning and education. It is generally believed that Dr. Ambedkar had completed the books entitled The Riddles of Hinduism, The Buddha and Karl Marx, and Revolution and Counter Revolution. All carry chapters on women entitled Elevation of Women and Degradation of Women which expose how Chaturvarna prioritised 'birth' instead of 'worth,' degraded women and is unable to from time immemorial, the women in this land of ours were treated as a sort of thing. Her placing in the society was not at par with other human being. She has no rights. She cannot move nor does anything at her will. In Hindu Shastras, she has been branded just like animals. From the verses of Ramayan as written by Mr. Tulsi Das, " Dhol, ganwar, shudra, pashu, naari—Ye sab tadan ke adhikari," one may easily draw inferences as to what status has been granted to our mothers.

In this direction Dr. B.R. Ambedkar has tried to brake down the barriers in the way of advancement of women in India. He laid down the foundation of concrete and sincere efforts by codifying the common Civil Code for the Hindus and the principle is capable of extension to other sections of the Indian society. Prior to these efforts of Dr. Ambedkar, the destiny of the Indian women depended upon the wrong notions and perceptions chalked out by the proprietors of orthodoxy.

The prevailing two schools of Hindu Law viz. 'Mitakshara' and 'Dayabhag, created and sustained inequality. According to 'Mitakshara' the property of a Hindu is not his individual property. It belongs to what is called coparcenary, which consists of father, son, grandsons and great grandsons by reason of birth. The property passed under Mitakshara by survivorship to the members of coparcenary who remain behind, and does not pass to the heirs of the deceased. Whereas Dayabhag recognised the property held by the heir as his personal property with an absolute right to dispose it of either by gift or by will or any other manner that he chooses. The chaotic conditions of the Hindu law were reduced to eat propositions in the form of judicial pronouncements and codification was the legislative recognition of the judge made law. Dr. Ambedkar himself had explained lucidly the reasons for consolidation and codification.

Article 25 of the Indian Constitution permits all the freedom. The reforms introduced by Dr. Ambedkar through 'Hindu Code-bill' have been adhered to and have been accepted by and large. He, by codifying Hindu Law in respect of marriage, divorce and succession, rationalized and restored the dignity to women. Prior to the Hindu Succession Act, 1956 and Hindu Marriage Act, 1955, the Hindu Law was uncodifyed in a large measure, though Hindu Women's Right to Property Act, 1937 was the subject legislative intervention. The Sharda Act is also worth mentioning. It has set the seal of authority upon that piece of social reforms, which the heads of orthodoxy were, imposing and impending. In Hindu Code Bill, the principles of codification covered: (*i*) Right to property; (*ii*) Order of succession to property; (*iii*) Maintenance, marriage, divorce, adoption, minority and guardianship.

Needless to say, the Bill was a part of social engineering via law. It was by any standard of any time a revolutionary measure. It was really a first step towards the recognition and empowerment of women in India. Under these revolutionary measures, a woman will have property in her own right and be able to dispose of her property.

In recent past, a lot hue and cry is being made over 'Women's Reservation Bill' by the different sections of the Indian society, different political or apolitical organizations but nobody seems to be honest in its perspectives. The political empowerment is a must for the all round development of the women, but as in the case of dalit politicians and legislators, our efforts may prove futile. We must concentrate on imparting social education before giving any concrete shape to their political empowerment to the women. Without academic and social education, the political empowerment of women in certain parts of the country had proved futile. In Panchayat Raj set up in U.P. and elsewhere in the country, the uneducated women are subjected to exploitation at the hands of government machinery. It will not be prudent on our part to restore the rights of the women belonging to the affluent section of the society only. Therefore, our efforts should be directed towards all round development of each and every section of Indian women by giving their due share. It is a must to maintain and protect chastity, dignity and modesty of women. It is the need of the hour to give due share to each and every section of the Indian women. I am sure, without removing social stigma, no progress or development could be achieved.

First of all we must try to treat our female child as par our female child as par with our male ones and thenceforth restore equality amongst them. No restoration of property right would be meaningful without making her mentally strong. We must allow them to think breathe and act independently and bring her out of the shackles of slavery. Do not impose the filthy rites, rituals and superstition citing the examples from our dated SHASTRAS. Don't treat women your slave or servant who has come to this world just to cook your food, wash your dirty clothes, and fulfil your other needs.

Conclusion

Ambedkar believed that socio-cultural forces artificially construct gender relations. He tried to show how the gender differences are constructed in the society and led to the submissions and passive positions of women. To elevate the status of women he believed that legal sanctions are necessary. He has given many provisions to women in our Constitution and also introduced the Hindu code bill in which, women are entitled to avail property Right, Order of Succession to property, Maintenance, Marriage, Divorce Adoption etc... Throughout his life Dr.B.R.Ambedkar fought for women's development and criticized many customs and systems which are responsible for the subjugation women in the contemporary society.

REFERENCES

1. *Ambedkar—A Critical Study,* W.N. Kuber, Published in Amazan.Com, 1992.
2. *Doctor Ambedkar Rachanalu-Prasangalu samputa*–11.
3. *Doctor Ambedkar Rachanalu-Prasangalu samputa*–12.
4. http://drambedkarbooks.wordpress.com
5. *Samatha India.* (An online Community of Dalits. A place for dalit news, articles, issues links.
6. *Valerian Rodrigues—The Essential Writings of Dr. B.R. Ambedkar*, Academic books, New Delhi.
7. www.ambedkar.org

CHAPTER

21

Women and Empowerment

Dr. G. Sandhya Rani

Women have been treated so long as ones lacking in ability and fit once for certain traditional tasks, that their confidence in themselves and in their abilities has shrunk greatly which further reinforced the prevalent attitudes. In order to help woman to come out of this vicious cycle, it is essential that they are supported and guided in the path of empowerment.

Social roles have cast women in a secondary position for such a long time that women themselves often perceive their own role as secondary and as such may not be comfortable with the idea of empowerment.

The concept of women's empowerment is the outcome of several important critiques and debates generated by the women's movements throughout the world, particularly be the third world feminists. Its source can be traced from the interaction between feminism and the concept of 'popular education' developed in Latin America in the 1970's (Walters : 1991).

In this chapter an attempt has been made to discus the various elements. Components and strategies involved in the process of women's empowerment.

Becoming powerful—the liberal meaning of the term 'empowerment' is being used today in all spheres of life as a process to strengthen the elements of society. It is both a process and the result of the process. It is transformation of the structures or institutions that reinforces and perpetuates gender discrimination.

The empowerment approach was first clearly articulated in 1985 by Development alternatives with women for a New Era (DAWN). This term received prominence in early nineties in western countries. In India the Central Government in its welfare programmes shifted the concept of development to empowerment in the Ninth Five Year Plan (1997 – 2002) and observed the year 2001 as 'Women Empowerment Year'.

The process of gaining control over the self, over ideology and the resources which determine power may be treated as empowerment. Empowerment is a process and the outcome of empowerment is redistribution of power.

Definition of Empowerment

According to Bandura (1986), "Empowerment is the process through which individuals gain efficacy, defined as the degree to which an individual perceives that her or she controls hir or her environment.

While discussing empowerment Jo Rowlands (1997) has identified four different forms of powers:

- *power over*—control or influence over others which is an instrumentation of domination;
- *power to*—generative or productive power which creates new possibilities and actions without domination;
- *power with*—a sense of the whole being greater than the sum of the individuals, especially, when a group tackles problems together;
- *power from within*—the spiritual strength and uniqueness that resides in each of us and makes us truly human. Its basis is self – acceptance and self-respect which extend, intern, respect for and acceptance of others as equals.

Empowerment is a process and there is no single method for measuring it. It should be understood and defined through indicators. These indicators should encompass personal, social, economic and political changes. It is also a process of challenging existing power relations and of gaining greater control over the sources of power. The goals of women empowerment are to challenge partnarchal ideology to transform the structures and institutions that reinforce and perpetuate gender discrimination and social inequality and to enable poor women to gain access to and control of both material and information resources. Empowerment cannot occur as a revolution but only as evolution.

Components of Empowerment

The following are identified as the components of empowerment:

- Sense of internal strength and confidence to face life;
- The right to make choices;
- The power to control their own lives within and outside the home; and
- The ability to influence the direction of social change towards the creation of a more just social and economic order nationally and internationally.

Process of Empowerment

Empowerment as an individual and collection process is based on the following principles:

- Self reliance
- Self awareness
- Collective mobilization and organisation
- Capacity building
- External exposure and interaction.

Empowerment has to pass through different stages. In the first stage, women should be trained to look into the situation from a different perspective and recognize the power relations that perpetuate their oppression. At this stage, the women share their feelings and experiences with each other and build a common vision and mission. In the second stage, the women try to change the situation by bringing about a change in the gender and social relations in the third stage, the process of empowerment makes them more mature to realize the important of collective action.

Empowerment could be placed at two levels:

- Individual; and
- Collective.

Individual empowerment is a process of personal empowerment involving self-esteem, dignity, self-respect and self-perception. Collective employment aims at transforming collective consciousness, values and attitudes. This requires effective organisation, mutual help and co-operation.

Empowerment can be classified into three broad categories :

- Social or socio/cultural.

- Economic
- Political

Social Empowerment

To create an enabling environment through various confired affirmative developmental polices and programmes for development of women besides providing them easy and equal access to all the basic minimum services so as to enable so as to enable them to realise their full potentials.

Economic Empowerment

To ensure provision of education training, employment and income generation activities with both forward and backward linkages with the ultimate objective of making all potential women economically independent and self-reliant;

Political Empowerment

To enable women to be politically more conscious, active and articulate.

Strategies

Empowerment can be activated through the following strategies. Education to promote the level of awareness, knowledge, information and skills of a women. Awareness is a pre-requisite for challenging the forces of oppression status que. It results in greater participation of women in decision making within and outside the family. The economic approach to empowerment seeks to alter the economic status of women by attacking the forces which cause gender division of labour, gender gap in wages, lack of control for women over their material resources etc.

It also emphasizes development of women's skills, promotion of their savings, and investment and enlarged economic opportunities.

The development approach attributer poverty to their powerlessness and the lack of adequate access to health care, education and service resources. Yet another approach believes that women's empowerment requires awareness of complex factors causing disempowerment of women. This approach advocates collective organisation of women as well as gender sensitization, gender planning and strategy and consciousness raising activities. More recently, an organizational approach has been advocated which believes that organised women can after the gender and social relations in favour of women both in public and private lives.

Finally, political approaches to empowerment believes that women can be developed on par with men, if politics are purged of violence, electoral malpractices, unscrupulous struggles etc, and were made value based. This would, however require greater participation of women in active politics.

Empowerment could place at two levels:

- Individual; and
- Collective.

Individual empowerment is a process of personal empowerment involving self-esteem, dignity, self respect and self perception.

Collective empowerment aims at transforming collective consciousness, values and attitudes. This requires effective organisation, mutual help and co-operation among women.

One of the most important things that women needs inorder to be successful in any activity is to become empowered. Women face many social barriers in their attempts to become successful. She needs persistence, determination courage, and support to succeed in her efforts.

Social roles have cast women in a secondary role for such a long time that women themselves often perceive their own role as secondary and as such may not be comfortable with the idea of empowerment.

Conclusion

Empowerment is a process and the outcome of empowerment is redistribution of power. The concept of women's empowerment has its roots throughout the world in women's movements. One of the most important things that woman needs in order to be successful in any activity is to become empowered. Women face many social barriers in their attempts to become successful. She needs persistence, determination, courage and support to succeed in her efforts.

REFERENCES

1. *National Policy for the Empowerment of Women 2001*, Ministry of Women and Child Development, Government of India.
2. Boserup Ester, *Women's Role in Economic Development*, St. Martin's Press, New York, 1970.
3. Karl Marilee, *Woman and Empowerment Participation and Decision-making;* Zed Books Ltd, London and New Jersey, 1995.

4. Leelamma Devasia and V.V. Devasia, *Empowering Women for Sustainable Development*, Ashish Publishing House, New Delhi, 1997.
5. Leslie J. Calman, *Towars Empowerment, Women and Movement Politics in India*, boulder, hest view press, 1992.
6. Margaret Hall C, *Women and Empowerment*, Hemisphere Publishing Corporation, Washington, 1992.
7. Mitra Jyothi, *Women and Society—Equality and Empowerment*, Kanishka Publishers, New Delhi, 1997.
8. Carr Marilyn *et.al.*, *Speakingout—Women's Economic Empowerment in South Asia*. Vistaar Publications, New Delhi, 1997.
9. Shanthi K. (ed). *Empowerment of Women*, Anmol Publications Pvt. Ltd. New Delhi, 1998.

CHAPTER 22

Social Forestry in India and Role of Women

Dr. G. Sandhya Rani

In developing countries of the world, women are considered the primary users of natural resources (land, forest and water), because they are the ones who are responsible for gathering food, fuel and fodder. Although, in these countries, women mostly can't own the land and forms outright, they spend most of their time working on the farms to feed the household. Shouldering this responsibility leads them to learn more about soil, plants, and trees and not to misuse them. Although, technological inputs increase male involvement with land many of them leave the farm to go to cities to find jobs. So women become increasingly responsible for an increasing portion of farm tasks. These rural women tend to have a closer relationship with land and other natural resources, which promote a new culture of respectful use and preservation of natural resources and the environment, ensuring that the following generations can meet their needs. Women's perspectives and values for the environment are some what different that of men's. Women give greater priority to protection of and improving the capacity of nature, caring for nature and maintaining ecological balance. Repeated studies have shown, that women have a stake in environment and this stake is reflected in the degree to which they care about natural resources. Eco-feminism refers to Women's and feminist perspectives on the environment—where the domination and exploitation of women, of poorly resourced people and of nature is at the heart of the eco-feminist movement.

Environmental Change and Women

Today, women struggle against alarming global trends, but they are working together to effect that change. By establishing domestic and international non-governmental organizations, many women have recognized themselves and acknowledged to the world that they not only have the right to participate in environmental dilemmas but they have different relationship with environment including different needs, responsibilities and knowledge about natural resources. Therefore, women are affected differently than men by environmental degradation, deforestation, pollution and over population.

Gender Perception of the Environment

Given the environmental degradation caused while men have had dominance over women, and women's large investment in environmental sustainability, some have theorized that women would protect the earth better than men if in power. Although there is no evidence for this hypothesis, recent movements have shown that women are more sensitive to the earth and its problems. They have created a special value system about environmental issues. Both women and nature have been considered subordinate entities by men which conveys a close affiliation between them.

Throughout history men have looked at natural resources as commercial entities or income generating tools, while women have tended to see the environment as a resource supporting their base needed. As an example, rural Indian women collect the dead branches which are cut by storm for fuel wood to use rather than cutting the live trees.

Any changes in the environment of these areas, like deforestration, have the most effect on women of that area, and cause them to suffer until they can cope with these changes.

While cutting a forest for income generation is something men would do, women are more likely to keep and protect a forest. For example in India in 1906, there was a conflict between men and women in the Lilly region Chipko. As forest clearing was expanding, the women protested by physically hugging themselves to the trees to prevent them being cut down, giving raise to what is now called the 'Chipko Movement' an environmentalist movement initiated by these women.

Social Forestry Programme—An Overview

The term 'Social forestry' was first used in 1973 by The National Commission on Agriculture, Government of India. It was then that India embarked upon a social forestry project with the aim of taking the pressure of currently existing forests by planting trees on all *unused and fallow land.*

Government forest areas that are close to human settlement and have been degraded over the years due to human activities needed to be afforested. Trees were to be planted in and around agricultural fields. Plantation of trees along railway lines and roadsides, and river and canal banks were carried out. They were planted in village common land, Government wasteland and Panchayat land.

Social forestry also aims at raising plantation by the common person so as to meet the growing demand for timber, fuel wood, fodder, etc, thereby reducing the pressure on the traditional forest area. This concept of village forests to meet the needs of the rural people is not new. It has existed through the centuries all over the country but it was now given a new character.

With the introduction of this scheme the government formally recognized the local communities' rights to forest resources, and is now encouraging rural participation especially women in the management of natural resources. Through the social forestry scheme, the government has involved community participation, as part of a drive towards afforestation, and rehabilitating the degraded forest and common lands.

Need of Social Forestry

This need for a social forestry scheme was felt as India has a dominant rural population that still depends largely on fuelwood and other biomass for their cooking and heating. This demand for fuel wood will not come down but the area under forest will reduce further due to the growing population and increasing human activities. Yet the government managed the projects for five years then gave them over to the 'village panchayats' (village councils) to manage for themselves and generate products or revenue as they saw fit.

Types of Social Forestry

Social forestry scheme can be categorized into groups: farm forestry, community forestry, extension forestry and agroforestry.

Farm Forestry

At present in almost all the countries where social forestry programmes have been taken up, both commercial and non commercial farm forestry is being promoted in one form or the other. Individual farmers are being encouraged to plant trees on their own farmland to meet the domestic needs of the family. In many areas this tradition of growing trees on the farmland already exists. Non-commercial farm forestry is the main thrust of most of the social forestry projects in the country today. It is not always necessary that the farmer grows trees for fuel wood, but very often they are interested in growing trees without any economic motive. They may want it to provide shade for the agricultural crops; as wind shelters; soil conservation or to use wasteland.

Community Forestry

Another scheme taken up under the social forestry programme, is the raising of trees on community land and not on private land as in farm forestry. All these programmes aim to provide for the entire community and not for any individual. The government has the responsibility of providing seedlings, fertilizer but the community has to take responsibility of protecting the trees. Some communities manage the plantations sensibly and in a sustainable manner so that the village continues to benefit. Some others took advantage and sell the timber for a short-term individual profit. Common land being everyone's land is very easy to exploit. Over the last 20 years, large-scale planting of Eucalyptus, as a fast growing exotic, has occurred in India, making it a part of the drive to reforest the subcontinent, and create an adequate supply of timber for rural communities under the augur of 'social forestry'.

Extension Forestry

Planting of trees on the sides of roads, canals and railways, along with planting on wastelands is known as 'Extension' forestry, (i.e) increasing the boundaries of forests. Under this project there has been creation of wood lots in the village common lands, government wastelands and Panchayat lands. Further schemes for afforesting the degraded government forests that are close to villages are being carried out all over the country.

Agroforestry

In agroforestry, silvicultural practices are combined with agricultural crops like leguminous crop, along with orchard farming and live stock ranching on the same piece of land. In lay man language agroforestry could be understood as growing of forest trees along with agriculture crop on the same piece of land.

In a more scientific way agroforestry may be defined as a sustainable land use system that maintains or increase the total yield by combing food crop together with forest tree and live stock ranching on the same unit of land, using management practices that takes care of the social and culture characteristic of the local people and the economic and ecological condition of the local area.

NGOs in Forest Development

The Government of India, issued policy instructions to all state governments on June 1, 1990 to muster support for greater participation of village communities and NGOs in regeneration, management and protection of degraded forests. The NGOs have been facilitators bridging gaps between forest dependent communities and forest departments in different states. This has been possible by adoption of a number of strategies by NGOs, which include meetings, training and workshops which have been instrumental in program implementation (Varalakshmi, 1999). In this process NGOs from time to time have published valuable Grey literature material in the form of seminar/conference proceedings, project reports, manuals, brochures, pamphlets, leaflets etc. reflecting their activities. The advances made in forestry depend largely upon superior and effective information sharing of research results and promotion of extension activities. To this extent, Grey literature in the form of miscellaneous publications released by NGOs plays a very important role in disseminating research results among villages and research institutions.

Role of Government Departments in Institution Building

Since 1989, the Regional Center of the National Afforestation and Eco-development Board (NAEB) under the Ministry and Environment and Forest (MOE &F), Government of India had been working in collaboration with the forest departments of the states of Uttar Pradesh, Rajasthan, Haryana and National Capital Territory of Delhi. For exchange of information, data and experiences amongst forest departments, research institutes, voluntary agencies, NGOs and village communities—workshops and consultation meets at different levels, had been providing necessary forum. During last decade ending in 1996-97, 32 such workshops were organized by the Regional Centre on a variety of topics such as technology, development and extension, policy and management issues, practical tools to carry out field activities, participatory rural appraisal (PRA), micro – planning , etc.

The Regional Center of NAEB at Mumbai in 1998, had conducted a study on women development vis-a-vis afforestation and eco-development in 31 villages in the four districts of Rajasthan (state). Their observations and findings have been documented in a report, which would help in formulating better-integrated projects.

The NAEB and MOE&F, have instituted the Indira Priyadarshni Vrikshamitra (IPVM) Awards for community development which consists a cash prize of ₹ 50,000, a medallion and a scroll. Individuals; panchayats (village community groups), village level institutions; voluntary agencies;

etc. who have made extraordinary contribution to the cause of afforestation and wastelands development during the preceding three years can apply for nominations of this award. (Hindustan Times 2002).

Role of Women in Community Development

Women play a crucial role in management and development of forests, as they are primary collectors of fuel, fibre, food from forests for domestic consumption and sale. A study was conducted to examine the extent to which women were able to contribute to family's food security through forestry activities and their roles in strengthening social forestry programmes. These results have been documented in a Grey Literature publication 'Role of Women in Social Forestry', published by the National Afforestation and Eco-Development Board, New Delhi in 1993. This document shows results of involvement of women in various forestry related activities, opportunities available to them, benefits flowing from the same and constraints faced by the women participants.

Chipko Movement

This revolt which took place in the early seventies in the Garhwal Kumaon Himalayas of Uttaranchal (state) is the best-cited example of confrontation between local people and state government on common forests. This movement had developed into a reconstruction effort under the management of women welfare groups who were largely responsible for protection and plantation in community lands and for fair distribution of grass and fodder among villagers. Quite contrary to this idea this region now has activists promoting 'PedKatao Andolan' or felling of trees for facilitating environmental clearance for road and water pipeline projects. (rawat, 1999).

Tree Growers Cooperatives

Tree growing on panchayat land, revenue land and degraded forestland by Producers Cooperatives in an organized manner has been practiced in the states of Gujarat, Rajasthan and Andhra Pradesh. The membership of these cooperatives included small marginal farmers, landless peasants and tribal groups who were mainly dependent upon common property resources. In Gujarat, the villagers planted *Casurina equisetifolia* as a part of the State Village Forest Scheme. The trees were felled in 1983-84 and village panchayat determined the distribution of benefits. The Internal Rate of Return was 35 per cent. The success of this project encouraged the villagers to undertake more planting in 1984-86 as a result of which 200 hectare of woodlot was established in the area. (Verma, 1988).

The National Dairy Development Board had launched a pilot project with 64 tree growers' cooperative with 8 districts of five states (saint Kishore, 1993). 55 cooperatives, with 5,000 members covering 25 hectare of land were functional. The scheme had been extended to six more states.

Arabari Project in West Bengal

The project involved regeneration and afforestation of degraded forest land. Several measures had been adopted to gain support of the local village communities. These included employment of villagers in afforestation work, availability of fuel wood on token payment, grazing cattle on a rotational basis and one-fourth share of the forest produce in the scheme. The project was highly successful, and within a span of 13 years the area turned rich, with produce worth Rs. 90 million per year. Overwhelmed by this commendable work the forest department brought more land under this scheme, through its commitment for 25 per cent share for the people was extremely tardy. In 1990, the Government of India issued orders to legalize joint forest management.

Aravalli Project

The unique feature with this Aravalli Hills Projects is that the common land was vested with the village panchayats and all social groups had access to this land. With the whole hearted support of the village communities about 24,250 hectare of land could be rehabilitated during a span of four years from 1991-94. The achievements of this project have been documented in a project report compiled by the Haryana (state) Forest Department (Srivastava, 1994). IT describes the formation of village forest committees in which women as well as men actively participated in decision making. The innovative plan for management, the microplan, developed in partnership with each community, is not a rigid document like the traditional Working Plan so familiar to Indian foresters. The Forest Department of Haryana, organized an experience sharing workshop, "Strategies for Institution Building for the Management of CPRs" in Feb. 1997 at Gurgaon in collaboration with the Agriculture Finance Corporation, New Delhi (NAEB, 1998).

Conclusion

Government of India embarked upon a Social Forestry Project with the aim of taking the pressure of currently existing forests by planning trees on all unused and fallow lands. The need for social forestry programme was felt since India has a dominant rural population that still depends largely on fuel wood and other biomass for their cooking and heating. Therefore the demand for fuel wood has been increasing along with population growth.

Women being home makers and managers have been playing a vital role in management and development of forests. The role of women in chipko movement is also highly significant. More over Women by nature always try to nurture the nature and protect the environment. Therefore for the successful implementation of social forestry programme, women should be involved in more numbers in the policy waking and execution bodies. There participation makes these programmes more effective and fruitful.

REFERENCES

1. Blatchford, O.N. 1972. Dissemination and Application or Research Information in the Field. Paper for presentation to the 7th World Forestry Congress, Buenos Airs, Oct. 1972. Forestry Commission Research and Development Paper 88. London, p. 4.
2. India Priyadarshina Vrikshamita Award 2001. *Hindustan Times, 28 September 2002*, p. 8.
3. National Afforestation and Eco-development Board, and Agricultural Finance Corporation. Ltd. Mumbai, 1993. Role of Women in Social Forestry. A Core Group Report. NAEB and AFC, New Delhi, pp. 57.
4. ———— 1994. Women and Social Forestry. Proceedings of Workshops 4-5 June 1993, New Delhi, p. 127.
5. ——1998. Women Development vis-a-vis Afforestation and Eco-Development in Rajasthan Aravallis. A Core Study Report. NAEB and AFC, New Delhi, pp. 58
6. Rawat, A.S. 1999. Forest Management in the Kumaon Himalaya—Struggle of the Marginalized People. Indus Publishing Co., New Delhi, pp. 291.
7. Saint Kishore 1993. Case Studies: Successful Community Efforts in Protection, recovery, restoration and management of CPRs. Community Management of Common Lands. Improving land management in Rajasthan. Practical guides series, p. 28-35.
8. Srivastava, J.P.L. and Kaul, R.N. 1994. Joint Management of Common Lands: The Aravalli Experience. Aravalli Project. Forest Department. Government of Haryana, p. 103.
9. Srivastava, J.P.L.(ed).1997. Strategies for Institution Building for Management of Common Property Resources. Aravalli Project. Forest Department, Government of Haryana, pp. 140.

10. Varalakshmi, V. and Kaul, O.N. 1999. Non-Governmental Organizations: Their Role in Forestry Research and Extension. Indian Forester, 125(1): 37-44.

11. Veeramani, N. Proposals for Improving Communication for Exchange of Technical Information Engaged in *Casurina* Cultivation Between Private Agencies and Forest Department. Forest Department. Government of Tamil Nadu, p. 1-6.

12. Verma, D.P.S. 1988. Some Dimensions of Benefits from Community Forestry – a Case Study Regarding the Flow of Benefits from the Dhanori Village Woodlot. *Indian Forester, 114(3): 109-127.*

CHAPTER

23

An Analysis of Growth Strategies Adopted in Recent Five-Year Plans

Dr. G. Sandhya Rani

Introduction

For the economic development of India, even before independence, the Indian National Congress set up the National Planning Committee (NPC) towards the end of 1938. The Committee conducted a series of studies on economic development. Besides this Committee, the Bombay plan by some leading industrialists and 'Gandhian Plan' by Shriman Narayan were prepared. Another People's Plan by M.N. Roy was also formulated but all these were only of historical importance and never implemented.

After attaining independence, the Prime Minister, Jawaharlal Nehru set up the Planning Commission in 1950. The basic aim of this Commission was to assess the country's needs of material capital and human resources and to formulate economic plans. The planning commission set long term objectives of planning. The First Five-Year Plan commenced in 1950-51 and it was followed by a series of Five-Year Plans.

According to B.S. Minhas, former member of the Indian Planning Commission, "Securing rapid economic growth and expansion of employment, reduction of disparities in income and wealth, prevention of concentration of economic powers, and creation of the values and attitudes of a free and equal society have been among the objectives of all our plans".

The strategy of planning deals with the reduction in absolute poverty, unemployment, income inequalities and a progress and improvement in the standard of living of the people.

Reduction in Absolute Poverty

For a country such as India with a majority of people steeped in poverty and misery, consistent increase in per capita income over a period is the yard stick, to judge the economic development of the country Continuous increase in these incomes would reduce and remove poverty. The following table presents the raise in per capita incomes from 1973-74 to 1999-2000.

Table 23.1 : Estimates of Poverty

Year	All India	Rural	Urban
1973-74	54.9	56.4	49.0
1977-78	51.3	53.14	45.2
1983	44.5	45.7	40.8
1987-88	38.9	39.1	38.2
1993-94	36.0	37.3	32.4
1999-2000	NA	NA	NA

Note : The 1999-2000 estimates are collected through different methodology of data.
Source : Ministry of Finance, Government of India, *Economic Survey*, p.13, (2000-01).

Indian planners aimed at reducing poverty and raising the standard of living of the masses. But when they found that growth and reduction in inequality are both indispensable, the objective of planning from the Fourth Five-Year Plan onwards was not simply economic growth but raising the standard of living of those who have been living in poverty for generations, nay, for centuries. The slogans of 'Garibi Hatao' and 'growth with justice' were coined to emphasise the removal of poverty.

Table 23.2 : Key Trends in Growth and Poverty in India

Sl.No.	Growth rate in poverty	Percentage
1.	Per capita Net State Domestic Product 2001	10306*
2.	Growth rate of SDP 1991-2001	5.6
3.	Projected SDP growth rate in Tenth Plan	8.0
4.	% poor in 1974	54.88
5.	% poor in 1999-2000	26.1
6.	Project % poor in 2006-07 at end of X Plan	19.34

*Per Capita NNP

Source: Economic Survey, 2000-01.

The important trends in growth and poverty in India are clearly explained in the table 23.2. The percentage of poor decreased from 54 to 26 during the years 1974 and 2000. At the beginning of eleventh Plan, it is projected as 19 per cent.

Reduction in Unemployment

One of the objectives of economic planning in all our Five-Year Plans is to reduce the unemployment by boosting employment. But it has never been given a high priority and unemployment has increased over the years. For the first time, the Planning Commission admitted in the Sixth Plan (1978-83) to accord employment, a pride of place in the Plan. But, not a single plan has been framed keeping employment generations as a primary objective and full employment goal is not achieved so far. In order to reduce poverty and employment, provide health and education for all sections of the community, the planners formulated a strategy of planned economic development:

1. Seek to attain the most rapid growth possible and sustain it over a decade so as to increase incomes and the demand for labour. The Tenth Plan aimed at 8 per cent GDP growth rate;
2. Ensure that the pattern of output is as labour-intensive and capital saving as possible. This will maximize the demand for labour and avoid rising unemployment;
3. Ensure that the best attainable growth rates are achieved by the states and areas with the largest concentrations of the poor;
4. Continue to give top priority to primary education enrolment and attendance, especially of girls;
5. Similarly, emphasis on primary healthcare and adequate nutrition, especially of children and women; and
6. Implement area-bases programmes where the problems of poverty are greatest or most intractable.

Mahalanobis Growth Model—trategy on Industrialisation

Prof. P. L. Mahalanobis was responsible for introducing a clear strategy of development based on the Russian experience. This strategy emphasised investment in heavy industry to achieve industrialization which was assumed to be the basic condition for rapid economic development. The core of the strategy adopted by Indian planners for the Second Plan and with minor modification for the subsequent. Three Plans (i.e. up to the Fifth Plan) was rapid industrialization through lumpy investment on heavy, basic and machine building industries.

(a) Strategy on Agriculture

With regard to agriculture Nehru stated that agriculture, "we shall find that this industrial progress cannot be achieved without agricultural advance and progress........Everyone knows that unless we are self-sufficient in agriculture, we cannot advance in industries.

(b) Strategy on Employment

Mahalanobis strategy adopted a "policy of encouraging labour intensive techniques in consumer goods industries even as the capital intensive sector of heavy industry was being expanded rapidly".

Table 23.3 : Growth and Unemployment Rates in India

GDP Growth Rates	Unemployment in 2001-02	Unemployment in 2006-07
6.5% without changes in policies and programmes	9.2	11.0
6.5% with changes	9.2	9.3
8% without changes	9.2	9.8
8% with changes	9.2	5.3

Source: Planning Commission, Government of India, 2006-07.

There has been a transformation of the Indian economy from a relatively persistent slow-paced growth in comparison with the more successful economies of East, South Asia and China to being one of the better performers in the world in the eighties and nineties. This change has led to renewed emphasis on achieving significant reduction in poverty and providing basic minimum services such as health and education to its citizens although India is still among the poor countries with a per capita GDP of US$ 460, its skilled labour force, strong technical capabilities and increasing openness to trade and investment have raised the potential for sustained faster economic growth. The X Five-Year Plan, which began in 2002-03, set a goal of eight per cent annual growth in real GDP over the next five years.

Drawing lessons from a variety of experiences over the years both within and globally, Indian policies have recognized the need for sustainability perspective in all its development efforts. This is evident from the expressions found in the policies on sustainability of development in terms of continued economic growth, social progress, protection and preservation of natural resources and environment. Since the cornerstone of economic policies is eradication of poverty, which is consistent with sustainable development, economic polices must focus on sustainable development as they do on poverty eradication.

The growth in average level of income, reduction in poverty, and improvements in health and education indicators are still below the levels seen in the developed economies and in several of the developing economies, as is evident from the low ranking of India in the Human Development Index. Poverty reduction, employment generation objectives were pursued through a variety of approaches. In the initial years of developmental planning, poverty was considered essentially as a rural problem and the strategies adopted focused on agricultural development. However, in recent years, attention has been given to the issue of urban poverty. Employment generation programmes in the context of poverty reduction have also been common.

The economic reforms of the 1990s have provided a greater role for markets in raising resources and allocating them for economic growth and development.

Models of Economic Development

(a) Nehru-Mahalanobis

This Model was based on long run development strategy which accorded greater preference to the long-term goals of development, rather than succumbing to the immediate and short-term goals. This strategy was adopted in the mid-fifties at the time of formulation of the Second Five Year Plan.

(b) The Gandhian Model

It was formed on the basis of Gandhian Plan in 1944 which was re-affirmed in 1949. It aims primarily at improving the economic conditions of the 5.5 lakh villages of India and therefore, it lays the greatest emphasis on the scientific development of agriculture and rapid growth of cottage and village industries.

(c) Cottage and Village Industries

The Gandhian Plan emphasizes the rehabilitation, development and expansion of cottage industries side by side with agriculture. Spinning and weaving are given the first place "Just as villagers cook their own roti (bread) and rice so they must make their own khadi for personal use. The surplus, if any they may sell"—Gandhian Plan". In 1910, village industries constituted 40 per cent of the labour force. By 1946, this had decreased to 10 per cent today, they remain at two per cent.

(d) Liberalization Privatization and Globalization (LPG) Model

The LPG Model of development was introduced in 1991 by the then Finance Minister Dr. Manmohan Singh. This model was intended to charter a new strategy with emphasis on Liberalization, Privatization and Globalization (LPG). LPG model of development emphasizes a bigger role for the private sector. It aims at a strategy of export-led growth as against import substitution practiced earlier. The experience of more than a decade of LPG model does not provide conclusive evidence of substantial improvement of these parameters.

(e) PURA—A Neo-Gandhian Approach to Development

Dr. Abdul Kalam has emphasized the adoption of PURA (Providing Urban Amenities in Rural Areas). He outlined the concept and strategy of PURA as the lever of economic upliftment of the villages. The PURA is Vision 2020 project and has to be spread over there Five Year Plans so that an investment of ₹ 100 crores in made in each development block.

Under the United Nations Development Programme (UNDP), countries have been ranked on the basis of Human Development Index (HDI). This index is based on life expectancy, adult literacy, and combined enrolment ratio. It is very distressing to note that India has been ranked at No. 126 on the basis of HDI in 2004. India has to still go a long way for reaching the stage of developed countries in terms of Human Development Index.

Table 23.4

Country	Life expectancy 2004	Adult Literacy (%) 2004	Combined Enrolment Ratio (%) 2004	Per capita real GDPs (PPP) 2004	HDI Rank
Canada	80.2	99.0	93	31, 263	6
USA	77.4	99.0	93	39, 976	8
Japan	82.2	99.0	85	29, 251	7
France	79.6	99.0	93	29, 300	16
UK	78.5	99.0	93	30, 821	18
China	71.9	90.9	70	5, 896	81
India	63.6	61.0	62	3, 139	126

Source: UNDP, Human Development Report (2006).

As a developing economy, India has been able to improve its GDP growth rate which was only 3.5 per cent during 1950-51 to 1970-71 to a level of nearly 7 per cent during 2000-01 to 2004-05. it has been able to

Table 23.5 : Socio-economic Indicators of Standard of Living (1999)

Country	Per capita daily intake			Per 100 persons	
	Fast (gms)	Protein (gms)	Calories	TV Sets	Physician (1998)
India	45	59	2, 496	69	0.4
China	71	77	2, 897	272	2.0
Japan	83	96	2, 932	707	7.3
USA	143	112	3, 699	847	2.5
UK	141	93	3, 276	645	1.5

Source: Tata Services Ltd., "Statistical Outline of India—1999-2000.

reduce poverty from a level of about 54 per cent in 1960-61 to a level of 26 per cent in 1999-2000. It has been able to improve literacy from a level of 17 per cent in 1951 to about 65 per cent in 2001. It has been able to raise the rate of capita formation from about 10 percent of GDP in 1960-61 to 30 per cent in 2004-05. Its life expectancy has improved from 32 years in 1951 to 63.3 years in 2003. According to Human Development Report (2005), India ranks at No. 127 in the world.

Table 23.6 : Trends of Real Economic Growth Rates at 1993-94 prices

Year	Growth Rate of GDP	Growth Rate of per capita NNP
1991-92	1.1	-1.5
1992-93	5.1	3.1
1993-94	5.9	3.4
1994-95	7.2	4.9
1995-96	7.5	5.2
1996-97	8.2	6.1
1997-98	4.9	2.6
1998-99	6.4	4.4
1999-00	6.2	4.3
2000-01*	4.3	2.4
2001-02**	6.0	4.3

*Provisional Estimates

**Quick Estimate

Source: GOI, Economic Survey, 2002-03, p. S-4.

The table indicates that not only annual average economic growth rates between 1992-93 and 1999-2000 exceeded six per cent but that the extent of fluctuation narrowed. The real GDP growth rates from 1992-93 to 1996-97 was 5.1 per cent, 5.9 per cent, 7.2 per cent, 7.5 per cent and 8.2 per cent respectively. This is really a secular and rising trend.

Women Development: Paradigm Shift from Women Welfare to Women Development

Women's Development has been a subject of great concern all over the world. The International bodies such as U.N. have taken great pains in focusing attention of the World community on this issue. It has been realized that Nation cannot develop rapidly if half of its population is backward. Inspite of this bitter truth, women all over the world have not progressed as they should have done.

The gender issues are linked to development through two distinct sets of conditions, namely, individual endowments and structural constraints for gender equity. Individual endowments refer essentially to the resources that a household will allocate to its women. Intra household allocations that discriminate against women cannot be attributed to particular macro policies. But the prevalence of inequitable gender relations in society definitely determines outcomes. Enhancing capabilities though state intervention like access to schooling; development work and health facilities do not address the broader gender structural constraints on women.

A perception of development as economic growth will forger that development is meant for people and that women are also people, they are simultaneously the means and the ends.

In taking the household as the unit of production and consumption the assumption is that there are no differences between members within the household regarding their capacity to decide as individuals for their own benefit.

Development process taking place in any an unequal society perpetuates these inequalities and unless these inequalities are addressed as part of development i.e., the elimination of inequality is viewed as a measure of development, women and other deprived groups will be at the losing end. It is admitted of course that elimination of poverty is its objective of development, but whose poverty? What is the indicator of poverty? It is only after three decades of women and development discourse that a Gender Index is arrived at by UNDP.

The Women in Development movement, whether in its scientific, political or popular form has definitely drawn the world's attention to the fact that women represent powerful human resources in development, that unnoticed they perform the major part of the labour and that they do so under very under privileged conditions.

Paradigm Shift in Women Development from Welfare to Empowerment

First Five Year Plan (1951-56)

- Establishment of Central Social Welfare Board in 1953.
- State Social Welfare Board in 1954.

Strategies

- To work for Women's welfare through all India Women Congress, National Council of Women, the YWCA etc. and NGOs.
- Organization of Women in Mahila Mandals or Women's clubs.
- 'Motherhood' and 'Women as mothers'—the main thrust.

Second Five Year Plan (1956-61)

- Issues of concern were social, moral, hygiene and post care and the problems of women workers.

Strategies

- Equal pay for equal work, policy provision of facilities for training, expansion of opportunities for part time employment.
- Women organized into Mahila Mandal to act as focal points for intervention.
- Factors which caused change in the attitude of Government of India.
- The report of the National Committee on status of women (CSWI) in 1974.
- The International Women's Year (1975).
- The International Women's Decade (1975-85).
- The Report of the National Plan of Action (1976) which provided the guidelines based on UN's World Plan of Action for Women.
- Setting up of the Women's Welfare and Development Bureau in 1976 under the Ministry of Social Welfare.

The Sixth Five Year Plan (1980-85)

- Shift in perspective from the traditional way of perceiving women as targets for welfare to partners and participants in development.
- A separate chapter devoted in the Sixth Five Year Plan document as 'Women and Development'.
- Advocated joint pattas (titles) and fair share in employment opportunities.
- Training centres for development of skills for women.
- Advocacy of poverty alleviation programmers for women.
- Integrationist approach.
- Positive discrimination in favour of women and the creation of cells within the administrative structure.
- But still the 'family' rather than 'women' remained the basic unit for intervention.
- When the Women's World Congress at Nairobi in 1985 laid down 'Forward looking strategies for the advancement of women up to the year 2000' India drafted and National Perspective Plan for Women (1988-2000).
- It advocates a multi-pronged and holistic approach.
- Special attention to rural women.
- Exclusive credit scheme for women.
- Homes for homeless women (IAY)
- 40% reservation for women in all anti-poverty programmes.
- In 1988 the Shramshakti Report was released by the National Commission on Self Employed Women and Women in Informal Sector.

Seventh Five Year Plan and Evolution of the Concept of 'Women's Empowerment (1985-90)

- Participatory approach.
- Twin concerns of 'equity and empowerment'.
- Establishment of Women Development Corporations.
- Bank loan legal facilities, work environment, technology.
- Setting up of Women's Study Centres.

Eighth Five Year Plan: (1992-97) the period of economic liberalization.

- 73rd and 74th Amendment Acts of 1993.

- Identified 27 beneficiary-oriented schemes some women specific and others common.
- Efforts at establishment of National Resource Centre for Women and Women's Information Network Systems.
- Country Report of the Fourth International Women's Conference September 4-15, 1995, Beijing.
- Drafting of the National Policy for the Empowerment of Women (Women Development Policy) in 1996.

Ninth Five Year Plan (1997-2002)

- Empowerment of women's as an objective of overall plan.
- Women have a sub-plan to accompany the main plan wherein the focus is on growth, equality and participation of women.
- Every department and state governments are to earmark funds for women's component.

Conclusion

India has lot of problems to solve. One of the most serious is being the absolute poverty, unemployment and income inequalities. The annual growth rate for foodgrain production in 1990s stagnated at 1.7 per cent, a much lower figure compared to the annual growth rate of 3.5 per cent of the 1980s. The strategies should be free from the dependence upon foreign capital or foreign technology. There should be aiming of avoiding inflation. For this, the money supply should grow at about the same average rate at which output and supply of wage-goods are growing. Functional and structural transformation of the economy should be brought in the task of strategy. Good strategies attempt to solve the triple problem of unemployment, poverty and inequality in India.

There is high probability that India will become a large political and economic power in not only Asia but also the world in the latter half of the 21st century.

The growth strategies adopted in various Indian Five Year Plans reveal that it has been one of balance growth and its main constituents have been a structural transformation of the economy so as to achieve a high and sustained growth rate of the economy. Indian planners aimed at reduced poverty and raising the standard of leaving of the masses, a clear strategy based on the Russian emphasis was introduced in India by P.C, Mahalanobis. Drawing lesson from a variety of experiences over the years both within and globally, Indian policies have recognised the need for sustainability perspective in all its development efforts.

In addition to this woman's development has been a subject of great concern all over the world. The gender issues are linked to development through individual endowments and structural constraints for gender equity.

REFERENCES

1. The Government of India, *Economic Services*, 2002-03.
2. Dutt and Sundaram, *Indian Economy*, S. Chand and Company Ltd. New Delhi, 2004.
3. V.K.R.V. Rao, *India's National Income* 1950-1983.
4. *Economic and Political Weekly* Research Foundation, National Accounts Statistics of India, (1950-51 to 2000-01)
5. World Bank, *World Development Report* (1997 and (1999-2000) and (2002).
6. Planning Commission, *The Approach Paper to the Ninth Five Year Plan* (1997-2002).
7. UNDT, *Human Development Report*, 2005.
8. Dreze, Jean and Sen, Amartya, *Indian Economic Development and Social Opportunity*. Oxford University Press Delhi.
9. World Bank, *World Development Report* 2003-04.

CHAPTER 24

Gender Mainstreaming in Budget Constraints and Strategies

Dr. B. Suguna Reddy
Dr. G. Sandhya Rani

Introduction

Women Empowerment Policy can be effective only when its principles and programmes get translated into a plan of action. For implementation of the plan, there has to be an efficient resource management by elected representatives and motivated civil servants, sincere financial commitments for women's schemes and programmes and consistent monitoring by the citizen's groups and women's bodies within the state apparatus and civil society.

Gender Impact of Budget

Understanding the relationship between macro-economic policies and the Union Budget, state budgets and the Panchayat Raj Institutions is a must as it impacts women's lives in several ways. It is good economic sense to make national budgets gender sensitive, as this will enable more effective targeting of government expenditure to women specific activities and reduce inequitable consequences of previous fiscal policies. The Gender Budget Initiative is a policy framework, methodology and set of tools to assist governments to integrate a gender perspective into the budget as the main national plan of public expenditure. It also aims to facilitate attention to gender analysis in review of macro-economic performance, ministerial budget preparations, parliamentary debate, and mainstream media coverage. It directly promotes women's development through allocation of budgetary funds for women's programmes and reduces opportunities for empowerment of women through budgetary cuts. The process of gender budgeting has undesirable gender specific consequences of the previous budget.

Women's groups have demanded allocations for women specific programmes of strategic nature to arrive at the desired goals in a shorter time span. They should target women of different age groups in terms of strategic interventions to take specific notice of adolescent girls, older women and women in difficult circumstances. Strategic gender tools like gender audits, gender impact assessments, gender analysis and gender budgeting to monitor implementation and impacts must be developed. Gender audit of plans, policies and programmes of various ministries with pro-women allocations has to be a part and parcel of the monitoring process to meet the strategic gender needs and practical gender needs.

There is a need for provisions in the composite programmes under education, health and rural development sectors to target them specifically at girls/ women as the principal beneficiaries and disaggregated within the total allocation. It may also be necessary to place restrictions on their re-appropriation for other purposes.

To effectively attain population stabilization, policies and plans need to empower women, promote their reproductive rights and involve men in reproductive decision making and household responsibilities. Particular attention should be given to improve women's access to quality reproductive health services, including adolescent girls to counselling on reproductive health and sexuality issues.

A women's budget statement can be an important tool for bringing together information on the implications of government expenditures for women. Such a statement does not produce a separate budget for women. Rather it attempts to disaggregate expenditure according to its impact on women. As pioneered in Australia, participating government departments were required to identify the impact of their proposed expenditure on women. A women's budget statement was then synthesized by the office of the status of women. The production of a women's budget statement thus requires a high degree of cooperation and some degree of commitment through the machinery of government. The creation of the conditions for this probably requires a substantial and well organized coalition of supporters both visible and outside of government.

Highlights of the Union Budget, 2002-2003 w.r.t. women

There was an increase in the Plan Allocation for the Department of Women and Child Development by 33 per cent. The plan allocation was ₹ 2200 crores and non-plan allocation was ₹ 53.64 crores. But in the revised budget the plan allocation was reduced to ₹ 2085 crores and the non-plan was reduced to ₹ 53.41 crores.

The budget 2002-03 provided :

- 100 scholarship a year in the department of Science and Technology to women scientists and technologists;
- National Nutrition Mission—Foodgrains at subsidized rate to adolescents girls and expectant and nursing mothers belonging to below poverty line families through ICDS structure.

Allocation of grants as per Demand number 58 of Department of Women and Child Development was as follows:

- Scheme 'Swadhar'—shelter, food, clothing and care to the marginalized women/ girls living in difficult circumstances who are without any socio-economic support 13.50 crores.
- Swayamsiddha Scheme to build training capacity—0.01 crore.
- Gender aware micro planning project for awareness generation, convergence of delivery, holistic empowerment of women economic empowerment—0.01 crore.
- Gender sensitization—dissemination of data/information of women's development, evaluation of existing programme on women and development—0.01 crore.
- National Nutrition Mission for Low Birth Weight (LBW) babies and for reduction of infant mortality rates, anaemia, iodine deficiency in adults etc.—1 crore.
- Self Help Groups for converging services, promoting micro enterprises—18.15 crores.

The National Institute of Public Finance and Policy did gender audit of the budget 2002.03. In their publication, "Gender Budgeting in India, the budgetary allocation for women specific schemes has increased only in the area of family planning (Ashok Lahira, Lekha Chakrabarty and P.N. Bhattacharya, 2002). The family planning schemes got additional 700 crores in the present budget.

For economic services concerning women, the budget (2002-03) had made provision of only 153.70 crores. For Rashtriya Mahila Kosh, the nodal agency for micro credit schemes, the budgetary allocation was reduced from earlier ₹ 3 crores to ₹ 1 crore. Budgetary allocation for providing drinking water and electricity connections for marginalized sections was inadequate. Women's groups severely criticized budgetary cuts on the schemes to provide foodgrains to adolescent girls as well as pregnant women and nursing mothers. Per capita allocation funds for nutritional support for girl children through mid day meal schemes declined from ₹ 112 to ₹ 70 per capita allocation of budgetary provision for girl's education was only ₹ 286.

Table 24.1 : Department of Women and Child Development, Demand for Grants, Demand Number 58

Items	2001-2002 ₹ in crores	2002-2003 ₹ in crores
Nutrition	9.45	7.92
Condensed course for Women's Education	2.00	1.80
Balika Samridhi Yojana	0.03	—
Hostel for Working Women	7.00	13.48
Support to Training and Employment programme	18.00	23.00
Mahila Samridhi Yojana	7.35	—
Socio-economic Programme	1.00	—
Centre Social Welfare Board	27.00	26.90
Training-cum-Production Centre	12.84	16.34
Short Staying Home	12.84	16.34
Awareness Generation Programme	4.00	3.80
National Commission for Women	5.00	5.40
Swashakti Project	15.00	25.00
Rashtriya Mahila Kosh	1.00	1.00
Indhira Mahila Yojana	6.73	—
National Nutrition Mission	—	0.05
Other Schemes	9.45	7.87
Reproductive and Child Health	441.40	571.53

Source: Annual Financial Statement of Central Government for 2002-03 (as laid before the Parliament on 28.2.2002), New Delhi.

There has to be coordination between launching of new schemes and the budgetary allocation. It does not serve women's interest if the funds are not available for the already launched scheme or funds are allocated for non-existing schemes as the funds will remain unutilized. In the absence of women specific educational schemes, ₹ 160 crores allocated for the National Programme for Women's Education remained unutilized.

Budget analysis from gender perspective should be introduced and promoted in all women's groups, educational and research institutions. Public debate on gender sensitive budget will help the country to tilt the balance in favour of area development and peaceful use of resources in the present atmosphere of jingoism.

Women's groups have DEMAND separate listing of women specific items and women's component and TRANSPARENCY in utilization of the allocated amount for women's programmes

Allocation and expenses of resources for women in Panchayat Budgets

To engender budgets at the Panchayat level, we need to analyse budgets scheme-wise, sector-wise, category-wise and year-wise with their budget estimates, revised estimates and the actual expenditure. It is also important to make thorough study of Economic Survey published by the Government of India and State Human Development Reports, State Policies for Women and allocation of resources in the State plans published by the state governments that guide programmes and budgetary allocations. This exercise helps us understand the working of macro policies in determining women's predicaments. Now, the women's groups are demanding that each and every ministry should allocate separate funds for women specific needs (Kaushik, 2002).

Each state has a detailed list of the programmes/schemes benefiting women under 4 categories

1. Women specific schemes where 100 per cent of the allocation is required to be spent on women.
2. Pro-women schemes where at least 30 per cent of allocation and benefits flow to women.
3. Gender neutral schemes meant for the benefit of community as a whole where both men and women avail these benefits.
4. The residual state specific programmes having profound effect on women's position/condition.

All India Institute of local Self Government, Mumbai gives details of all schemes under these 4 categories through its publications and through its workshops and training programmes. Moreover, it also teaches the elected representatives the efficient ways of programme implementation through budgeting from below (Virmain, 2002).

The gender budgeting statement presented in the union budget for 2004-05 covers a significant number of ministries/departments and is hence a welcome step. However, many of the figures given in the statement reflect highly questionable assumptions, which on the one hand and unjustifiable and on the other quite patriarchal. In the union budget 2004-05, it is stated that report of the expert group on 'classification system of Government transactions' to be examined and it possible, to be implemented from the budget for 2005-06.

In budget 2005-06, the Union Government of the first time included a statement on gender budgeting, which presented the magnitude of allocations for various programmes/schemes under the 10 demands for grants that were expected to benefit women substantially (and hence eligible to be a part of the gender budget). The total allocations included in the gender budgeting statement (Statement No.19, Expenditure Budget Vol. I, Union budget 2005-06) constituted about 2.8 per cent of the total expenditure. With budget 2005-06, this gender budgeting exercise has been expanded to cover 24 demands for grants under 18 ministries/departments of the Union Government and give union territories. The total magnitude of the gender budget (i.e., women-specific allocations) has now gone upto 4.67 per cent of the total in the 2005-06 budget estimates (BE) (as a much higher number of departments and their schemes have been included under the gender budgeting exercise presented this year and the total magnitude of gender budget shows a rise to 5.1 per cent of the total in the budget estimates for 2006-08. While this step from the government to expand the scope lf gender budgeting is indeed welcome, there are some serious drawbacks in this exercise (Statement No.20, Expenditure Budget Vol.I, union budget 2005-06), which must be rectified by the government.

The inclusion of a gender budget in the union budget is a rather nascent development and women's activism needs to be given a lot of credit for it. The demand for a gender budget is not a demand for a separate budget for women, rather, an attempt at dissecting the budget for its gender specific impact since gender based differences and discrimination are built into the entire social economic political fabric of almost all societies. A gender neutral or gender blind national budget ignores the different, socially determined roles and responsibilities of men and women and is bound to reach and benefit the men more than the women unless concerted efforts are made to correct gender based discrimination.

The gender budgeting statement presented in the budget 2004-05 indicates the budget provisions for programmes/schemes that are substantially meant for the benefit of women in two parts (Part A and Part B). While Part A presents women-specific budget provisions under the schemes in which 100 per cent provisions (or allocations) are meant for women, Part B presents women-specific budget provisions under schemes where such allocations constitute at least 30 per cent of the total provisions. The gender budget allocations, as presented in Part A and Part B of the said statement, add upto ₹ 28,736.53 crore for the budget estimates of 2004-05, which as we mentioned above constitutes 5.1 per cent of the total government expenditure of ₹ 5,63,991 crore in 2004-05 BE.

This table reveals the following:

- According to the gender budget statement, almost 65 per cent of total budget provisions under the department of health and family welfare are meant substantially for the benefit of women. This seems unrealistic and needs to be looked at carefully. It is quite disturbing to note that in the 2005-06 BE, the entire (i.e. 100 per cent) allocations for Safdarjung Hospital, Vardhaman Mahavir medical College and AIIMS (all three are in New Delhi), under the department of health and family welfare, have been included as women specific allocations in the gender budget. It must be noted here that it might have been the intention of the government to include in the gender budget statement only the allocations for gnyaecology and obstetrics out of the total allocations for these institutions, but if that is the case the total allocations for these institutions as mentioned in the Expenditure Budget Vol. II.
- Demand No. 46 (Department of Health and Family Welfare) are incorrect figures which must be rectified by the government.
- Out of the total allocations for ministry of social justice and empowerment (Demand No.87) in 2005-06 BE, which is ₹ 1817.6 crore, 96 per cent allocations (i.e ₹ 1743.15 crore) have been included in the gender budget for 2005-06 BE, which is simply unacceptable. Does the government intend to say that almost entire outlays of this ministry are going towards the benefit of women? We must note here that according to Statement 21 of Expenditure Budget Vol.I (2005-06), which presents the budget provisions under the programmes/schemes that are meant

Table 24.2. Women-specific shares (or Gender Budget Component) in Total Allocations under various Departments of Union Government

Demand No.	Ministry / Department	Total Allocations for the Department (₹ Crore)		Women-specific Allocations (Per Cent share in Total Allocations)	
		2005-06 BE	2005-06 RE	2005-06 BE	2005-06 RE
1	2	3	4	5	6
1	Department of Agriculture and Cooperation	4589.83	4300.51	1.00 (0.02)	3.75 (0.09)
12	Department of Industrial Policy and Promotion	640.27	490.60	5.00 (0.78)	5.00 (1.02)
15	Department of Information Technology	965.30	916.00	5.70 (0.59)	5.70 (0.62)
46	Department of Health and Family Welfare	10281.13	9675.83	6631.53 (64.50)	6368.66 (65.82)
47	Department of AYUSH	405.98	364.00	38.24 (9.41)	36.95 (10.15)
52	Police	14772.00	14945.00	11.04 (0.07)	6.71 (0.04)
54	Ministry of Home Affairs, Transfer to UT Government	838.05	946.71	2.03 (0.24)	1.71 (0.18)
55	Department of Elementary Education and Literacy	12536.53	12536.33	5949.37 (47.46)	5946.50 (47.43)
56	Department of Secondary Education and Higher Education	5800.50	5800.00	1277.94 (22.03)	1349.55 (23.27)
57	Department of Women and Child Development	3931.11	3931.34	3922.49	3922.47 (99.77)

...(Contd.)

1	2	3	4	5	6
59	Ministry of Labour and Employment	1192.09	1265.00	125.05 (10.49)	115.76 (9.15)
64	Ministry of Non-conventional Energy Sources	605.38	356.43	5.00 (0.83)	0.01 (0.002)
76	Department of Rural Development	18353.87	21354.27	4359.00 (23.75)	4800.00 (22.48)
81	Demand No.81, Department of Science and Technology	1636.00	1446.00	4.00 (0.24)	4.00 (0.28)
83	Department of Bio-technology	458.6	402.6	5.00 (1.09)	5.00 (1.24)
86	Ministry of Small Scale Industries	460.3	470.62	0.40 (0.09)	0.40 (0.08)
87	Ministry of Social Justice and Empowerment	1599.7	1599.7	1550.03 (96.90)	1510.35 (94.41)
94	Andaman and Nicobar Islands	1672.69	1617.31	0.45 (0.03)	0.45 (0.03)
95	Chandigarh	990.96	971.84	0.73 (0.07)	0.73 (0.08)
96	Dadra and Nagar Haveli	113.01	114.63	0.47 (0.42)	0.47 (0.41)
97	Demand No. 97, Daman and Diu	114.3	114.8	0.29 (0.25)	0.29 (0.25)
98	Demand No. 98, Lakshadweep	240.95	250.95	0.06 (0.02)	0.06 (0.02)
102	Ministry of Urban Employment and Poverty	512.03	409	-	29.00 (7.09)
104	Ministry of Youth Affairs and Sports	506.99	478.01	131.18 (27.45)	128.99 (26.98)

Note: Figures in the parentheses indicate the percentage of women—specific allocations within total allocations for respective ministry/department.

Source: Compiled from Expenditure Budget, Vols. I and II, Union Budget 2005-06.

substantially for the benefit of scheduled castes and scheduled tribes, as much as 73 per cent of allocations under the ministry of social justice and empowerment are SC/ST specific.

- Entire (100 per cent) allocations for Nehru Yuva Kendra and Promotion of National Integration under ministry of youth affairs and sports (Demand No. 104) have been included in the gender budget, which is quite unjustificable.

Need Assessments

Need assessments attempt to establish what is needed and where it is needed and are typically carried out by gathering quantitative dates on the demographic characteristics, income levels, and services available in localities throughout the country and combining these into poverty indicators of various kinds. The problem is that the data are often not disaggregated by gender, and the needs are not defined from the point of view of the users of services. Moreover, the need for to be is not generally considered and to me poverty is neglected.

There is an unpaid economy (which has been variously labelled domestic social reproduction, reproductive) in which women do most of the work of caring for and maintaining the labour force and the social framework or social capital (neighbourhood networks, and voluntary organizations, formal and informal) both vital services for the paid economy.

- Likewise almost 100 per cent allocations under the department of women and child development have been included as women-specific, which could imply an assumption that welfare of children is the sole responsibility of women. The government must explain on what basis they have included almost the entire allocations under the department of women and child development as women specific.

Conclusion

Budget is not just an annual statement of receipts and expenditures it is an instrument for fulfilling the obligation of the state. Budgets are a political statement of the priorities set by government in resource allocation. Thus if addressing gender needs is the priority of the government then it can be best reflected through its budgets.

Gender responsive budgeting is thus a concept to analyse the impacts of actual government expenditure and revenue on women and girls as compared to an men and boys. In the union budget 2002-03 the plan allocation for the Department of Women and Child Development increased by 33 per cent to ₹ 2,200 crores. In 2005-06 budget, Mr. Chidambaram, Finance Minister included a separate statement highlighting the gender sensitiveness of the budgetary allocations under 10 demands for grants. However, the preparation of gender sensitized budget needs the cooperation and coalition of supporters both inside and outside of government.

REFERENCES

1. 'Gender Budgeting Statement: Misleading and Patriarchal Assumptions', *Economic and Political Weekly*, July 29, 2005.
2. Chapter 4, *Women, Children and Development*, Mid-Term Appraisal of Tenth Five year Plan.
3. Chapter 4, Women, Children and Development, Mid-Term Appraisal of Tenth Five Year Plan.
4. *Times of India*, March 8, 2007.
5. *Union Budget Statements*, 2003-04, 2004-05, 2005-06, Ministry of Finance, Government of India, New Delhi.

CHAPTER

25

Sericulture

A Tool for the Socio-economic Development of Women

Dr. B. Suguna Reddy
Dr. G. Sandhya Rani

Women in India have been generally considered as 'Home makers' but not as those who also look for livelihood to support their families. Women also form more than half of the agricultural labourers in our country. Although most rural women spend 16 to 18 hours working at home and outside, their importance in the development of the family has not been fully recognized and appreciated. The basic fact is that the income generated by the rural women in the family is generally utilized more profitably for the socio-economic development of the family.

It is often seen that men migrate to the nearby urban areas in search of employment leaving the entire burden of maintaining the household on women. Moreover in rural areas even if a family has some land, the women out of necessity must work on other's fields to supplement their family income. Further with the introduction of more farm machinery women's labour is getting further and further pushed in the unskilled category.

If the rural areas are made economically viable and self-sustaining units, the employment and income generation for rural women need to be given utmost priority. This can improve the socio-economic development of women in a balanced manner. In fact, in developing countries like India, the economic status of rural women may be accepted as an index of the social development and the progress of the country.

Therefore in this article an attempt has been made to highlight the importance of 'Sericulture' for the socio-economic development of women in our country.

Rural women have to be made economically self-dependent through the application of science and technology appropriate to the socio-economic conditions of the rural area. While selecting programmes and technologies all care is to be to ensured that these programmes enable the women to do productive work, alongwith their other family responsibilities. It is in this context sericulture has proved to be and excellent occupation for the development of women.

Sericulture being an agro-based rural industry is highly suitable to the countries which are an agricultural based and problems of providing employment to the rural landless labourers especially women. Sericulture in its various operations creates employment throughout the year. The development of sericulture would generate employment to all the family members including women children and aged persons. It also removes seasonal migration and unemployment among farmers. It is mainly rural and labour intensive industry requiring relatively low investment and offering high profit potential and foreign exchange earning. Mulberry, which is a feed to silkworms, could be raised using the land unsuitable for other crops while waste by-products from sericulture can be of good value.

Sericulture being a family-oriented occupation women play a major role in various activities of this industry. Nearly 60 per cent of the labour requirement is met by the women in general in almost all the traditional sericulture agencies of the world. Women's precision and patience make silkworm handling easier. Traditional and customs of the Indian society, rural context do not encourage the majority of the women to work outdoors. But an increase in the literacy rate and some awareness made women to participate in decision making in farming practices and involve themselves actively in the subsidiary enterprises and took up additional responsibilities which could supplement their family income and raise their standard of living. Here, sericulture proves to be a boon where in women can carry all the work within the house itself after attending to their own regular household chores. Thus sericulture is ideally suited for women in the rural areas. In fact, employment opportunities for women are very high in sericulture enterprise. Various operations in the production of 'silk' beneficially engage women. These operations do not require hard labour and almost all the sericulture activities (expect such tasks as digging, ploughing and carrying heavy loads) can be carried out by women very penitently. It is observed that women's share of operations in sericulture is about 90 per cent in mulberry cultivation, 100 per cent in silk worm rearing and about 80 per cent in silk reeling, dyeing, etc.

Especially, silk worms being delicate have to be handled with proper care. Thus the entire process of rearing needs expertise, high skill and patience. Women process these qualities to an eminent degree and therefore they are more suitable than men. It is worked that about 2,760 women work days comprising about 60 per cent are generated per annum out of a total of about 4,631 man days in all the activities in sericulture per hectare of irrigated garden.

Reeling is another activity usually undertaken by using hired labour. About 65 per cent of labourers engaged in reeling are females usually from families living below the poverty line.

Sericulture provides scope for direct involvement of women in the process of production of 'silk' the final product of sericulture industry. This enhanced role of women in sericulture is significant since it is contrast to other agricultural or agro-based professions where the participation of women is comparatively lower.

Thus the role of women in sericulture in India is so crucial that we cannot plan for the growth of this industry without making every effort towards up grading the skills of women sericulture is. Therefore appropriate intervention and assistance can add new dimensions to the participation of women in this activity.

Conclusion

Out of 6.29 lakh villagers in our country sericulture is being practiced in about 59,528 villages employing 60.30 lakh persons. It has been showing an enormons growth potential and also proved as an activity which transfers money from rich sections to the poor. In this context to improve the effective participation of women and for their socio-economic development the Government of India has implemented 'National Sericulture Project' with World Bank Assistance. Under this project the Directorate of Sericulture has taken up various programs like Formation of Women Groups, Financial Assistance to Women Groups, Extension Support Activity, Study tours to Women. Farmers, improve access to Credit to Women Entrepreneurs, Silk Weaving Training to Women Weavers and finally Increased Access to Market etc.

Therefore is can be concluded that sericulture has vast potential in developing women in rural areas by providing them opportunities for improving their socio-economic status. Awareness among women should be developed by providing suitable knowledge and training. The Governmental programmers should be strengthened by taking necessary measures to increase women's participation in sericulture. Moreover, the training programmes should help women to develop confidence to take up skilled works and make decisions independent of women. Employment of a few women in gainful activities like sericulture will act as a catalyst and set the pace for other women in the neighbourhood who possess similar aptitudes and necessary skills to follow. This brings a change in the status of women at village level which is so important for sustainability of women's development programmes.

REFERENCES

1. Acharya. J. Sericulture and Development, Development Sociology Series–1. Indian Publishers and Distributors. Delhi. 1993.
2. Charsely, S.R. *Culture and Sericulture*, Academic Press, New York, 1982.
3. Ganga, G. & Sulochana Chetty. J., *'An Introduction to Sericulture'*, Oxford & IBH Publishing Company (Pvt) Ltd., New Delhi. 1991.
4. Hanumappa, H.G., *"Sericulture Society and Economy"* Himalaya Publishing House, Bombay, 1993.
5. Koshy, K.D *"Silk Exports and Development"*, Ahish publishing House, New Delhi, 1993.
6. Raj Purohit, A.R, & Govinda Raj K.V. "Employment and Income in Sericulture" Shiny publications, Bangalore, 1981.

CHAPTER

26

Environmental Education for Sustainable Societies

Global Responsibility

Dr. B. Suguna Reddy

The people from all parts of the globe should be devoted to protect life on earth and recognize the central role of education in shaping the values and social action and commit themselves to a process of educational transformation aimed at in creating equitable and sustainable societies. In doing so the people should seek to bring new hope to our beautiful planet.

We consider that environmental education for equitable sustainability is a continuous learning process based on respect for all life. Such education affirms values and actions, which contribute to human and social transformation and ecological preservation. It fosters ecologically sound and equitable societies that live together in interdependence and diversity. This requires individual and collective responsibility at local, national and planetary level.

We consider that preparing ourselves for the required changes depends on collective understanding as the systemic nature of the crises that threaten the world's future. The root causes of such problems as increasing poverty, environmental deterioration and communal violence can be found in the dominant socio-economic system. This system is based on over-production and over consumption for some and under consumption and inadequate conditions to produce for the great majority.

We consider that inherent in the crises are an erosion of basic values and the alienation and non-participation of all individuals in the building as their own future. It is as fundamental importance that the world's communities design and work out their own alternative to existing policies. Such alternatives include the abolition of those programmes of development, adjustment and economic reform, which maintain the existing growth model with its devastating effects on the environment and its diverse species, including the human one.

We consider that environmental education should urgently bring about change in the quality of life and a greater consciousness of personal conduct as well as harmony among human beings and between them and other forms of life.

Some Principles of Environmental Education

- Education in the right of all; we are all learners and educators.
- Environmental education, whether formal, non-formal or informal should be grounded in critical and innovative thinking in any place or time promoting the transformation and construction of society.
- Environmental education is both individual and collective. It aims to develop local and global citizenship with respect for self determination and the sovereignty of nations.
- Environmental education is not neutral but it is value based. It is an act of social transformation.
- Environmental education must involve a holistic approach and hence an interdisciplinary focus in the relation between human beings, nature and the universe.
- Environmental education must stimulate solidary, equality and respect for human rights involving democratic strategies and provide a climate for cultural interchange.
- Environmental education should treat critical global issues; their causes and interrelationships in a systemic approach. Fundamental issues in relation to development and the environment such as population, health, peace, human rights, democracy, hunger, degradation of flora and fauna should be perceived in this manner.
- Environmental education must facilitate partnership in the processes of decision-making at all levels.
- Environmental education must recognize respect, reflect and utilize indigenous history and local cultures as well as promote cultural, linguistic and ecological diversity.

- Environmental education should empower all people and promote opportunities for grass roots democratic change and participation.
- Environmental education values all forms of knowledge. It must be designed to enable people to manage conflicts in just and humane ways.
- Environmental education must stimulate dialogue and cooperation among individuals and institutions to create new life styles regardless of ethnic, gender, age, religious, class, physical or mental differences.
- Environmental education must integrate knowledge, skills, values, attitudes and actions.
- Education must help to develop an ethical awareness of all forms of life with which humans share this planet, respect all life cycles and impose limits on human's exploitation of other forms of life.

Evaluation Systems

- Distribute and promote the treaty on Environmental Education for sustainable societies and global responsibility in all countries through Joint Companies by NGO's social movements and others.
- Stimulate and create organizations and groups of NGO's and social movements to initiate, implement, follow and evaluate the elements of this treaty.
- Produce materials to publicise this Treaty in the form of texts, educational Courses material, research, cultural events, programmes and other means.
- Form an international co-ordination group to give continuity to the proposals in this Treaty.
- Stimulate credit and develop net works of environmental educators.
- Ensure the 1st planetary meeting of Environmental Education for sustainable societies.
- Co-ordinate action to support social movements which are working for improving the quality of life extending effective international solidarity.
- Foster links between NGO's and social movements to review their strategies and programmes on environment and education.

Groups to be involved

- Organizations of social movements – ecologists, women, youth, ethnic, farmers' union, neighbourhood, artistic groups and others.
- NGO's committed to grass roots social movements.
- Professional educators related to environmental issues in formal education system and other educational activists.
- Those responsible for the mass media who are ready to accept the challenge of openness and democracy thus initiating a new concept of mass communication.
- Scientists and scientific institutions to take the ethical positions to the work of social movements and organizations.
- Religious groups interested in working with social organizations and movements.
- Local and national Governments to act in tune with the aims of this Treaty.
- Business people committed to work within a rationale of recoverv, conservation and improvement of the environment and the quality of life.

Resources

- Allocating a part of their resources to the development of educational programmes related to environment and quality of life.
- Demanding the Governments allocate a significant percentage of Gross National Product (GNP) to environmental education in all sectors of public administration with the direct participation of NGO's and social movements.
- Propose economic policies that stimulate business to develop appropriate technology for environmental education programmes.
- Encouraging funding agencies to prioritise and allocate resources to environmental education and ensure its presence in projects wherever possible.
- Contributing to the formation of a co-operative decentralized global banking system for NGO's and social movements in using financial resources for environmental education programmes.

To sum up the Environmental education is unique in the history of Civil society shows commitment of change and at the same time a demand that Governments change for a new world order.

REFERENCES

1. Krishna Ahooja Patel, Women and Sustainable Development—An International Dimension—Ashish Publishing House, New Delhi, 1995.
2. Centre for Environmental Studies, Environment and NGO's in Developing Countries, 1985.
3. NGO Working Group of the Treaty on Environmental and Education for Sustainable Societies and Global Responsibility, 1992.

SECTION–IV
WOMEN'S ENTREPRENEURSHIP

CHAPTER

27

Need for Entrepreneurship Development Programmes for Rural Women

Dr. B. Suguna Reddy
Dr. G. Sandhya Rani

Entrepreneur is the spark plug who transforms the economic scene. Entrepreneurship development has therefore become a matter of great concern in all developed and developing countries all over the world. Especially in countries like India development of entrepreneurship has attained greater significance in recent years. In India, majority of people live in villages (72.8 per cent as per 200 census) and the dependence of people on agriculture sector for livelihood is still high in our country.

Women in Rural India

Nearly 73 per cent of Indians live in villages, out of which women occupy 50 per cent. Poverty is widespread and employment opportunities in public and private sectors are beyond the reach of these women due to their illiteracy and unskilled nature. Therefore, there is no end to their suffering unless and until some support is extended from the society as well as from the government.

Usually rural women are highly hesitant to take up any new activities. Due to illiteracy and ignorance and due to age-old beliefs and blind superstitious and customs, they hesitate to come out freely to accept the changing trends.

In this context, here it is necessary to remember Gandhiji's words—"My greatest hope is women. They want a helping hand to lift them out of the well in which they have been kept. The slightest thing will work wonders. They are waiting to be organized".

The effort of the Government of India to bring women into the main stream of economic development supports Gandhiji's opinion.

Considering 'human capital resource', as the most vital aspect, the Government of India has initiated entrepreneurship development programmes for women in rural areas. These programmes do contribute social transformation since they absorb rural women in income generating activities either on full or part time basis. Thus the development of grass root entrepreneurship among rural women is imperative for an economy envisaging active participation and contribution of women.

But the inadequacy of entrepreneurship amongst the rural women may be attributed to the absence of congenial and appropriate entrepreneurship climate. It is an established fact that some psycho-social factors are hampering the growth of women entrepreneurship in rural area. For example :

- Lack of motivation
- Illiteracy
- Economic backwardness
- Lack of awareness about opportunities.
- Agriculture as main occupation
- Lack of family and community support
- Preference for traditional occupations
- Family burdens and responsibilities
- Shyness and inhibitions
- Preference for secure jobs
- Less mobile
- Lack of entrepreneurial awareness and promotional knowledge.
- Unawareness
- Migration of family members.

Women in Small Scale and Tiny Industries

'Small is Beautiful', runs as a western saying. 'Small Red peppers are Hotter'—Korean saying. Means what is small may well be stronger and vigorous. The Government of India has recognized that for faster development of industrial/service sector small and tiny industrial development is necessary. Further motivating more women to take up entrepreneurship in these sectors is also a pre-requisite for Indian economic development.

To encourage women towards entrepreneurship especially rural women the foremost necessity is creating an environment in which they function very well with enthusiasm and creativity. This includes administrative policies and programmes to provide women, access to essential finances, raw materials, right technology, training, creating new opportunities and market. Therefore, in order to encourage women into the economic scenario, specialized schemes have to be designed and implemented.

But how to develop entrepreneurship among women. In this context the entrepreneurship development training programmes play vital role particularly to encourage rural women to develop their entrepreneurial competencies.

Traits or competencies are underlying characteristics of the entrepreneurs which result in superior performance. Here, arises a crucial question—"whether these characteristics are in born in the entrepreneurs or can be induced or developed—"Entrepreneurs are born or made?.

Whether Entrepreneurs are Born or Made

A well known behavioural scientist David McClelland (at Harvard University) made an interesting investigation and gave answer to this question. He said that 'the need for achievement' was the answer. His trails to induce the 'need for achievement among young persons gave very good results (Kakinada Experiment).

The success of this experiment made people to appreciate the need for and importance of the entrepreneurial training, now popularly known as'EDP' to induce motivation and competence among the prospective entrepreneurs.

The EDP course consists of

- General introduction to entrepreneurship
- Motivation training
- Managerial skills
- Support system and procedure
- Fundamentals of project feasibility study, and
- Plant visits.

On the whole, the ultimate objective of EDPs is to make the trainees prepared to start their own enterprise after the completion of the training programme.

Almost all the governmental programmes are concentrating on the development of rural women entrepreneurship. But to motivate these women to start, to continue and to develop their enterprises EDPs are necessary. During initial stages, EDPs help rural women to start their ventures with confidence on systematic base. EDPs further provide:

1. Assistance in product selection for new ventures
2. Suitable organizational arrangements for technology and selection of equipment and machinery.
3. Preparation of project report and financial arrangements.
4. Adequate information to women about the various rules and regulations connected with the setting up of new industrial ventures. Also helps in registration and licensing work and provides adequate information regarding marketing of products.

Some Institutions Offering EDPs

1. SBI—Street Sakshi
2. Indian Bank—Priyadarshini Yojana
3. National Institute of Entrepreneurship and Small Business Development, New Delhi.
4. Indian Council of Women Entrepreneurs, New Delhi
5. National Standing Committee on Women Entrepreneurs, New Delhi.
6. State Financial Corporation.
7. National Institute of Small Industry Extension and Training, Hyderabad.
8. ALEAP—in A.P. (Association of Lady Entrepreneurs of Andhra Pradesh)
9. AWAKE—in Karnataka
10. SEWA—in Ahmedabad (Self Employed Women's Association)

Some of the above institutions have been offering EDPs free of cost or at very nominal fees. Moreover free training material will also be provided. But majority or rural women are beyond the reach of this information. Rural women, encouraged by the officials and NGOs usually start their enterprises. But majority of rural women who have already started self-employment ventures or those who are going to start do not know about this EDPs. Most of them without taking any training, starting their own ventures and suffering a lot for sustainability and growth of enterprises. Due to lack of systematic, scientific and technical knowledge about raw material, technology to be adopted and marketing of products, these women have been incurring losses and they are slowly demotivating and withdrawing themselves from entrepreneurship. This type of experiences of women is adversely affecting the growth of entrepreneurship in rural areas.

This emphasises the need to impart training to rural women in entrepreneurship development to overcome certain problems. Therefore for developing entrepreneurial competencies among the rural women EDPs have to be made compulsory. Keeping in view the background of rural women EDPs must be arranged suitable to their requirements and provide necessary training, information and support for starting their own units.

They have to undergo training (EDPs) atleast for one week or 10 days to develop entrepreneurial skills. If necessary another training in product manufacturing techniques, should also be given to upgrade their existing skills as well as technical know-how.

Information about these programmes must be disseminated among rural women.

- First of all women should be motivated towards EDPs.
- Gram Panchayat have to take the responsibility of providing and dissemination the information about EDPs.
- While providing financial assistance priority must be given to the EDP trained women.
- EDPs should be arranged in the nearby Panchayats or at mandal headquarters during the leisure time of women.
- Free accommodation and transport facilities should be provided.
- Adequate follow-up support is to be given to these rural women even after completion of their training.
- Most advisable is arranging EDPs as non-residential day time training, so as to enable women to go back to their houses by evenings.
- Stipend, technology, procurement of raw material, and marketing facilities should be arranged by the organizers.

For the proper development of rural women entrepreneurship in India many more strategies have to be evolved to suit to the various conditions in different communities and regions. In addition to some concessions already given to women entrepreneurs some more concessions are warranted to rural women entrepreneurs. Formalities should be reduced and assistance should be provided to rural women entrepreneurs for completing documentation and preparing proposals for assistance.

Conclusion

Entrepreneurship is a process and the entrepreneurs have to play a significant role in this process. The social structure has been an instrumental to the emergence of entrepreneurs from among the women folk. But the task of integrating women especially rural women in development requires simultaneous efforts to improve their managerial skill and working conditions from both social and economic angles. The Herculean task of rural women entrepreneurship development can be accomplished well, when EDPs are brought to the reach of all women who have hidden entrepreneurial talents but could not explore these potentialities for lack of proper support.

REFERENCE

1. Arvindrai N Desai, *Women's Work and Society*, New Delhi: Ajantha Publication, 1986.
2. Ajit Kantikar Nalinee Contractor In Search of Identify : *The Women Entrepreneurs of India*, Ahmedabd: Entrepreneurship Development Institute of India, 1992.
3. Dhubhashi Medha Vinze, *Women Entrepreneurs in India*, New Delhi Mittal Publications, 1987.
4. Khanka S.S., *Entrepreneurship in Small Scale Industries*, Bombay: Himalays Publishing House, 1990.
5. National Commission of Self Employment of Women in the Informal Sector, *Shram Sakthi*, New Delhi: Govt. of India, Dept. of Labour, 1989.
6. Shanta Kohli Chandan, *Development of Women Entrepreneurship in India: A Study of Public Policies and Programmes*, New Delhi: Mittal Publications, 1991.
7. Sinney S Ruth, *Towards a Typology of Women Entrepreneurs: Their Business Venture and Family,* Hawaii: East West Centre, 1997.
8. Sami Uddin, *Entrepreneurial Development in India*, New Delhi : Mittal Publications, 1989.
9. Sahay Sushma, *Women and Empowerment—Approaches and Strategies*, New Delhi: Discovery Publishing House, 1989.
10. Vasant Desai. *Entrepreneurial Development*, The Vol. 1 & II, New Delhi: Himalaya Publishing House, 1991.

CHAPTER

28

Development of Women Entrepreneurship Role of Commercial Banks

Dr. G. Sandhya Rani

Introduction

In recent years entrepreneurship has been a new impetus for economic development and growth of the developing countries. Entrepreneurship promotion and development have been identified as one of the key components of our nation's economic strategy. Entrepreneurial resource, have been considered as a crucial input in the process of economic development.

It is evident that the economic development of any developing nation like India is mostly dependent on its entrepreneurs to bring a foster change. In every society entrepreneurs are playing an important role. An entrepreneur acts as a mediator between his / her operating unit and the large society. An entrepreneur has to play multiple roles like an organizer a creator, a competitor, a manager, a planner, a visualisor etc... .

The term entrepreneur was used to describe some one, who manages production projects. But in due course of time the portrayal of an entrepreneur is further developed through business, managerial and personal perspectives. In the view of an economist an entrepreneur is one, who brings resources, labour material and other assets together that makes their value greater than before and also one, who introduces changes, innovations and a new order.

Women and Entrepreneurship

Women in any nation constitute half of its country population. But, their contribution to the nation's development throughout the world is meager.

Though women are associating with small scale industries and business, they were kept away from the mainstream of economic development.

It is clear that from the beginning that the role of women in Indian economic system is minimal. Their participation was restricted to the labour activities in agriculture, agro-based industries, cottage industries and in construction work. Besides the women's employment in the above mentioned unorganized sector women are invariably associated with petty trading of fruits, vegetables, milk and milk products, readymade eatables etc. Women's participation in the productive activities of the Indian economy is a recent phenomenon. Of the total India's entrepreneurs population women entrepreneurs are very few. Women entrepreneur have to overcome opposition from the family front, constraints from the society, then only she can develop into a successful entrepreneur. Women have to face more challenges and to encounter public criticism. There is a lot of scope for the women entrepreneurs to diverge from their traditional dress making, papad making activities towards the fields of science and technology, for which a women should be developed by giving appropriate education, training to develop entrepreneurial skills and needs financial assistance. The Government has undertaken various developmental measures and have brought about a perceptible improvement in the general socio-economic conditions of women. As a result number of women are associated not only with domestic industrial enterprises or business, but also making a remarkable success in such industries which needs technological skills.

But still it is evident from the statistics in industrial sector, women constitute an average of 27 per cent, of the industrial task force. Even in the present situation, women's contribution is considered low and much of their contribution goes unrecorded, being outside the market economy or in the informal sector.

In fact, women are major producers and consumers of industrial and other goods. They are prime contributors, as well as beneficiaries of the process of industrial development.

Definition of Women Entrepreneur

In general women entrepreneurs may be defined as a woman are group of women who initiate, organise and run a business enterprise.

In terms of Schumpeter concept of entrepreneurs, women who innovate, imitate or adopt a business activity are called 'Women Entrepreneurs'.

The Government of India has defined women entrepreneurs based on 'women's participation in equity and employment of a business enterprise'.

Importance of Entrepreneurship

Entrepreneur plays a vital role in economic development. Economic development is essentially a process to increase in real per capital income of the country over a period of time. Entrepreneurs serve as catalysts in the process of industrialization and economic growth. They put to use capital, labour and technology and act as economic agents. The rate of economic progress of a nation depends upon its rate of innovation which inturn depends on the rate of increase in the entrepreneurial talent in the population. These entrepreneurs are key agents for the creation of enterprises. They play a vital role in the economic development of any country.

Entrepreneurship

According to A.H. Cole, 'entrepreneurship is the activity of an individual or a group of associated individuals, undertaken to initiate maintain or earning profit by production or distribution of economic goods and services'.

According to B. Higgins—'entrepreneurship means the function of seeking investment and production opportunity, organizing an enterprise to undertake a new production process, raising capital, hiring labour, arranging the supply of raw materials, finding site, introducing new techniques, and communities, discovering new sources of raw materials, selecting top managers of day to day operations of the enterprise'.

Importance of Capital

Investment is very important in any business. It is very much needed to purchase raw material, machines, tools and implements. Hence investment is given top priority to establish or develop any enterprise. In this regard the banks and financial institutions have been playing a significant role in providing financial assistance to entrepreneurs.

Role of Commercial Banks in Financing Women Entrepreneurs

The commercial banks in our country comprise of the following:

The State Bank of India an its associated Banks, other Nationalized Banks, Private Sector Banks and Regional Rural Banks.

For a long period, commercial banks did not come forward to extend financial assistance to Small Scale Industries (SSIs) because of their weak economic base. The first lead in this regard was taken by the State Bank of India, in the consultation with the Reserve Bank of India in March (1956) by setting up a scheme for the provision of credit for entrepreneurs. The Commercial Banks started taking initiation in financing small scale industries (SSIs) in a greater way only after the nationalisation of banks.

Entrepreneurship development is a driving force of the entire development process and lies at the heart of national development. From times immemorial, new entrepreneurs were dependent on private money lenders for supply of finance. The money lenders used to exploit their ignorance, illiteracy and need. To relive them from the clutches of money lenders, commercial banks started to help them. Since the nationalization of major banks they were directed to extend credit to entrepreneurship development both direct and indirect. Several entrepreneurship development schemes were stated by the commercial banks. Commercial banks made tremendous progress but still it is felt, inadequate to satisfy the credit needs of new entrepreneurs of the society. The banks also aims at creating self employment opportunities among women in small business ventures. Banks are pioneers in many socio-economic upliftment projects, now pursuing the women entrepreneurship development programmes. They have been extending support in the form of loans concessions, subsidies and guidance at various levels. They have introduced different kinds of packages to cater to every category of entrepreneurs and enterprises.

Women Entrepreneurship Development

In Andhra Pradesh entrepreneurship among women is slowly developing. Many organizations and institutions are coming forward to help the women to start an enterprise. At present there are a number of Entrepreneurship Development Programmes for women in Andhra Pradesh. Entrepreneurship development is recognised as an important component by the Andhra Pradesh government. In many districts the number of women entrepreneurs have been raising gradually as a result of favourable industrial policies of the government.

Women Entrepreneurship Development in Tirupati Town

Number of women entrepreneurs are very few in past in Tirupati Town. But now their number is gradually increasing in town area as well as in rural areas also. Many institutions and commercial banks have been coming forward to help them and giving support to the entrepreneurship development among women.

Many commercial banks in Tirupati Town have been providing financial assistance to women entrepreneurs through a number of programmes and schemes.

The Main Objectives of the Banks are

1. To encourage entrepreneurship among women
2. To provide quick and liberal facilities to small entrepreneurs and other weaker sections.
3. To develop women through entrepreneurship and remove the discrimination between males and females.
4. To increase employment opportunities by encouraging entrepreneurship and self employment.
5. To save the new entrepreneurs from the private moneylenders.

In the following pages a detailed description of women entrepreneurship development programmes of two commercial banks State Bank of India and Union Bank of India is presented.

State Bank of India

State Bank of India was established on 31st August, 1956 in Tirupati Town. The Zonal Office of State Bank of India is also located in Tirupati. There are many women entrepreneurship development schemes in the State Bank of India.

They are also providing financial assistance for SHG women and government scheme beneficiaries. They sanctioned One Crore Rupees for SHG women during the last 6 to 7 years. There are two types of schemes for providing financial assistance to SHG women. They are 'short term loan' and 'long term loan'.

State Bank of India is providing financial support for Govt. Schemes beneficiaries. These schemes beneficiaries are repaying the loan on monthly basis. They are taking loans for the purpose of working capital, term loan etc. State Bank of India is providing financial assistance to the following Governmental Schemes :

1. Scheduled Caste Action Plan (SCAP)
2. Prime Minister Rojgar Yojana (PMRY)
3. Rajiv Yuva Sakthi Pathakam (RYSP)
4. Swarna Jayanthi Rojgar Yojana (SJRY)
5. Financial Assistance to Minorities etc.

In addition to the above there are many women entrepreneurship development schemes in State Bank of India (SBI).

Schemes for Women Entrepreneurs

Whatever may be their dream project State Bank of India offers the right support to women entrepreneurs. Their slogan is as follows : *"She has dreams, aspirations, ambitions. She's enterprising, a go-getter set to create a world of her own. What she needs is the right support for her dream projects. State Bank of India gives them a future".*

State Bank of India is a pioneer in many socio-economic upliftment projects, now pursues the women entrepreneurship programmes. Their mission is to encourage and develop entrepreneurship among women.

State Bank of India extends its support in the form of loan concessions and guidance at various levels. They have a loan package which aims at developing entrepreneurship among women. The SBI schemes for women entrepreneurship development are given below :

1. Stree Shakti Package
2. Entrepreneur scheme
3. Liberalized scheme
4. Small Business Finance
5. Scheme for professionals and self-employed
6. Business enterprises.

Stree Shakti Package

This package provide financial assistance to Small Scale Industrial (SSI) units managed by women entrepreneurs with a substantial share capital. This scheme offers loans along with concessions like lower margin and lower interest rates. The loan package aims at developing entrepreneurship among women.

Entrepreneur Scheme

This loan scheme provides assistance to technically qualified, trained and experienced entrepreneurs to set up new variable industrial projects. This loan scheme provides assistance to technocrats, including those unable to meet the normal margin requirement under liberalized scheme, to set up variable industrial projects.

Liberalised Scheme

It is a general scheme. It finances to the need based appraisals for productive purposes. Comprehensive credit facilities for acquisition of fixed assets, working capital, bill facility, etc will be given.

Small Business Finance

The scheme aims at creating self-employment opportunities in small business ventures. This is beneficial to a larger section of people with lower investment needs. Credit is offered on liberal terms to priority sectors like retail traders, professionals, self-employed, business enterprises and transport operators.

Scheme for Professionals and Self-employed

This scheme is tailored to suit to the needs of individuals or a group of individuals (not being a company or co-operative society) in various categories like doctors, chartered accountants, cost accountants, lawyers and solicitors, management consultants, journalists or other such professionally qualified persons.

Business Enterprises

Under this scheme loans will be given for setting up business enterprises like restaurants, xerox centers and computer centers. All schemes which are available for general category borrowers are also applicable for women entrepreneurs.

Rate of Interest

The rate of interest is fixed separately for long-term loan and short-term loans, 12 per cent is for long-term loan and 11 per cent is for short-term loans.

Repayment Structure

The repayment procedure for long-term loans is 3-5 years, in special cases the maximum limit is 7 years. For working capital or short-term loan the period is for 12 months or on demand.

In some cases, particularly in government sponsored schemes borrowers are defaultingly repaying. The reasons are as follows :

1. Willfull defaulting.
2. Not getting sufficient income.
3. Unable to expand the market for their goods and services.

In case of defaulters the bankers usually undertake such type of action like oral communication, issuing legal notices, securitization notices, appealing to Lok Adalut etc.

Other Information

State Bank of India is having consultancy service for women entrepreneurs. Recently this bank has set up a separate cell for processing the loan requirements to avoid undue delay.

They have established a separate "Entrepreneurship Development Training Cell for Women", in Hyderabad. All the State Bank of India bank braches have been recommending women entrepreneurs to take training in entrepreneurship development cells to develop their entrepreneurial skills.

Union Bank of India (UBI)

Union Bank of India was established in 1981. It was located in AIR Byepass road in Tirupati. The regional Office of Union Bank of India is in Vijayawada.

They have been providing financial assistance for women entrepreneurship development. Especially they have been giving financial assistance to Self Help Group women. This bank had sanctioned ₹ 2,48,29,734 for SHG (Self Help Group) women till February, 2008. They have been giving loans to Self Help Group Women for establishing petty business activities.

The Union Bank of India also finances to the following Govt. Schemes beneficiaries :

1. Prime Minister Rojgar Yojana (PMRY)
2. Swarna Jayanthi Swarajgar Yojana (SJSRY)
3. Swarnajayanthi Grameena Swaraj Yojana (SGSY)
4. Rajiv Yuva Sakthi Pathakam (RYS)
5. SC/ST Action Plan etc.

So for Union Bank of India has given loans for 210 women members from these schemes upto 2007.

Repayment Structure

The repayment of loans is on monthly basis. The interest rate is 8.75 per cent for below ₹ 50,000 and 9.75 per cent for above ₹ 50,000.

Union Bank of India has given ₹ 2,48,29,734 to SHG women. This Bank is financing to SHGs from 10 years i.e., since 1998.

Though this bank is not having any specific women entrepreneur development schemes, there are many women entrepreneurs in Tirupati Town who have got financial assistance from Union Bank of India.

Union Bank of India has also given financial assistance to 214 self help groups (SHGs) i.e., to 2900 members, for both individual as well as group entrepreneurship, activities.

The repayment of loans taken by women entrepreneurs is almost regular. In case of irregular repayment they are following the measure like, personal follow up and issuing legal notices. The bankers said that the main reason for irregular repayment of loans is miss-management of money by the beneficiaries.

Inspite of all these Banks are doing a remarkable service by providing financial assistance to women entrepreneurs and encouraging them to establish their own units.

Conclusion

In recent years the Commercial Banks have come forward to help the prospective women entrepreneurs due to the changes in their policies. They have been giving financial assistance as well as guidance to establish self-employment ventures. Almost all the Commercial Banks have started Entrepreneurship Development Programmes especially for women entrepreneurs. This is a welcoming trend on the part of the Commercial Banks to bring women in to the mainstream of economic development. A positive and favourable attitude of these banks also help women to become socially and economically empowered.

REFERENCES

1. Heggade, O.D. *'Developing Rural Women Entrepreneurship',* Mohit Publications, New Delhi, 1998.
2. Karmakar K.G. *'Rural Credit and Self Help Groups',* Sage Publications, New Delhi, 2002.
3. Natarajan, S. *'Indian Banking',* Sulthan Chand and Company Ltd, New Delhi, 2004.
4. Rangachary H.P. *'Banking and Financial System',* Kalyani Publishers, New Delhi, 2003.
5. Vasant Desai *'Small Scale Industries and Entrepreneurship',* Himalaya Publishing House, Hyderabad, 2001.

CHAPTER 29

Entrepreneurship Development Among Women Through Modern Technologies

Dr. G. Sandhya Rani
Dr. B. Suguna Reddy

Introduction

More profoundly that at any previous stage of history, technology has entered into almost every aspect of human life. The futurists decade back, announced the arrival of 'Scientific and Technological Revolution (STR)' in the society with Super-Industrial Power. Technology is now regarded as the fifth factor of production after land, labour, capital and organization/entrepreneurship.

In any economy 'technological advancement is a pre-condition for development. It is in general defined as "an integrated set of techniques pertaining to modes of living and mediating between society and environments" (Dickson, Fourteenth Congress of the Universities of Commonwealth, 1988: 386), Science develops new ideas of controlling and utilizing nature and each new idea paves the way to new technological invention. Thus, technology deals with everything that impinges on the life of people.

Science is a Theory
Technology is a Practice

But, technology had differential impact on people, communities and nations and on categories in terms of gender. More markedly the existing inequalities between men and women have been exacerbated, due to technological innovations.

History offers a different picture in the case of women in production and women as contributors to the advancement of technology. 'Autumn Stanely' explains the link between women and technology from the single focus of food technology. Then the mode of production was domestic and the form of technology was handicraft. With industrialization technology enters the mechanistic stage and pushed women to the back seat and inscribed the status of consumers.

There is a very close association between technology and industrial progress. Industrial development is the key for economic development of any country. In almost all countries it has always started with individual enterprises.

Technology and Entrepreneurship

The emergence of entrepreneurs in a society depends to a great extent on the economic, social, religious cultural and psychological factors prevailing in the society. Though, women were the inventors of technology, they lost control over productive resources for centuries together.

The phenomenon of female entrepreneurship is only a recent one. Women owned businesses are the fastest growing segment of the small business population world over. Women entrepreneurs have been making a significant impact in all segments of the economy, particularly in India, women entrepreneurs represent a group of women who have broken away from the beaten track and are exploring new vistas of economic participation. Their rask has been full of challenges and yet they have steered clear of public prejudices family opposition and cynical remarks of co-workers in a thorny way they have established themselves as independent entrepreneurs.

The modern technology in this process helped them a lot to fulfil their dreams. Women entrepreneurs with the spread of education and new awareness are spreading their wings to higher levels of '3Es' namely engineering, electronics and energy though the number of such units is not as large as it should be.

The Outstanding Leadership Qualities of Women Entrepreneurs

With the education and training women have gained confidence to do all work, which was the prerogative of man and do it excellently rather better than men. Over the years the educated women have become ambitious, acquired experience and basic skills, competency and self-assurance.

Some of the outstanding leadership qualities of women entrepreneurs are given below:

1. Accept challenges
2. Adventurous
3. Ambitious
4. Conscious
5. Drive
6. Educated
7. Enthusiastic
8. Skillful
9. Determination to excel
10. Patience
11. Industrious
12. Intelligent
13. Studious
14. Hardwork
15. Keenness to learn and imbibe and
16. Unquenchable optimism

Women's economic potential may be constrained by both direct and indirect discrimination. Direct discrimination may occur, for example, in accessibility to support mechanisms such as credit and training. On the other hand, indirect discrimination is generally due to a lack of recognition of women's differing roles in society and its impact on employment and thus, a corresponding lack of appropriate accommodations to combat this (International Labour Conference Conclusions, concerning Decent work and the informal economy P-2) In the International Labour Conference (ILC). Seven barriers were identified.

- Women's more demanding role in the family relative to that played by men.
- Negative attitudes towards women in business.
- Relatively lower education levels, including limited access to vocational training opportunities.
- Fewer opportunities on the formal sector for skill development.
- Insufficient access to technology, support services and information by women entrepreneurs.

- Women often have fewer opportunities than men to gain access to credit due to lack of collateral, she small amounts of credit requested and negative perceptions of female entrepreneurs by loan officers and registering an enterprise under their name as well as accessing formal business development service and other SME development programmes (in cases where enterprises are jointly run with a male relative, there are registered under the name of the latter, thus decreasing the perceived status of women's contribution and their participation in decision making. There is also evidence of male appropriation of female run businesses once they become profitable.

Problems of Women Entrepreneurs

The basic problem or difficulty of a women entrepreneur is that she is a woman. She has responsibilities towards family, society and work. On the other hand the attitude to society toward her and constraints in which she has to live and work are hostile. In spite of the constitutional equality and legal equality, in practice majority of women in Indian society are still suffering from male reservations about a women's role and capacity.

The problems of women-entrepreneurs are listed below:

1. Need for achievement, economic independence and autonomy are absent
2. No- risk bearing capacity
3. Lack of education
4. Family involvement
5. Male dominate society
6. Lack of information and experience
7. Lack of training to use modern technology
8. Inadequate size of loans
9. Margin money requirement
10. Ignorance of Banking procedure
11. Lack of marketing skills
12. Lack of facilities and reluctance of society in training women

As a result of these problems women entrepreneurs are frequently in debt to middle men or money lenders and this is leading to demotivate prospective women entrepreneurs to withdraw from this field.

Prospects of Modern Technology and Women

Though Indian Society is traditional bound, now it is in the stage of transition. There is a steady and gradual change in the attitudes of people and their outlook towards women. The modernised technological innovations paved way for the entry of women into the field of a business as entrepreneurs. Today women entrepreneurs are not only restricting their talents in the traditional industries or small scale industries. They have entered into non-traditional occupations—A revolutionary shift from 3Ps to 3Es (pickle, papad, and powders to engineering, electronics and energy) with the help of modern technology.

Modern technology is like a double edged knife. It can be used for both purposes: Constructive as well as distructive. Similarly, in the same way with regard to women modern technology on one hand has helped to develop confidence and to establish individual enterprises. On the other hand it has led to the displacement of thousands of women from jobs due to their illiteracy and unskilled nature. Especially in the agrarian sector majority of women lost jobs drastically.

But, for skilled, trained educated and enthusiastic women, the modern technology opens new vistas. There are a good number of opportunities for women entrepreneurs. Though at present the number of women engaged in non-traditional manufacturing units is less there is a positive reaction from the side of society towards these women. There are associations and organizations imparting training, technical assistance credit and marketing facilities for the product manufactured in women' enterprises.

Women entrepreneurs are forming into associations and establishing their own Industrial Estates and Business Empires. Modern technology is within the reach of women entrepreneurs and the assistance to use these technologies in the process of production and marketing is available through various Governmental and non-governmental organizations. The 'Entrepreneurship Development Programmes' which are being offered by these organizations are also playing a significant role in developing entrepreneurship among women.

Today, in Indian society we can witness women entrepreneurs in a variety of occupations. In the following pages case studies of successful women in various modern technological industries / trades at different scales of operations is presented. For example there are women entrepreneurs starting from agro-based food product industries to electronic and engineering products.

Though there are some problems and constraints in the way of women entrepreneurs, the opportunities available in the market-oriented economy are very encouraging. The modern technology is highly helpful to grab these opportunities and to capture the market. Therefore, prospective women entrepreneurs have to make use of these opportunities.

Strategies

The following have been identified as suitable strategies to develop entrepreneurship among women:

- Literacy levels of women have to be enhanced and education of women should be made compulsory;
- All women entrepreneurs should join together and form Co-operative societies to see their industries run effectively;
- To motivate women to come out of their traditional perceptions and responsibilities some psychological and social changes have to be inculcated;
- The tendency of women portraying themselves as 'poor me' should be changed;
- Successful women in the field of entrepreneurship have to help other women in starting and sustaining in their businesses whole-heartedly;
- To become a source of simulation the women as well as the society are to be highly motivated stimulation is partially a responsibility of organizations (Government and Non-Government) and partially women themselves;
- Promotion of women entrepreneurship as an important and valued component has to be taken care of;
- Entrepreneurship education and training at all levels has to be introduced;
- The Government policy-makers have to re-evaluate strategies on women education and their entrepreneurial development and it should be planned and implemented;
- To support and supplement women entrepreneurship, it should be in the form of training—skill upgradation, managerial skills, production and marketing along with development programmes like health and nutrition, women and child welfare etc.
- Women should be made aware of various credit facilities, financial incentives and subsidies.

- For effective sustainable development and technology transfer to women entrepreneurs, proper training based on scientific inputs, suitable product ideas, product identification, market survey, project formulation and necessary approvals from the government at the right time with less of legal formalities, soft recovery rules are of utmost importance.

Case Studies

1. Burning Flame

Starting with 'Smruthi Gas' the only liquid petroleum gas agency, Indira Tripathy is also the proprietor of 'Tripathy Traders' and 'Indira Incorporation' in the city of Bhuvaneswar. She has now established herself as a successful business woman and has earned the distinction of the only woman L.P. gas agent in the city. Being a woman, she faced many problems. When she stepped out her house after the death of her husband in search of employment to support herself and two little kids, people misunderstood her intention and wanted to take advantage of the situation. But she tackled the situation with tact. Initially people were skeptical about her abilities. But things have changed now. She recently expanded her business and along with a friend she started a small scale industry. This unit purchases chrome ore and turns it into power. Today, she is a successful women entrepreneur and she is not dependent on anybody for her livelihood.

2. Capacity for Capacitors

Radha, a post graduate in Applied Nutrition, manufactures capacitors, motors and motor stamping successfully in her unit, applied Electronics Corporation. She underwent training in 'Entrepreneurship Development Programme' Organised by the 'Industrial and Technical Consultancy of Andhra Pradesh, to learn about procedures, formalities and other aspects involved in setting up an managing a small scale industrial unit. She said that 'EDP' training is highly useful.

She went into partnership with a friend and formed an 'Electric Industry' and started manufacturing metalized polypropylene capacitors for fans, motors and other electronic applications. The turnover in the beginning was ₹ 2.5 lakhs and now it has gone upto ₹ 25 lakhs. She told that through she experienced many problems in the initial stages, with small children and other household responsibilities, she had very good co-operation from her parents, husband and friends. She feels that a certain percentage of government requirement of items manufactured by small scale industrial units should be reserved for women so as to encourage them to enter into this field as entrepreneurs.

Source: (Adopted from the book—Published by the Entrepreneurship Development Institute of India, Ahmedabad—1992, p. 77, p. 167)

Conclusion

There is a very fast change in the Science and Technological field today. As potential contributors for the economic development of women have to play a significant role, making use of the avenues open for them in the economy. Modern Technology has reduced the drudgery on the part of the labourers as will as entrepreneurs to a considerable extent. It has opened up doors and there is a good number of opportunities to the entrepreneurs.

Women of tomorrow will have to fit into emerging technologies to participate more in public sphere, become active entrepreneurs and be involved in larger number in the work force.

Women entrepreneurship in India is a recently fast growing concept that is applauded in several quarters of our National life. For giving a great fillip to the cause of women entrepreneurship development, the state and Central Governments have initiated a number of measures which includes training in modern technology and providing necessary technical assistance. Further Modern Technology is also helpful in reducing gender inequalities and gender discrimination in the economy.

REFERENCES

1. Adiseshaiah Malcom (s) (ed) *Science and Technology for Women*, Madras: Tamil Nadu State Council for Science and Technology, 1985.
2. Ajit Kanitkar and Nalinee Contractor *In Search of Identity: The Women Entrepreneurs of India*, (Ahmedabad: Entrepreneurship Development Institute of India), 1992.
3. Burck, Charles *'The Real World of Entrepreneurs'*, Fortune, April 5, 1993.
4. Department of Women and Child Development, Ministry of HRD, Government of India, *National Perspective Plan for Women* (1988-2000).
5. Dorai Swamy. R. Women and Self Reliance, SEDME, September 1995.
6. International Labour Conference Conclusions Concerning Decent Work and the Informal Economy, p. 20.
7. National Commission on Self Employment of Women in the Informal Sector – *Shram Sakthi* (New Delhi: Government of India, Department of Labour, 1989.
8. Pillai Jaya Kothai, *Women and Empowerment,* New Delhi, Gyan Publishing House, 1995.

9. Report V (1) *General Conditions to Stimulate Job Creation in Smart and Medium-sized Enterprises*, 85th session, p. 62, 1997.
10. Seed Working Paper: Promoting Women's Entrepreneurship Development Based on *Good Practice Programmes: Some Experiences from the North to South*, Paula Kantor, p. 6, 2001.
11. Sinney S Ruth, *Towards a Typology of Women Entrepreneurs: and Their Business Venture and Family* (Hawaii; East West Center) 1977.
12. Umesh C. Patnaik, *Entrepreneurship Education in Canada: An Observation*, SEDME, UNE; 1994.
13. Vinze, Medha, D. *'Women Entrepreneurs in India'*, 'Mittal Publication, Delhi, 1987. Whyte, Judith Girls into Science and Technology, London: Routledge &Kegan Paul, 1986.
14. Zimmerman, Jan *"Technology and the Future of Women: Haven't We Met Somewhere Before"* in Rothschild, Joan (ed). Women Technology and Innovation.

CHAPTER

30

Support Systems
A Ray of Hope in the Lives of Women Entrepreneurs

Dr. G. Sandhya Rani
Dr. N. Rajani

The process of socio-economic change is an intrinsic part of human civilization. Industrialisation is also a process which accelerates economic growth, induces social change and promotes entrepreneurship.

The primary objective of our country is to achieve rapid, balanced and sustained rate of economic growth. Therefore efforts are directed towards the creation of conditions in which a faster development of productive human as well as material resources can take place.

In any country entrepreneur is the spark plug who transforms the economic scene. Entrepreneurship development has therefore become a matter of great concern in all developed and developing countries all over the world. Especially in countries like India development of entrepreneurship has attained greater significance in recent years. The Government of India has recognised that to faster industrial and service sectors, development of small and tiny industries is necessary. Further motivating more women to take up entrepreneurship is also a pre-requisite for Indian economic development.

The Government of India has accepted various challenges to fight against poverty on all fronts to improve the lot of the weaker sections of the society. By way of decentralizing the economic and the industrial concentration, in order to ensure the equitable distribution of the national wealth, particularly in rural areas, new strategies have been designed by our Policy Makers and Planners.

The development of rural industries is one such strategy. Rural industrialization is not only crucial for accelerating industrial growth but also for achieving the social objective of dispersal of industry and equitable distribution of wealth. The rural industries will encourage the new class of entrepreneurs, particularly technocrats, and the educated unemployed to start their own industrial ventures.

The New Industrial Policy 1992 of the Government of India, envisaged that more stress has to be given to the Small Scale Industries (SSIs) in rural as well as in urban areas, which aims at providing all essential services, support and guidance to SSIs and tiny sector under one roof.

In India nearly 73 per cent (As per 2001 census) of people live in villages and out of which women occupy 50 per cent. Indian society is still male dominated and women are not treated a equal partners both inside and outside four walls of the house. As such the Indian women enjoys a disadvantageous status in the society. Age old socio-cultural traditions, systems, customs and taboos are arresting the women within four walls of their houses and also making their conditions more vulnerable. These factors combinedly serve as non-conducive conditions for the emergence and development of women entrepreneurship in the country. Given these unfavourable conditions the development of women entrepreneurship is expectedly low in the country.

The Government of India has been assigning increasing importance to the development of women entrepreneurship in the country recent years. The Seven Five Year Plan, moved a step forward by including a Special Chapter on, 'Integration of Women in Development'. The Chapter suggested.

- To treat women as specific target groups in all development programmes.
- To devise and diversify vocational training facilities for women to suit to their varied needs and skills.
- To promote appropriate technologies to improve their efficiency and productivity.
- To provide assistance for marketing their products.
- To involve women in decision making process.

In this context, it is necessary to remember Gandhiji's words—"My greatest hope is women. They want a helping hand to lift them out of the well in which they have been kept. The slightest thing will work wonders. They are waiting to be organised".

Women entrepreneurs represent a group of women who have chosen to wipe off the beaten tract and explore new avenues of economic participation. Among the reasons for women to run organized industries are their skill and knowledge and abilities in business and of all a compelling and increasing desire to achieve economic independence. Various attempts have been made to understand the emergence of entrepreneurship. Psychologically, one attempts to explain it on the basis of personality traits or characteristics such as desire for achievement, creativity, risk taking, independence and leadership. However, women entrepreneurs should be regarded as individuals who take up challenging role, in which they would like to adjust their personality needs, family life, social life and economic independence. It is disheartening that women entrepreneurs suffer from personal and environmental factors such as lack of self confidence and family support, social pressure and perception towards women who desire to become business owners etc. This situation eventually projects the need to provide an appropriate and supportive environment to potential entrepreneurship among women.

Therefore with a view to improve the participation of women in the industrial sector in her recent Policy 1992, the Government of India further stressed the need for conducting Special Entrepreneurship Development Programmes for women, with a view to encourage women to enter industrial sector. Product and process-oriented courses enabling women to start small scale industries are also recommended in the Policy statement. These programmes do contribute for the social transformation since they absorb all categories of women in income generating activities either on full or part time basis.

The first generation women entrepreneurs were deprived of such facilities as there were no such organizations to come to their help. But in course of time, gradually different support systems not only provide the financial assistance but also provide training in science and art of entrepreneurship, technical know-how, consultancy services etc. The relationship between the support system and women entrepreneurs should be mutually beneficial and sustainable to achieve the set goals in entrepreneurship. As such, it becomes pertinent to examine as to what extent these support systems are alive to their duties and to motivate the women entrepreneurs to come forward to compete with their male counterparts in different types of enterprises. Normally, a women entrepreneur in a society is perceived as a maker of pickles, papads, masalas and other household activities. However, with changing scenario of women development they are assuming the role of ownership and decision-making in non-traditional enterprises such as preparation of decorative articles, rope making, basket making and also making other such articles where growth and employment generation are imminent.

There is therefore a need to promote entrepreneurship among women. There is a need for greater commitment and involvement of financial and other support systems to promote entrepreneurship among women. There is need to draw up a concrete action plan to help women to solve problems of finance, production, marketing, generating loans for land/ buildings.

There is no systematic and descriptive analysis of forces activating support systems for creation of congenial environment for the development of functional entrepreneurship. It is imperative to examine as to what extent the support systems are operating to motivate the women entrepreneurs to utilize the available opportunities and also to establish sustained entrepreneurship.

In order for women to achieve their potential, according to Kantor, "policies and programmes must address the various constraints acting on their abilities to succeed".

Within the International Labour Organisation's (ILO's) core mandate for the promotion of social justice, the protection of women workers and the promotion of equality between men and women in employment have been areas of long standing concern. Whilst the principle of equal opportunity and treatment between men and women at work is widely accepted in most countries, inequalities persist on a global basis. Such inequalities are particularly prevalent in the small and medium industries sector, where women entrepreneurs are mainly found in the informal economy.

In this context the relationship between micro enterprises and poverty reduction is coming up for serious consideration among the Policy makers and Development Programme Implementers. Micro enterprises have been playing a significant role and the potential for micro enterprises is becoming quite apparent.

Micro enterprises are an important source of income and employment for a significant proportion of rural poor. In fact this sector is perceived to be an essential part of survival strategy of poor households. The growing commercialization of rural economy, increasing dependence of agriculture on external inputs and growing educational opportunities have opened up new vistas for the micro enterprise sub sector.

As per 2001 census, micro-enterprises sub sector accounts for 25 per cent of employment of all main workers. The growth prospects of this sub sector are highly promising. Certain product lines such as brick making, dairy products, retailing of electronic entertainment, soft toys making, chalk piece making, mushroom culture, coir products, candle making, agarbatti making etc., are considered to have very encouraging market.

Methodology

An explorative sample of 50 women entrepreneurs from two support system (IKP and RASS) in Tirupathi were selected for the study.25 women entrepreneurs from each support system were interviewed using the tools and their profiles were prepared. Four of the above cases benefited through the support systems were presented and analysed for indepth study.

Salient Feature of Micro, Small and Medium Enterprises Development (MSMED) Act, 2006

Salient features of Micro, Small and Medium Enterprises Development Act, 2006 are as follows:

1. *Need for A New Law:*

- SSIS earlier dealt only in two sections of ID&R Act, 1951
- Different issues related to SSIs dealt by multiple laws
- Need for a single legislation pointed out by different committees and voiced by industry associations
- Absence of any statutory Consultative and recommendatory body
- Most of the policies such as purchase preference policy, registration of SSI, etc., not having statutory basis
- Need to strengthen laws to check delayed payments
- Need to provide a statutory basis to credit availability for the sector
- Simplification of registration process
- Need to define the MSME concept
- Need to promote the service sector
- Need for facilitating Closure

2. *Classification of Enterprises*

The earlier concept of 'Industries' has been changed to 'Enterprises'

- Enterprises have been classified broadly into:

(*i*) Enterprises engaged in the manufacture/production of goods pertaining to any industry; and (*ii*) Enterprises engage in providing/rendering of services.

- Manufacturing enterprises have been defined in terms of investment in plant and machinery(excluding land and buildings) and further classified into:
  - — Micro Enterprises—Investment up to ₹ 25 lakh.
  - — Small Enterprises—Investment above ₹ 25 lakh and up to ₹ 5 crore
  - — Medium Enterprise—Investment above ₹ 5 crore and up to ₹ 10 crore.
- Service enterprises have been defined in terms of their investment in equipment (excluding land & buildings) and further classified into:
  - — Micro Enterprises—Investment up to ₹ 10 lakh
  - — Small Enterprises—Investment above ₹ 10 lakh & up to ₹ 2 crore above ₹ 2 crore and up to ₹ 5 crore

How to Register a Large and Medium Industry:

- The entrepreneur should file and IEM application with secretariat for industrial licenses, Government of India, incase the line of activity is not covered under the licensable category.
- The entrepreneur should file an Industrial License (IL) application with secretariat for industrial licenses, Government of India, incase the line of activity is covered under the licensable category.
- The IEM/IL applications are available at www.dipp.nic.in
- The entrepreneur should file an application with the commissioner of industries, Hyderabad for getting clearances various departments under single window system.
- After commencement of the production the unit should submit part B application to the Government of India in respect of IEM proposals.
- On implementation of the project and before commencement of the production the entrepreneur should approach the Government of India for conversion of the letter of intent to industrial license in respect of Industrial license proposals.

How to register 100 per cent EOU

- The entrepreneur has to file an application in the prescribed format with the development commissioner of export processing zones.

Challenges and strategies to develop micro entrepreneurship among women

1. Micro enterprises require some entrepreneurial skills.

Some of these can be acquired through training programmes like Entrepreneurship Development Training Programmes. Government and non-governmental organizations have to motivate women to undergo these training programmes so as to develop their entrepreneurial skills and capacities. Specific training in manufacturing/service sector are available for the prospective women micro entrepreneurs in Governmental as well as in non-governmental organizations and universities.

2. The growth of micro entrepreneurship mainly depends on creativity and innovative ideas.

Women have to execute their talents in bringing out new products/ services depending on the demand and requirements.

3. Since the markets are highly dynamic, price and demand fluctuations are very common.

Therefore for the sustainability and growth of micro enterprises women must be able to understand the behaviour of markets and respond appropriately to meet the challenges thrown by the markets.

Entrepreneurship Development Training Programmes

The Entrepreneurship Training Programme is popularly known as EDP. The programme consists the following:

- General introduction to entrepreneurship
- Motivation Training
- Managerial Skills
- Support System and Procedure
- Fundamentals of Project Feasibility Study, and
- Plan Visits.

On the whole, the ultimate objective of 'EDP's is to make the trainees prepared to start their own enterprises after the completion of the training programme.

Almost all the governmental programmes are focussing their attention to develop entrepreneurship among grassroot women especially on Scheduled Tribe women. But to motivate these women to start, to continue and to develop their enterprises EDPs are necessary. During initial stages EDPs help these women to start their ventures with confidence on systematic base. EDPs further provide:

1. Assistance in product selection for new ventures
2. Suitable organisational arrangements for technology and selection of equipment
3. Preparation of Project Report and financial arrangements.
4. Adequate information to women about the various rules and regulations connected with the setting up of ventures and marketing of products.

Institutions offering EDPS

State Bank of India—Stree Sakthi Pathakam

Indian Bank—Priyadarshini Yojana

Entrepreneurship and Small Business Development, New Delhi

Indian Council of Women Entrepreneurs, New Delhi

State Financial Corporations

ALEAP—Association of Lady Entrepreneurs of Andhra Pradesh—Hyderabad

Self Employed Women's Association—SEWA–Ahmadabad

Some of these Institution have been offering EDPs free of cost or at very nominal fees. Moreover free training material will also be provided. But majority of women are beyond the reach of this information. Usually encouraged by the officials and NGOs women start enterprises. Self Help Groups consist of women with heterogeneous background and majority of them without any training start their own ventures and have been suffering a lot for sustainability and growth of enterprises. Due to lack of systematic, scientific and technical knowledge about raw material, technology to be adopted and marketing of products these women have been incurring losses and they are slowly demotivating and withdrawing from the entrepreneurship. This type of experiences are adversely affecting the growth of entrepreneurship among women.

This emphasises the need to impart training to women in entrepreneurship development to overcome certain problems. Therefore for developing entrepreneurial competencies among women EDPs have to be made compulsory. Keeping in view the background of women (their education, interest, motivation etc), EDPs must be arranged to suit to their requirements and provide necessary training in skill development and information support for starting their own units.

Different institutions offer different time period for EDPs. But atleast one week training is necessary for developing entrepreneurial skills. After the preliminary training depending upon the response of the trainees another training programme in product manufacturing techniques should also be designed to upgrade their existing skills as well as technical know-how.

Short Description of Support Systems

RASS (Rashtriya Seva Samithi)

RASS was registered as a non profit, non political and non religious organization. RASS has growth over years both in its understanding and the implementation of development programmes in rural areas of Rayalaseema initially which is one of the most backward region of the state and spread to all over state. Women's organization is one of the most important programmes of RASS. A special women's development program was started with an objective to equip women with an understanding of the need for an organized effort which will enable them to approach situations in rational manner. As part of the women development programme, RASS provides skill training in different fields. At the end of each training course, efforts are made by RASS to enable the trainees to secure government subsidy, margin money and bank loans towards a self-employment scheme.

IKP

Society for Elimination of Rural poverty (SERP) is implementing Indira Kranthi patham(IKP) in all the 22 districts of Andhra Pradesh. Under the scheme, it is envisaged to organize the female beneficiaries into small groups and provide them additional financial assistance together with the necessary supporting services so as to enable them to take up income generation activities. Thus through special efforts and necessary input, the scheme seeks to enable rural women to participate more effectively in the rural development programme, in particular. Thus this scheme is actively involved in making rural women entrepreneurs.

Results and Discussion

Case 1

Nagamma is a 50 year old lady married and blessed with two children, She is involved in rope making and selling business since three years.

Nagamma and her husband were working as labourers in the fields of a landlord before they started the business. They worked there nearly

15 years. Land lord was very unkind and used to extract heavy work from them. He does not even pay enough money for their work. They used to get only ₹ 7 per day per person for their heavy work. Though Nagamma has started her rope making business three years back, she used to sell ropes through the landlord. He was acting as a middlemen to market the ropes from which he would be benefited maximum where as the people who are spending all their time, energy in getting the raw material and preparing the ropes would be getting almost nothing. Along with many other women Nagamma was innocent about the deeds of landlord. They were very unhappy with the least margins of profits in their business.

RASS officials identified some potential women in remote villages which need development. Nagamma was one among them. They were astonished looking at their status. They have recognized their productive skills and helped them to help themselves to stand on their own feet. It took nearly one year to convince the group and the group leader Nagamma to trust RASS and its initiative. With the support and motivation from RASS , Nagamma took initiative to form a sangh along with five other fellow women interested in the same venture. She took leadership in organizing the group and the common venture with financial assistance from RASS. The group is conducting the sales by themselves nominating few of their men.

Nagamma is quite happy with her income now though she doesn't get much profits. She is getting ₹ 1 per rope where as she was getting only 40 paise per rope previously, when landlord was acting as middleman. This change was not appreciated by landlord and started troubling them by not allowing them to enter into his fields for getting water etc. But she is managing the situation with the help of RASS at every stage. She is very much grateful for awakening her. She is interested in her children taking up entrepreneurial ventures because she doesn't want them to work as bonded labour and suffer the miseries of exploitation.

Case 2

Lakshmi Devamma, a 41-year old lady is married and blessed with three daughters and a son. Of the four, two daughters got married few years ago and one daughter and son are in schooling. She belongs to a middle economic class family and her husband is a farmer. Lakshmi is hard working and is trying to help others in need. She maintains very good relations not only with her village women but also with women of neighbouring villages.

Since her husband's income is insufficient to feed her children, Lakshmmi Devamma started bulk buying and selling business with the encouragement of RASS. When RASS officials noticed Lakshmi Devamma's skills and talents of communications and making relations, They are very much pleased. With minimum efforts, they were able to convince Lakshmi Devamma to be the leader of a group of women and to start the business. Many people in that village were involved the same business before as well. But they were exploited by the middlemen who were doing the business by taking the products from the villagers and making more profits. The RASS officials recognized this exploitation and decided to enlighten people about this. Their task became simple due to Lakshmi Devamma as she is an active leader of the women group.

As her business is seasonal in nature, she has to buy groundnut/ jaggery/red chillies in bulk from villagers and she usually spends nearly ₹ 12000 of a group, spending ₹ 1000 for transportation and ₹ 2000 are kept as savings. The intial finance came from RASS, a non governmental support system. She did not plan initially suitable marketing and sales strategy, however, she did enquire about market rates and decided on her customers and also calculated how much to sell in order to make profits. Of the initial investment of ₹ 13000, the group was able to get ₹ 5000 as profit in their first endeavour.(72.2%).Only the profit was reinvested in some other profitable business. The remaining capital was distributed among themselves.

Lakshmi Devamma feels grateful to RASS officials for bringing out her talents and encouraging her and also the villagers to start the business on their own by forming into a group which is worth while.

Case 3

Chandralakshmi, a 35 year lady is married and has two children. Both of her parents in bamboo basket business. She has only primary education i.e., upto 5th class. Her husbands qualification is also same. He is running a nursery school from which he only getting only ₹ 300 a month which is not at all sufficient for running the family.

In order to supplement the family income Chandralakshmi started basket making business. She took credit from a private person for initial investment with an agreement to keep him as middleman to sell her finished product. Almost all the women in the village are facing the same situation. IKP authorities decided to select potential women interested in starting a group venture and provide loan. As the expectations of the middleman was observed in that village during their visit, they were pleasantly surprised looking at the skills of women. They wanted to organize them into groups depending upon the tasks they are performing. So initially They formed a group of 11-member under the leadership of chandralakshmi. Since she has good communication skills and also has courage and dynamism, She volunteered to be the leader of the group. Each member of the group got ₹ 1000 as loan. Apart from providing loan they were also made to realize the exploitation of middlemen. After IKP officials came into the picture, they never depended on middlemen to market their products.

Before joining IKP group Chandralakshmi hardly fed her children with the income in business as middlemen was taking a large profit at the cost of poor women. But after joining the group, she started making profits within two years. She repaid the entire loan in monthly instalments.

Case 4

Savithramma, a 35 year old lady is married and blessed with three children. Her husband is a labourer and his income is hardly sufficient to meet their minimum basic needs. As the family of five lives in rural areas Savithramma used to supplement her family income by preparing decorative items. This work requires great skill which she possess. She never had the conception that her skill could be a source of business. When IKP officials initiated efforts to group rural women to create an income generation activity, Savithramma took the responsibility to mobilize rural women capable of skilled work as she does. She was able to form a nine member group. Each member has provided with a loan of ₹ 1000 with total investment of ₹ 9000 they bought thr raw material and started the enterprise.

Savithramma being a illiterate does not have even any idea that she could supplement to the family income through an enterprising ventures. When IKP officials noticed her skills and routed the idea to start the business, she accepted the proposal. At that time IKP officials gave her full support by counseling as how to start the business and how to sell the finished products. They gave her full courage to start the business as she is very skillful and hard working lady she could develop her business very fast.

Savithramma stated that with the encouragement given by IKP she was able to support financially the family and feed her children satisfactorily. She is also educating her children and saving some amount for future needs. She reveals that IKP is a very useful scheme for human resource development of women. Besides all the developmental activities, Income generation activity is quite relevant and purposeful to the rural women which enabled them to become entrepreneurs. She is highly grateful to the personnel of IKP for providing her all facilities and encouraging rural women to start the business.

Inferences Drawn from the Cases

It was observed that most of the women in rural areas are illiterates, have low education, ignorant and not explorative due to social and cultural pressures. However, They are very entrepreneurial and hardworking due to demand and models in their respective families. Middlemen and landlord in such societies started exploiting the need and skills of women which eventually model them to lose their interest and entrepreneurial spirit. Under these circumstances, two selected support systems are playing critical as well as catalytic role in identifying the potential rural women and making them as successful entrepreneurs and thus become models to others in the community.

With the efforts of these support systems, some of the women recognized and realized their hidden talents and improved their managerial and entrepreneurial skills. They started their own ventures and started marketing their products without depending on middle men and landlord. This not only improved their economic status and also helps gain their self confidence.

Conclusion

Discrimination practices exist in all countries whatever may be their development level and the discrimination faced by particular groups may vary from country o country.

Considering human capital resource as the most vital aspect, the Government of India has initiated EDPs for women especially in rural and tribal areas. The development of grassroot entrepreneurship among women is imperitive for an economy envisaging active participation and contribution of women.

Entrepreneurship is a process and the entrepreneurs have to play a significant role in this process. The social structure has been an instrumental to the emergence of entrepreneurs from among the women folk. But the task of integrating women especially tribal women in development requires simultaneous efforts to improve their managinal skill and working conditions from both social and economic angles. The Herculean task of tribal women entrepreneurship development can be accomplished well, when EDPs are brought to the reach of all women who have hidden entrepreneurial talents but could not explore these potentialities for lack of proper support. Recognising the need, both government and non government support systems are created to open a variety of ventures. These support systems are not only sharpening their skills but also financing their ventures. Yet, there are many constraints on both sides to bring out optimum entrepreneurial potential from women. Sensitization for commitment and conscious efforts on both parties will go a long way in achieving success and gaining confidence.

REFERENCES

1. Anne/Marie Gaston. *Bharat Natyam: From Temple to Theater*, Vedams, New Delhi, 1996.
2. Biswajit Sinha and Ashok K. Choudary, *'Encyclopaedia of Indian Theatre'*, Vol. 2.
3. Biswajit Sinha, Major Sanskrit Dramatists, Raj Publications, New Delhi, 2002.
4. Biswajit Sinha, *Sanskrit Theatre: Encyclopaedia of Indian Theatre*, Raj Publications, New Delhi, 2005.
5. Deepika Biswas, *Classical Dances in India*, ABD Publishers Jaipur, 2009.
6. Hemendra Nath Das Gupta, *The Indian Theatre,* Gian Publishing House, Delhi, 1988.
7. Hemendranath Das Dupta, The Indian Theatre, Gian Publishing House, Delhi, 1988.
8. Horace Hayman Wison, Select Specimens of the Theatre of the Hindus, Translated from original Sanskrit Vol – I, Asian Educational Services, New Delhi, 1984.
9. Jacquelire M. Smith, *Dance Composition, A Practical Guide for Teachers*, Lepus Books unwin Brothers, Ltd, Surrey, 1976.
10. Manjul Gupta, *A Study of Abinavabharati on Bharatas Natyasastra and Avaloka on Dhananjaya's Dasarapaka* – Dramatical Principles Gian Publishing House, New Delhi, 1987.
11. Prameela Gurumurthy, Kathakalaksepa, A Study, *International, Society for the Investigation of Ancient Civilisations*, Madras, 1994.
12. Prof. V. Subramaniam (edt) *The Sacred and the Secular India's Performing Arts* – Ananda K. Coomaraswamy Centenary Essay, Ashish Publishing House, New Delhi, 1980.
13. Projesh Benerji, *Art of Indian Dancing*, Sterling Publishers (private) Ltd, New Delhi, 1985.
14. Regional Massey, *India's Dances, Their History, Technique and Repertoire*, Abninav Publications, New Delhi, 2004
15. S.S. Janaki (edt) *The Samskrita Ranga Annual* IX 1988-90 on Indian Classical Theatre Tradition, The samskrita Ranga, Madras, 1991.
16. Sarah Stanton and Martin Banham (edt) *Cambridge Paperback Guide to Theatre*, Cambridge University Press, Cambridge, 1996.

17. Sreenivasa Rao Kolachelam, *The Dramatic History of the World*, Asran Educational Services, New Delhi, 1986.
18. Sudhanva Deshpande (edt) *Theatre of the Streets—The Jana Natya Manch Experience.* Janam, New Delhi, 2007.
19. Suresh Chandra Benerji, *A Companion to Indian Music and Dance*, Raga Natya Series No.4, Sri Satguru Publications, A Division of Indian Books Centre, Delhi, 1990.
20. Tarlekar G.H. Studies, *in the Natyasastra – with special Reference to the Sanskrit Drama in performance,* Moti Lal Banarsidass Varanasi, 1975.
21. Utpal K. Benarjee, *"Indian Theatre in Twenty Fist Century"*, Shubha Publications, New Delhi, 2009.
22. Varadapande M.L., *'History of Indian Theatre: Classical Theatre'*, Vol – III, Abinav Publications, New Delhi, 2005.
23. Varadpande M.L, *History of Indian Theatre*, abinav Publications, New Delhi, 1987
24. Varadpande M.L, *History of Indian Theatre, Loka Ranga Panorama of Indian Folk Theatre,* abhinav Publications, New Delhi, 1992.
25. Varadpande M.L., *Traditions of Indian Theatre*, Abinav Publications, 1979.
26. Vera Mowry Roberts, *The Nature of Theatre*, Harper 2 Row, Publishers, New York, 1971.

CHAPTER 31

Appropriate Technology to Save Rural Women from Drudgery *Constraints and Recommendations*

Dr. G. Sandhya Rani

Introduction

The role of women in all kinds of economic activities in any country has largely been ignored until recent years. In India the place of women in rural economy is strongly conditioned by overall socio-economic and cultural factor. Therefore, the existing statistical profile on the role and contribution of women to rural life presents a distressing picture. The common view is that somehow women have a genetic rather than a cultural inability to interact with technology. But this is merely a fallacy. In fact today's advancements in technology are originally due to women's ability to domestic and hybridized high protein plan, which allowed the formation of permanent settlement and civilization. But in modern society the role of women has been most grossly unrecognized for example the rate of skill formation among females in the rural areas has been estimated at 3.3 per cent. The female work participation rate in rural areas as per 2001 census works out to be 16.5 per cent as against 52.2 per cent for males.

This low statistical profiles is because of poor conceptualization of female work styles and mistaken female economic roles.

Women explicitly are not made participate in the development activities in rural areas. In fact, there is no utter disregard or under utilization of the services of women in the rural improvement strategies of the country. Integration of women into technology transfer programmes is confronted with several constraints. Cultural constraints play vital role in restricting women in the introduction and use of technology. Religion is another formidable force to reckon in connection with the only of women into technology. Inadequate education has also its influence on women's ability to participate in new technological activities. In some developing countries government policies are also restricting women in technological involvement.

Therefore, it can be asserted that women by and large, are discriminated against in most of the developed and developing countries. Hence efforts must be made to solve this present problem which is restricting women's entry into technology and to allow women to participate effectively on par with men. Though there are some physical differences, basic intelligence and eagerness to participate in developed process is very high among women.

Objectives

1. To change rural women's attitude towards technological skills.
2. To provide increase training and skill development facilities so as to enable rural women to increase their own capacities to be effective economic agents.

The Impact of Privatization on Women's Employment

In recent years the privatization craze has reached its zenith. There is a made scramble in almost all the states to disinvest and privatize all public sector undertakings. All public sector undertakings are being handed over in a platter to the private sector—even profit making units and those with a long history of effectively and reputation for professional management.

The public sector in India has played a very vital role in developing the economy. Its purpose is not merely profit making but to provide services to the common man and to develop the core sector. In fact, some of the public sector undertaking such as BHEL, HAL, CMC, C-DOT and ISRO are functioning very efficiently. But most of the public sector undertakings are being criticized for the reasons that interference of politicians in management, nepotism in appointments etc and not due to economic viability of the enterprises and inefficiency of personnel. In fact, some of the best trained professionals and staff in India are employed in the public sector.

But the Government of India is planning to hand over the core industries such as electricity, Telecommunications, Railways, Transportation etc to the private sector.

Hence, whether privatization is a panacea for all the ills of the public sector undertaking is debatable.

As women from half of the total population in India, the impact of privatization on women's employment is an important issue whether privatization of all government undertakings open avenues for women to join in or due to lack of skills and technical know how women will be pushed down/displaced from employment becomes a serious question. Majority of the women (except a few) are unskilled because of various socio-economic and cultural reasons. As it is well known that in the imperfect market situation when there are many substitutes for a single commodity both in input and output market, the competition between and among them becomes very tough. Usually, private sector firms are capital intensive. Unless they maintain quality and show efficiency in their performance they cannot withstand in the market. Hence, private sector, looks for that kind of labour input, who are able to work with specific skills and talents in various fields of the manufacturing process.

Appropriate Technology for Women

Both these policies have kept rural areas on the periphery of the main currents of human development and prevented the emergence of a genuine indigenous scientific temper and appropriate technology which could sustain and be sustained by the new organization institutions which alone could generate and support development.

The virtual separation of modern science and technology from the socio-cultural milieu has led to a multi-dimensional division of the society usually referred to dualisms, industrial versus agricultural, urban versus rural, science versus religion, poor versus rich, intellectual versus manual. The modern science and technology, appropriated as it is by the upper stratum of the society under one pretext or the other have give rise to a number of human development problems. In the first place, its own growth and advancement has remained stagnant, and in the second place it has kept the societal development at a low ebb. The technology for rural development has remained a preserve of the honoured few, its accessibility to the rural populace continues to be meager. Rural areas have been treated as potential markets for industrial goods and the terms of trade have been unfavourable to them. Man has become a factor of production, and not the end of production.

Science and technology, indigenous to developing countries, has not been allowed to intermingle, with the one borrowed remained stunted and the external technological doses have remained alien-productive but not generative and useful but not usable by the masses.

The end-product of all development is the flowering of human personality. Human beings have basic needs, food, shelter, clothing, health and education. Any process of growth that does not lead to their fulfillment or even worse, disrupts them is a travesty of the idea of development. The primary purpose of economic growth should be to ensure the improvement of conditions all sections. A growth process that benefits only the wealthiest minority and maintains or even increases the disparities between and within countries is not development. It is exploitation and the time for starting the type of true economic growth that leads to better distribution and to the satisfaction of the basic needs for all is today.

Development should not be limited to the satisfaction of basic needs. There are another needs, other goals and other values. Development includes freedom of expression and impression, the right to give and to receive ideas and stimulus. There is a deep social need to participate in shaping the basis of one's own experience, and to take some contribution to the fashioning of the world's future. Above all, development includes the right to work, by which we mean not simply having job but finding self-realization in work, the right not to be alienated through production processes that use human beings simply as tools.

The Need for Appropriate Technology

For women, technology would mean better living and working conditions. For them, technology has bettered existing skills. The need today is for technologies that are simple non-polluting, socially and culturally acceptable of being used by the people for whom it is intended and economically appropriate in the long term and less dependent on exhaustible resources. The advantages of using appropriate technologies are: (*a*) reduction of the drudgery in the occupation and life of women by improving traditional skills; (*b*) promotion of stability in productivity, quality and income; (*c*) increase in the work efficiency of women; (*d*) saving of time which can be utilized for some other constructive purposes; (*e*) improvement of sanitary and environmental conditions, health and nutritional status of women; (*f*) protection of women from hazards in their occupation in home and outside.

Technologies for Development

Technological application has both direct and indirect benefit. The direct ones are those which can be adopted straightway like improved tools, improved chulas etc. The indirect ones are those which need to be promoted as manufacturing/production unit like production of iodised salt, balahar—a cheap nutritious food for children etc. S.C. Jain (1985) identified five areas for the interaction of science and technology.

Food

(*a*) Smokeless chulah designs; (*b*) solar dehydration box for drying selected fruits, vegetables, chillies etc. Fruit and vegetable preservation and utilization; (*c*) techniques for extending the life of perishables, like milk, eggs, fruits like bananas, etc.; (*d*) solar oven cooker for cooking food on the farm while engaged in farm work; (*e*) alternate fuel in cooking, i.e., the biogas plant which provides smokeless fuel for home cooking, light and use of slurry as fertilizer; (*f*) pellatization of coal dust (where coal is available) and making it available at subsidized rate through rural depots. This fuel could also be used as warmer in cold months; (*g*) recipe of balance food for pregnant mother and during lactation period; (*h*) Balanced/nutrient (protean rich) food for mother and child; (*i*) fortification of salt with iodine by submersion process for prevention and control of goiter disease.

Water for Drinking

(*a*) Production of chlorine capsules/tablets for disinfection of well water; (*b*) production of ceramic filter—candles for providing bacteria—free drinking water for infants; (*c*) production of improved, easy to handle hand pumps for drawing underground water; (*d*) improved well with light drawing well, parapet wall and improved outlet for waste water (leading to kitchen garden); (*e*) solar water heaters for rural dispensaries; (*f*) windmill for lifting water for meeting community water needs.

Shelter

(*a*) Fire-proof thatch roof; (*b*) water proof mud plaster for walls; (*c*) stabilized earthen flooring; (*d*) providing scientific ventilation and layout of household needs; (*e*) improved houses for low income groups; (*f*) techniques for construction of simple hygienic latrines with septic tanks; (*g*) scientific disposal of waste and used water; (*h*) improved kerosene lantern and deva for smokeless lighting; (*e*) construction of rural houses in Seismic zones; (*f*) use of ferry-cement for storage of water and food grains, manager of cattle and for roofing; (*g*) use of agricultural wastes for making boards and corrugated sheets for partition walls and roofing.

Mitigating Drudgery

(*a*) Production of improved and accident free chaffcutter for cutting cattle fodder; (*b*) technique for heat-treatment of sickle used for harvesting;

(*c*) grinding wheel light and more efficient for work by hard based on ball bearings for making flour and powder and for processing dal (pulses, grain); (*d*) improved pulley with ball bearing for making water drawing process easier; (*e*) improved hard tools for inter culture like hand-hoe and similar other agricultural tools; (*f*) improved design for wheel barrows to lighten the burden of draft; (*g*) improved and cheap packaging for packing eggs and fruits for transporting to market; (*h*) cooking stove requiring no pumping, using less kerosene, more energy, and no danger of bursting; (*e*) identification of symptoms of diseases and first aid for home and cattle; (*f*) improved design for bullock carts incorporating novel features like low friction bearing, adjustable draw-bars, pneumatic wheels, wooden, wheels, lighter loading platform, and breaking systems; (*g*) improved wheel barrow for scavenging work; (*h*) improved load carrying suspended on shoulders: (*i*) improved pullies—for drawing water from the well; (*i*) improved rope lift.

Economic Projects

Improved cottage, scale hand spinning and weaving machines for cotton, wool and other organic fibres. Cottage match box and match sticks making. Mushroom cultivation. Cultivation and processing of spices. Handicrafts design and development techniques. Improvement techniques for processing of leather and preparation of leather goods including book binding. Soap making (home scale). Preparation of bangles and beaded ornaments. Sericulture, epiculture, aquaculture, animal husbandry including milk, egg and meat production and primary preservation, mini rice mill, tailoring and garment making. Preparation of breakfast ingredients for self-consumption and sale, organization of collection of non-edible oil seeds, its primary processing for possible value adding and grading. These are major raw materials for many industries. Rearing of sheep, goat and pig, groundnut shelter and decorticator, paddy husker, coconut scrapper, use of bamboo for handicrafts and convenient furniture to economise space.

In order to reduce the drudgery of women various technologies for improving the status of women have been developed by several rural development organizations and voluntary agencies. The Department of Science and Technology prepared a 'Compendium of Technologies' and this gives the outline of various technologies which would benefit women. According to this report the drudgery reducing technologies are categorized under four headings like technologies for drawing and fetching water, technologies for cooking, technologies for repair and maintenance of the house, and technologies for working farms.

Conclusion

The role of women in all kinds of economic and productive activities has been ignored in many countries. In India the status of rural women is strongly conditioned by many factors such as social, economic and cultural. But in fact today's advancements in technology are originally due to women and their ability to grow the crops, which allowed the formation of permanent settlement and development of human civilization.

For women technology would mean better living and working conditions. The advantages of using appropriate technologies are very high. This technological application has both direct and indirect benefit. The utilization of appropriate technologies by rural women considerably reduces their drudgery and improving their standard of living.

REFERENCES

1. Acharya and Patkar, Technological Infusion and Employment Conditions of Women in Rice Areas, *Conference Paper, Women and Rice Farming System*, IRRF, Philippines.
2. Asha, 'Women and New Technology in India', *ILO Information*, Vol.19, No.2, ILO, 1211, Geneva, 22, Switzerland, 1993
3. Dayal, R., Schemes for Rural Development: Scope for Women, *A Handbook of UNICEP*, Dept. of Rural Development Publication, 1982.
4. Dept. of Rural Development, Government of India, *Annual Report*, 1986-87.
5. Govt. of India, Planning Commission, New Delhi, Ninth Five Year Plan, 1992-97.
6. Gulati Leela, *Fishing Technology and Women*, DS Publications, Trivendrum, 1983.
7. Iftikhar Ahmed, *Technology and Rural women: Conceptual and Empirical Issues*, George Allen and Unwin, London, p. 1-6, 1985.
8. Ram Jeth Malani, 'A Women's Place', *Indian Express*, Sunday, October, 1980.
9. Sadhu, A.N. and Mahajan, R.K. *Technological Change and Agricultural Development in India*, Himalaya Publishing House, Bombay, pp. 175-203, 1985.
10. Thabwala Lenana, *'Women Workers in the Cotton Textiles Industry of Ahmedabad'*, SEWA, Ahmedabad, 1983.

CHAPTER

32

Entrepreneurship Development among Women for Better Future

Dr. G. Sandhya Rani
Dr. B. Suguna Reddy

Introduction

Women account for a nearly 50 per cent of the Indian population. Indian society being conservative for ages with male domination women have been oppressed lot and at least in the modern democratic India they should have received a better deal with equal status, opportunities and dignity. However efforts and achievements in this regard are grossly inadequate during the past fifty years of our independence.

India has ratified various international conventions and human rights instruments committing to secure equal rights for women. However, there still exists a very wide gap between the goals enunciated in the constitution, legislation, policies, plans, programmes and related mechanisms on the hand and the situational reality of the status of women in India.

We have now entered into the 21st century and the threshold of the third millennium. Therefore, the approach towards women's development and the scope for their participation in the national development should be more refined. In this context it is necessary to recollect the approaches of Government of India towards women's development. These has been a significant shift in the approach towards well-being of women, from 'welfare' during 'fifties' to 'Development during seventies and 'Empowerment' during 'Nineties'.

Therefore an integrated approach should be adopted towards empowering women. This underscores harmonization of various efforts on different fronts viz., social, economic legal and political.

After independence, India embarked on a system of economic planning with higher priority on Industrial development especially in the Second and Third Five Year Plans. Women constitute half of the population in India and majority of women live in rural areas. Out of the total population, 27 per cent of the rural women live below the poverty line.

It is increasingly being realized by decision makers that widespread poverty and stunted development cannot be tackled without providing adequate opportunities for productive employment to women. Therefore the government has been giving preferential treatment to women in finding them employment and facilitating them to become women entrepreneurs. Despite the encouragement given by government and other developmental agencies, the progress of entrepreneurship development among women in the country has not been satisfactory.

Therefore, in this chapter an attempt has been made to highlight the myths and reasons why women in India do not take easily to entrepreneurship.

In traditional societies women confined to the four walls of houses and in modern societies they are coming out of the four walls to participate in all sorts of activities. Recently they started plunging into industry and also running their enterprises successfully. At this juncture to make women economically independent, to be empowered and to act with self confidence it is necessary to provide them opportunities to become entrepreneurs.

Entrepreneurship Meaning

It involves strong use of business skills and is mainly market, oriented. It also involves employment of at least one person, and managing personnel is an important factor in entrepreneurship. All entrepreneurs are self employed and income generating persons.

Definition

According to Joseph. A.Schumpeter; "A person one who introduces innovative changes is an entrepreneur. He treated entrepreneur as an integral part of economic growth".

Some people described entrepreneur as a changing agent.

Entrepreneurship Development among Women

In the light of the present day conditions, entrepreneurship development among women occupies a significant place.

But the socio-economic and cultural traditions and taboos are restricting women's movement and arresting their development as entrepreneurs. Given these unfavourable conditions, the development of women entrepreneurship is expectedly low in the country. This is well indicated by a dismally low level of women (5.2%) in total self-employed persons in the country. Further, women entrepreneurs in India accounted for 13 per cent of the total two million during 1999-2000.

Women Entrepreneurs

"An enterprise owned and controlled by a woman having a minimum financial interest of 51 per cent of the capital and giving at east 51 per cent of the employment generated in the enterprise to women"—Definition of the Government of India.

In nutshell, women entrepreneurs are those women who think of a business enterprise, initiate it, organize and combine the factors of production, operate the enterprise and undertake risks and handle economic uncertainly involved in running a business enterprise.

The slow pace of the propensity to enterprise is mainly due to the existence of a set of barriers prohibiting the process of entry into, continuity in and eventual exit from a business venture of a would be entrepreneur is a function of forces that one may view as barriers limiting the fullfledged business performance.

These barriers are:

1. A cultural bias in identifying and management the entrepreneurial development process;
2. Limited industry specific data and insufficient market information;
3. Limited effectiveness of the infrastructural base;
4. Existence of visible and invisible obstacles to allow the entry of a specific societal group (i.e., women) into business;
5. Unorganised capital market and traditional feasibility assessment processes;
6. Unsympathetic and cumbersome government attitude;
7. Limited access to technology.

Characteristics of Women Entrepreneurs

Some of the outstanding characteristics of women entrepreneurs are as follows:

1. Accept changes
2. Adventurous
3. Ambitious
4. Conscious
5. Educated
6. Enthusiastic
7. Determination to excel
8. Hard work
9. Patience
10. Industrious
11. Intelligent
12. Motivator
13. Skillful
14. Studious
15. Keenness to learn
16. Unquenchable optimism.

Some recent researches conducted indicated that several women are now wiling t become entrepreneurs due to various factors. With the spread of education and new awareness, women entrepreneurs are spreading their wings to higher level of 3 E's namely engineering, electronics and energy, from the traditional items of 3P's namely pickles, papads and powders (Masala).

Hence, today no field is unapproachable to trained and determined modern Indian women. But, women entrepreneurs encounters two sets of problems viz.: General problems of entrepreneurs; and problems specific to women entrepreneurs. They are as follows:

1. Problem of finance
2. Scarcity of raw material
3. Stiff competition
4. Limited mobility
5. Family ties
6. Lack of education
7. Male-dominated society
8. Low risk bearing ability
9. Lack of proper training facilities
10. Social attitude etc.

As a result of these problems some women entrepreneurs are de-motivating and leaving their ventures. Women entrepreneurs of small scale industries are frequently in debts to middlemen or moneylenders who provide raw material or credit at extremely high rates of interest. To relieve women entrepreneurs from this vicious circle of exploitation, indebtedness and social disabilities, necessary changes have to come in the attitudes of people. Secondly the credit policies of the Banks, government and other financial institutions should be liberalized to extend loan to the prospective women entrepreneurs at confessional terms.

Recent Trends

The general consensus that is emerging in all discussions relating to the development of women is that promotion of women entrepreneurs should form an integral part of all developmental efforts. The experience of developed countries where the share of women of owned enterprises is continuously on increase strengthens the view that the future of small-scale industries depends very much on the entry of women into industry. Several National and International Organizations and agencies have appreciated the need and importance of developing women entrepreneurs in recent years. The declaration of UNO the decade 1975-1985 as the Decade for women paved way to take up a number of measures for women's Development.

The meeting held at Vienna in 1978 on 'the role of women in Industrialization in developing countries' identified several constraints such as social, attitudinal, and institutional barriers, inadequate training, employment opportunities and insufficient information and so on which held women back from participating in industrial activities. The World Conference of the United Nations Decade for Women held at Copenhagen in Denmark in 1980 also adopted a programme aimed at promoting full and equal opportunities and treatment of women in employment and their access to non-traditional skilled trades.

In India, the National Conference of Women Entrepreneurs held at New Delhi in 1981 advocated the need for developing women entrepreneurs for the overall development of the country. It called for priority to women in allotment of land, sheds, sanctions of power, licensing etc., the Government of India is also assigning increasing importance to the development of women entrepreneurs in the recent years. Since Sixth Five year plan onwards there has been an increasing concentration towards the promotion of women as entrepreneurs. In the recent Industrial policy, the Government of India further stressed the need for conducting special Entrepreneurship Development Programmes for women with a view to encourage women to enter industry.

Product and process-oriented courses enabling women to start small-scale industries are also recommended in the policy statement. Several institutional arrangements are made both at the centre and the state levels like Nationalized Banks, Financial Corporation, Training Institutes, Consultancy services, Infrastructure support etc. A number of Voluntary Organizations have also been engaged in protecting and developing women entrepreneurs in our country.

Further, the policy Government of India to eradicate poverty and to reduce unemployment is promoting self-employment among women in rural, urban and semi-urban areas. Several programmes of Govt. of India as well as state Governments are focusing their attention on women entrepreneurship development with a view to provide them a better future.

There is a major business revolution across the nation and women are a significant part of it. The impact of this will be definitely on the society particularly on women.

Women's economic potential may be constrained by both direct and indirect discrimination. Direct discrimination my occur for example, in accessibility to support mechanisms such as credit and training. On the other hand, indirect discrimination is generally due to a lack of recognition of women's differing roles in society and its impact on employment and thus, a corresponding lack of appropriate accommodation to combat this.

In International Labour Conference (ILC) six barriers were identified:

1. Women's more demanding role in the family relative to that played by men;
2. Negative attitudes towards women in business;
3. Relatively lower education levels, including limited access to vocational training opportunities;
4. Fewer opportunities in the formal sector for skill development;
5. Insufficient access to technology, support services and information by women entrepreneurs;
6. Women often have fewer opportunities than men to gain access to credit due to lack of collateral, the small amounts of credit requested and negative perceptions of female entrepreneurs by loan officers and registering an enterprise under their name as well as accessing formal business development services and other SME development programmes (in cases where enterprises are jointly run with a male relative these are registered under the name of the latter, thus decreasing the perceive the status of women's contribution and their participation in decision making. There is also evidence of male appropriation of female run business once they become profitable.

Conclusion

The new thrust given to the process of economic development of the country by the new dynamic policy resolutions has created an all-round enthusiasm and the new slogan of 'March towards the twenty first century' had gained popularity. This new enthusiasm has also recognized the vital sector of the society which can contribute substantially towards the economic development of the country. This vital sector is women entrepreneurs. In fact the Harvard school experts fell that the basic quality of efficient management is futuristic out look and a capacity to nurture and plan for the future or unknown. This comes naturally to women. Therefore they feel that successful managers will be those who combine this feminist attribute of nurturing and futuristic planning with male aggressiveness. But this inherent management talent of women and her entrepreneurial skills go unrecognized and unaccounted as it does not show profit or loss in monetary terms.

In order to ensure the development of entrepreneurs among women at a faster rate there is a need to set up separate industrial cooperative estates for women in different regions. Women entrepreneurs in rural and backward regions need special assistance and incentives from the government. If proper guidance and training is provided to women to run their enterprises efficiently they will definitely overcome all the barriers which are obstructing their progress. Moreover the entrepreneurship development among women will help them to design for a better future.

REFERENCES

1. Ajit Kanitkar & Walince Contractor, In *Search of Identify the Women Entrepreneurs of India* (Ahmedabad, Entrepreneurship Development Institute of India), 1992.
2. Arvindrai N. Desai, *'Women's Work and Society'*, Ajantha Publication Institute, New Delhi, 1986.
3. Department of Women and Child Development, Ministry of HRD, Government of India, *National Perspective Plan for Women* (1988-2000).
4. Dhubhashi Vinze Medha, Sinney S. Ruth. *'Women Entrepreneurs in India'*, Mittal Publications, New Delhi, 1987.
5. Dorai Swamy, R., *'Women and Self Reliance'*, SEDME, September, 1995.
6. *International Labour Conference Conclusions Concerning Decent Work and the Informal Economy*, p. 20.
7. Kanka, S.S., *'Entrepreneurial Development'*, S. Chand & Company Ltd., New Delhi, 1999.
8. Kanka, S.S., *'Entrepreneurship in Small Scale Industries'*, Himalaya Publishing House, Bombay, 1990.
9. National Commission on Self-employment of Women in the Informal Sector—Sharam Sakthi (New Delhi, Government of India, Department of Labour), 1989.

10. Pillai Jaya Kothai, *'Women and Empowerment'*, New Delhi, Gyan Publishing House, 1995.
11. Report V(i) *General Conditions to Stimulate Job Creation in Smart and Medium-sized Enterprises,* 85th Session, p.62, 1997.
12. Sami Uddin, *'Entrepreneurship Development in India',* Mittal Publications, New Delhi, 1989.
13. Seed Working Paper: *'Promoting Women's Entrepreneurship Development-Based on Good Practice Programmes: Some Experiences from The North to South,* Paula Kantar, p. 6, 2001.
14. Shanta Kohli Chandal, *'Development of Women Entrepreneurship in India'*—A Study of Public Policies and Programmes, Mittal Publications, New Delhi, 1991.
15. Sinney, C. Ruth, Towards a Typology of Women Entrepreneurs, and Their Business Venture and Family (Hawaii, East West Centre), 1977.
16. Swarajya Lakshmi, C. *'Development of Women Entrepreneurship in India—Problems and Prospects'*, Discovery Publishing House, New Delhi, 1988.
17. Umesh C. Patnaik, *Entrepreneurship Education in Canada*: An Observation, SEDME, UNE, 1994.

CHAPTER

33

Efficacy of Entrepreneurial Training on Self Help Group Women

Dr. N. Rajani

Introduction

Approximately 1, 2 billion people have to survive with less than one dollar a day (World Bank report 2008). Different studies conducted by Planning Commission of India and other agencies state that more than 42 per cent of Indians are earning less than ₹ 45 per day. The incidence of poverty in the world is unimaginably high. The millennium goals drafted by United Nations stress on the reduction of poverty in the world by 2015. Worldwide all the countries from developing to underdeveloped nations initiated different policies and programmes of their choice to bring down the poverty rate in their countries.

Poverty alleviation effort, supported by providing credit through small cooperatives or Self Help Groups (SHGs) was introduced in India long back. Group lending, it was felt, could ensure a much higher level of loan repayment. Self Help Groups are small co-operatives mostly credit co-operatives. This type of groups functions effectively, which was initially stipulated by Prof. Mohammed Yunus in Bangladesh and funded through Grameena Bank.

In India, the concept of group lending or small credit co-operatives was brought on a pilot basis through programmes like the "Development of Women and Children in Rural Areas (DWCRA)" and the "Maharashtra Rural Credit Project (MRCP)". Seeing the success of these pilots in terms of repayment of the loans taken and participation by women, the concept was brought in, in the mainstream poverty alleviation effort through the programme, "Swarna Jayanthi Gram Swarajgar Yojana (SGSY)", as a substitute for IRDP, the earlier poverty alleviation programme.

The Self Help Groups have paved the way for economic independence of rural and urban poor women. These SHGs, have now become a popular instrument world over, especially in developing countries for poverty alleviation. Micro-finance in India in this form of small, women's credit co-operatives has increased its outreach in several states. The number of SHGs is increasing rapidly. Some estimates put these at currently 2.5 million SHGs in India. (*Economic Survey of India*, p. 67).

A study on self help groups of WIGS, RASS by Ramamohan (1996) indicates that self-help groups broader socio-economic opportunities and provide space for poor of the poor women to function effectively in their Micro enterprise through group efforts.

The SHG's have excellent opportunities to work together to initiate small business or extend various essential services.

Now many Government and NGO's are involved in the development of women by motivating them to form into SHGs and providing training inputs in awareness generation and capacity building through transfer of knowledge and skills to further self-initiatives at the grassroots.

National social service (1998) survey found that technical training for literate women is essential and enhances their earnings three times those of illiterate women, though they too can double earnings with technical training.

Dr. D. Padmavathi's (2002) study on Training Women, for entrepreneurship, indicates that training of women entrepreneurs develops good managerial skills, helps to know the available financial resources, to select cheaper and good quality raw material, to tap the market facilities to sell their products etc.

Entrepreneurial training and development can be defined as "a programme designed to help an individual in strengthening his/her entrepreneurial motive and in acquiring skill and capabilities necessary for playing his/her entrepreneurial role effectively.

A baseline study was conducted with the objective of gathering the SHG women opinion on the requirement and duration of training on entrepreneurship, specific to their needs.

Sample

Sample selection was purposive in nature with the specific objective of training, active and already entrepreneurially engaged SHG women.

The reason was that such women would be able to grasp the training inputs much better when compared to other SHG women who may not be so involved in their economic activity.

The sample selection was from Tirupati urban area where numerous SHGs were already operating. Total sample selected for the sample was 100 numbers.

Training Process

One and half month entrepreneurship development programme was conducted for the selected self help group women. An entrepreneurship development programme is a process wherein the entrepreneurial and managerial capabilities of the potential entrepreneur are developed. The training content was balanced in terms of theoretical and practical orientations. The training content included self-appraisal of participants, entrepreneurial qualities, market survey, business plan development, Government programmes, schemes and incentives for women entrepreneurs and interface with the successful women entrepreneurs.

Pre-Training Phase

Specific training content was developed for the benefit of the members based on the experience of the investigator in organising entrepreneurship development programme in India and exposure to the same abroad.

Training Phase

During the training phase the self-help group women were trained to strengthen the existing traits and to develop latent traits using a variety of participatory techniques such as self appraisal, brain storming, simulation games etc. They were exposed to several case studies of women entrepreneurs in the region. An interface was also arranged between the trainees and support systems and also with successful women entrepreneurs. The trainees were trained to do market survey and develop business plan.

Post-Training Phase

Women have to overcome many social cultural problems. They need support and encouragement on all these fronts. Therefore enterprise training should be holistic and the parent institution which found the self-help groups should strengthen the follow up activities to empower the self-help group women and to utilize the benefits available to them.

Tools

The following tools were used to collect the data.

- Interview schedule—to collect the socio-economic profiles and other related data of self-help group women.
- Self-rating questionnaire—to assess the entrepreneurial qualities of self-help group women. (developed by Udai, Pareck)
- Self-assessment exercises. (developed by Udai Pareck)
- Interview schedule—to study the impact of entrepreneurship development programme on self-help group women.

Procedure

The research tools were used on self-help group women to collect the required information and to assess their entrepreneurial personality. The collected information was scored and analysed. Results were tabulated and discussed accordingly.

Results and Discussion

Table—33.1 presents the distribution of respondents according to their age.

Table 33.1 : Distribution of the Respondents according to the Age, Educational status, Marital status, Economic status and Type of family

Characteristics	Respondents = 100	Per cent
Age		
Upto 30 years	14	14
31 to 40 years	58	58
41 and above	28	28
Educational Status		
Illiterate	27	27
Below 10th class	69	69
Intermediate	4	4
Marital Status		
Unmarried	–	–
Married	84	84
Widow	16	16
Divorced		
Economic Status		
Below ₹ 2,500	86	86
2,501 to 5,000	14	14
Type of Family		
Nuclear	69	69
Joint	31	31

Table—33.1 presents the distribution of respondents according to their age educational qualifications, marital status, economic status and the type of family.

Age

The data shows that irrespective of their age, women joined in the self-help groups to supplement the family income. It appears that generally women enter into any Income generating activity which will help them to improve their standard of living in their thirties. By that time normally they would have settled in life and time to supplement family income.

Education

It was observed from the study that 27 per cent of 69 per cent studied below 10th standard, 27 per cent SHG women were Illiterate but they are able to put their signature but they could not read. The illiterate members learnt signatures after joining the SHGs and they were helped in this by the literate members of the SHGs. By regularly practicing it they learned this skill and only 4 per cent had better educational qualification i.e. up to intermediate.

It was observed, though 27 per cent of the women were illiterate still they have their own system of accounting and manage their petty trades i.e., vegetable vending, thread making, flower vending etc. Hence, it may be said that not having literacy did not prevent the members entry into income generating activities to support their families.

Marital Status

Majority of the SHG members (84 per cent) were married. It is quite obvious that in poor families married women shoulders heavy responsibilities for the economic viability of the families, hence it is but natural for the married women to join SHGs to gain economic benefit to their respective families.

Economic Status

The study further shows that 86 per cent of the respondents monthly income was below ₹ 2,500 and 14 per cent SHG women income was between ₹ 2501 to ₹ 5000. In the present study the members families total monthly income is less than ₹ 5000. No wonder that the women from these families became members of SHGs with the fond hope of improving their economic position.

Type of Family

The study revealed that majority of women 61 per cent came from nuclear families while 31 per cent were from joint families.

Table 33.2 : Distribution of Respondents according to type of IGA

Type of business	Respondents	
	Number	Per cent
Trade-sector	50	50
Production	25	25
Service	25	25
Total	**100**	**100**

From the Table 33.2 it was clear that half (50 per cent) of the women SHG members who were involved in income generating activities belong to trade sector which includes businesses like purchase and sale of products with little or no processing, like small provision stores, saree business, vegetable vending etc.; 25 per cent women are in the small scale production sector which involves manufacturing of products like thread making and pot making; and another 25 per cent of them belonged service sector which included activities like ironing, tailoring and tiffin centres etc.

Previous Business experience

Majority of the SHG members who are involved in Income Generating Activity (75 per cent) did not have any previous business experience before embarking into the Income Generating Activity, and only 25 per cent had some experience before starting the income generating activity.

Reasons for starting Income Generating Activity

SHG members started Income generating activity to supplement their family income. Schwartz (1979) expressed that 'economic necessity' was found to be one of the most prime motivations for women to take up the entrepreneurship. It is evident from the table—33.3, the SHG women had given the following reasons for starting income generating activity in decreasing order of importance. It was also true that most of the SHG members family income is low. All of tlhem expressed that they entered into the income generating activity to supplement their family income. 77 per cent started to provide good life to children. 75 per cent started the income generating activity as a result of encouragement received from family members and friends and 52 per cent started to get financial liberty.

Table 33.3 : Reasons of the respondents in starting the Income Generating Activity

Sl.No.	Reasons	Respondents	
		Number	Per Cent
1.	To supplement the family income	100	100
2.	To provide good life to children	77	77
3.	Encouragement by family members/friends	75	75
4.	To get financial liberty	52	52

Despite difference in the reasons for starting income generating activities, for all of them the main reason is to earn something extra to supplement their family incomes.

Awareness of Self-Help Groups members on Entrepreneurship Development Programme (EDP)

The items on the aspect "Awareness of Self-Help Groups members on EDP" were answered in terms of Yes/No and there were a few open ended questions related to entrepreneurial qualities and awareness on self-employment schemes and subsidies offered by the Government for the benefit of women empowerment and about the EDP training.

Entrepreneurship in the economic field refers to identifying innovative ideas, product services, mobilizing resources and finally marketing them, covering the risk with constant striving for growth and excellence (Akhouri, 1990). Majority of the group members (64 per cent) were not aware of the concept of entrepreneurship development programme and its importance. Without this knowledge some of the members perform certain activities involved in entrepreneurship. But the difference between knowing and not knowing will reflect in skill development. A person who knows about the entrepreneurship will capture the resources immediately than the person without the knowledge. In order to perform a business venture smoothly, there is a intense need for the awareness of EDP.

Opinion about the entrepreneurial qualities

The women SHG members were asked their opinion about the entrepreneurial qualities needed in an individual to succeed in their income generating activities and the data was given in table. It is clear from the table—33.4 that 28 per cent of the SHG members expressed that the individual should have the qualities of risk taking, hard work (28 per cent). 18 per cent of the women expressed that leadership qualities must be essential for a person to succeed, and only 8 per cent of the respondents said that Initiative is one of the qualities required. Remaining 18 per cent have expressed that Money, Education are the qualities.

Table 33.4 : Distribution of the respondents according to their opinions on entrepreneurial qualities

Qualities	Number of members expressed
Hard working	28
Initiativeness	8
Leadership	18
Risk taking	28
Others	18

Training

Information was also collected on the training of the SHG members whether they have undergone any training. If so, what type of training, duration and objective of the training programme? The SHG women did not have any training experience earlier. Training is essential to make themselves more visible and to strengthen their skills. Either way lack of training appears to be the main deterrent to be a successful entrepreneur.

Information was elicited whether there is a need to undergo EDP training and the results were shown in table—33.5. The data reveal that 61 per cent of the respondents expressed that the training is essential for them to improve their knowledge, skills and only 39 per cent couldn't explain the need for training. The most significant problem that women entrepreneur had to face in running their business was reported as lack of business training (Watkins and Watkins 1986). Hence, appropriate training and interventions are needed to bring qualitative changes in the situation.

Table 33.5 : Need for training

Need for training	Respondents
Yes	61
No	39

Details on EDP Organised for SHG Members

With the increasing realization that women enterprise is important, many organizations/institutions are now developing and administering training programmes aimed at fulfilling women's specific requirements. Most such programmes recognize that: (*a*) family is prime for women; and (*b*) environmental, financial and knowledge constraints usually prompt women to look for home-based business, they can run using their traditional skills. Therefore the training programmes should concentrate on imparting or enhancing traditional skills to the point that they can be developed into a business. This gives the business the advantages of: (*a*) greater familiar acceptability because of minimal change in life-style; and (*b*) quicker start up since skill enhancement resources needed are limited.

The training programmes those aimed at the poorer section, concentrate on skill enhancement on the basis of 'income generation' motive without dealing specifically with the attitudinal autonomy motive.

A one and half month (3 days in a week) EDP was organised for 100 women SHG women members. The training inputs were :

1. Entrepreneurship and entrepreneurial qualities;
2. Assessment of entrepreneurial qualities of women SHG members;
3. Communication skills;
4. Market survey;
5. Steps to start small business unit;
6. Business plan development;
7. Government programmes implemented for women empowerment and subsidies, incentives given to women;
8. Interface with successful women entrepreneurs.

The women SHG members were oriented toward the concept of Entrepreneurship and most important entrepreneurial qualities like—initiative, persistence, information seeking, Risk taking, systematic planning, problem-solving, assertiveness and self confidence.

Assessment of entrepreneurial qualities

To gain an insight into their own motivation and behaviour a set of following exercises were used:

- Self-rating questionnaire
- Ring toss
- Tower building

- Boat making
- Broken squares

This part of training was imparted as a part of behavioural input. In this input the focus is on the entrepreneur, the aim of the training was making the participants aware of their strengths and weaknesses which would help them to improve their strengths and eliminate their weaknesses.

All these exercises revealed that the women SHG members had average and low average levels of entrepreneurial traits like initiative, self-confidence, systematic planning, fear of failure, information seeking, concern for quality at work, problem-solving, confidence, persuasion.

This training was directed primarily to reinforce behaviours like concern for excellence, learning from feedback, moderate risk taking ability, self confidence etc. In this session the participant individually got opportunity and help not only to understand his own behaviour but also to internalize the implications of such of behaviour.

The present-day 'knowledge explosion' in the world has also necessitated communication explosion, otherwise knowledge explosion has no meaning. Certainly in rural development, nothing is morc important than the transfer of useful information from person to person. Good communication plays an important role in passing the required information to create awareness. On the need and importance of communication skills, a lecture was organized to the SHG members. This lecture helped them to understand how to communicate, what to communicate and why to communicate for an effective management of their income generating activities and to deal with support systems.

Market survey

Market survey helps to understand the demand for the product in the area, and feasibility of marketing of the product, specifications of the customer and market structure and it would also will be helpful to control the problems like difficulty in procuring raw material, consumer dissatisfaction, unavailability of equipment etc.

All this information was given to the members and they were asked to conduct a market survey on their own. Members were divided into 10 groups to do this task. The groups conducted survey demand for Tiffin centre, flour grinding, fancy shop and provisional stores in their areas only. During the market survey the members collected information about the number of families, income levels of the people in their area and their needs. The illiterate SHG members also made their effort in collecting all this information satisfactorily. This session helped them to have a practical knowledge on market survey.

Steps to start Business

In order to make the venture a dynamic and growing organism, the new entrepreneurs should plan the enterprise systematically. The SHGs were exposed to lecture on steps to start a small business unit to give a final shape to business idea.

Business Plan Development

A business plan is a document which provides flesh and blood to the business idea. It focuses on the steps or decisions the individual need to take prior to the starting of the business becoming operational. The business plan helps to take strategic decisions on business and whether to implement their business idea or not, and to get advanced knowledge for enterprise management.

The above information on business plan development given to SHG members through lecture method and they were asked to develop the business plan of their own business idea to understand to what extent they acquired knowledge from previous lecture.

The business plans prepared by the SHG members included the contents like type of business, details of customers (who would be customers, how many of the SHG members are expected per day), raw materials needed, and raw materials needed based on their expected customers, cost of the raw materials, capital needed to start the business. A high per cent (73) of SHG members tried to prepare their business plans incorporating all this information. The remaining (27) per cent found difficulty in preparing the business plans due to their illiteracy.

Impact of SHG members on EDP

The impact of EDP studied through the expressions of the SHG members in verbatim.

When the SHG members were asked to comment on the balance between theory and practicals, 80 percent of the SHG members reported that there was a balance between theory and practicals, whereas 20 per cent felt that it was more practical-oriented.

The SHG members were asked whether they were satisfied with the training given to them and also the duration of the training programme, all of them (100 per cent) expressed their satisfaction.

The SHG members were questioned to list out the entrepreneurial qualities necessary for a person to succeed. 75 per cent of them listed all the qualities. The remaining 25 per cent of them listed five to six qualities.

77 per cent of the SHG members expressed that most interesting session of the training programme were, self analysis exercises and business plan development. They expressed that self analysis session helped them to analyze their entrepreneurial trails and they formed that need to strengthen their trails. Business plan development helped them to understand the requirements to do a business.

The session on communication skills, steps to start small business were found to be satisfactory in 23 per cent due to their theoretical nature and all the (100 per cent) SHG members expressed that the session on Government programmes, subsidies and incentives created awareness among them.

The interface with successful entrepreneurs and support systems was also appreciated by all the SHG women.

In the present study due to time limitation only the immediate impact in terms of absorption of knowledge was studied, the parent institution which is playing key role in empowering the women through SHG formation should take the responsibility of further follow-up providing training inputs to strengthen and motivate them to start their own enterprise.

Conclusion

Women Self-Help Groups are considered as the most powerful means to strengthen the socio-economic development of women through integrated approach. It is treated as a platform to provide opportunity to women for all over development through group efforts.

Women empowerment is a pre-requisite for creating a good nation. If a woman is empowered her captaincies towards decision-making will surely influence her family's and society behaviour. There is an emerging need to train women towards empowerment. Imparting entrepreneurial training in all the aspects of entrepreneurship go a long way in ameliorating their socio-economic lot. The Government has emerged as a major catalyst by way of providing training incentives and other facilities to succeed particularly for poor women to empower them.

REFERENCES

1. Akhouri MMP, 1990, "Entrepreneurial Economic Success Index for Assessing Entrepreneurial Success", *Sedme*, 4 (1); pp. 36-39.
2. *Economic Survey of India*, 2007-08.
3. Prasada Rao, M., 2010 *"Impact of SHG based Microfinance on Women Empowerment".* Amazar.com/widgets
4. Sathiabama, K., 2010 *"Rural Women Empowerment and Entrepreneurship Development"* http://www.esocialsciences.com/data/articles/document 1942010230. 524502.doc
5. Schwartz, EB, 1979, "Entrepreneurship—A New Female Frontier", *Journal of Contemparary Business* (Winter); pp. 47-76
6. Dr. R. Srinivasan, 2010 *"Entrepreneurial Training and Development —Some Thoughts".* Html:file://F:/ENTREPRENEURIAL%20Teaching %20 DEVELOPMENT-SOME%20WHO...10/2/2010.
7. Udai Pareek, 1991 *"Developing Motivation through Experiencing".* Second edition, published by Oxfort and IBH Publishing Pvt. Ltd., New Delhi, pp. 81-145, 177-187.
8. Vijayalakshmi, R., 1996, "Women Micro-entrepreneurs in the Food in the Food Industry : A Study in A.P." *Proceedings of the all VII All India Meeting of Women in Science* "Role of Women in Science Society Interaction", pp. 193-200.

Index

D

G

H

I

R

S